# The Hasidic Community of Williamsburg

# Judaica and Hebraica Series

# The Hasidic Community of Williamsburg

## A Study in the Sociology of Religion

With a new introduction
by William B. Helmreich

# Solomon Poll

Transaction Publishers
New Brunswick (U.S.A.) and London (U.K.)

Library of Congress Catalog Number: 2006040412
ISBN: 1-4128-0573-2
Printed in the United States of America

Library of Congress Cataloging-in-Publication Data

Poll, Solomon.
  The Hasidic community of Williamsburg : a study in the sociology of religion / Solomon Poll ; with a new introduction by William B. Helmreich.
      p. cm.
  Includes bibliographical references.
  ISBN 1-4128-0573-2 (alk. paper)
    1. Hasidism—New York (State)—New York.  2. Jews—Social life and customs.  3. Jews—New York (State)—New York.  I. Title.

BM198.2.P65   2006
305.6'9683320974723—dc22                                   2006040412

*For Ruth Z., Leah P., Erno C., and Seema B.*

# Contents

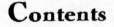

# Contents

# Introduction to the Transaction Edition

## Cultural Isolation, Accomodation, and Integration: How Minorities Preserve Their Culture

I n his book, *The Hasidic Community of Williamsburg*, the sociolo gist, Solomon Poll, wrote: "The Hasidim of Williamsburg try to sepa rate themselves not only from non-Jews and 'unreligious' Jews but also from 'religious' Orthodox Jews....These 'Hasidim' create a socio-logical wall between themselves and other Jews" (vi).

These words, first penned in 1962, are still, more or less true, of today's Hasidic, or Ultra-Orthodox, community in Williamsburg. Though much has changed indeed, a walk through the community's streets pro-vides ample evidence of its insularity. Yiddish remains the dominant lan-guage there and is spoken, not only by older residents, but by small children, teenagers, and young adults. The garb is of the old-European Hasidic variety and the stores are almost all owned by Hasidim. Yeshivas and dozens of small synagogues, known as *shtibls*, may be found along the tree-lined streets, nestled between quaint and well-preserved brownstones, home for the thousands of Hasidim, mostly of the Satmar group, who live there.

Today it seems a given that a community proud of its heritage would flourish in the United States. Certainly in New York, which, as the histo-rian, Mike Wallace said, was an experiment to see if "all the peoples of the world could live together in one place," there ought to be room for even the most different of ethnic groups. Yet this view certainly was not commonly held by "experts" at the time Poll's book appeared. Most knowledgeable observers, including the eminent sociologist of the Jew-ish community, Marshall Sklare, did not at the time predict a bright future for Orthodoxy.

The ability of Orthodoxy to survive into the twenty-first century as a dynamic movement capable of attracting and retaining young people is one reason why Poll's book remains a significant contribution to the literature. Although he focused on the most sectarian segment of the community, the fact is that it, when combined with the "Strictly Orthodox" Lithuanian-style yeshiva community, which it closely resembles, makes up about half of today's Orthodox community. The other half, the "Modern Orthodox," while different from the Hasidim are, nevertheless, as practicing Jews, still part of the same broader community in many ways, sharing the overall goal of strengthening and preserving religious Jewish life and culture.

There are many reasons why Orthodoxy is today a thriving movement within the Jewish community. First, the Orthodox community's numbers were greatly augmented by the arrival from Europe, after World War II, of thousands of Jews committed to it. Poll provides us with an ethnographically rich account of the Hasidim who were part of this group and who settled in Williamsburg. He also tells us, as the following quote makes clear, how they were seen by the more moderate and smaller group of Orthodox Jews who had been living in Williamsburg before the Ultra-Orthodox arrived: "As I walked down the stairs I met two Hasidic children. One said to the other, 'Look at that Jew. He has already completed the evening service when our *rebbe* did not even start with the afternoon service.' To this the other Hasidic child replied: 'Oh what do you want from him, he is surely a *goy*.' Well, I do not wish to live in a community where I, an observant Jew, am considered a *goy*." (p. 27)

One can just imagine what non-observant Jews or gentiles thought of these newcomers. In any case, the fact that the Hasidim entered the community all at once, over a period of five or six years, increased their feelings of group solidarity and a belief that their way of life could easily be transplanted the new land in which they found themselves.

Another factor was the general attitude towards cultural identification on the part of the government and people in general. Whereas the interwar period was characterized by the view (sometimes referred to as "Americanization") that immigrants should give up their old ways and assimilate, the postwar approach, known as cultural pluralism, took the position that forcing people to abandon their ways was counterproductive. It was bound to be stiffly resisted and was, in any case, wrong because it failed to consider that retaining the "old" culture helped immigrants bridge the gap between what was and what could no longer be.

This was a framework in which Orthodoxy could survive and Poll masterfully demonstrates the myriad ways in which the Hasidim adapted to life in the U.S. without really changing their beliefs and practices. In fact, this is the heart of his thesis. As Poll explains, the Hasidim created an economic system that enabled them to thrive as a religious community. This included specialized occupations, shops, markets for religious goods, and jobs outside the community in areas like retail clothing and manufacturing and diamonds.

Some might think that such communities have a greater chance to survive if they are located far from the temptations of the larger society, perhaps in rural areas. The Amish come to mind as a case in point. But Poll argues persuasively that this is not always or necessarily true. In the case of the Hasidim, the urban environment exerted a positive influence. As Max Weber pointed out long ago, the Jews were throughout history a generally urban people who adjusted well to life in cities. Such a milieu provided larger markets for their goods and diverse economic opportunities.

Poll raised the question (p. 256) as to whether or not the Hasidim could succeed in a rural area and responded in the negative. Citing the case of New Square, in Rockland County, he pointed out that the community still depended on Williamsburg and New York City in general for its sustenance and in this he was and remains correct. Since then the Satmar have established a successful and numerically large community in Monroe, New York. However, like New Square, it remains tied to New York City in the sense that so many of its residents commute to the city to earn their living. On the other hand, those that staff the community's many schools and who run the local shops are more rooted in Monroe. What Poll could not have anticipated is the current struggle for political power now raging between the Monroe and Williamsburg factions, one beyond the purview of this brief introductory essay.

Nevertheless, what is remarkable is that the Williamsburg he studied is still largely intact almost half a century later, eloquent testimony to its long-range appeal. Because of the explosion in population, other Hasidic communities have sprung up too, most notably in Brooklyn's Boro Park section. This area is home to numerous sects such as Bobov, Ger, Nadverne, Tchortkov, Satmar, Tzelem, and Pupa, but that diversity has no effect on the overall urban spatial configuration of the community. Williamsburg has Lee Avenue as its main thoroughfare and Boro Park has 13th, 16th, and 18th Avenues. Both communities have yeshivas, shtibls, wigmakers, religious booksellers, kosher restaurants and supermarkets, etc., etc.

As a result, Poll's book is as relevant today in many ways as it was when it first appeared. This should perhaps not be surprising inasmuch as it tells the story of a community that prides itself on not being affected by the winds of change, that sees in its beliefs and lifestyles confirmation of what it believes to be eternal truths and values that have been transmitted for centuries, primarily through its holy religious books. This point was succinctly expressed to me when I studied the educational institutions of the rigorously Orthodox, by one of its major scholars and sages, Rabbi Yitzchak Hutner. He was responding in almost mystical fashion to my query as to how the yeshivas had survived for thousands of years:

> "They'll give you all sorts of reasons, but in reality it's a mystery just like the mystery of the Jews. How did the Jewish people survive? And this question about the yeshivas is a mystery within a mystery. And all the reasons are junk. It was the work of God...The Jew has a deep mysterious connection to Torah that we don't fully understand, although we know it's there." (*The World of the Yeshiva: An Intimate Portrait of Orthodox Jewry,* p. 320)

There is a certain duality at work here that goes a long way towards explaining the community's vitality. Even as they go about their daily affairs, working as diamond cutters, appliance salesmen at stores like B & H, managing small clothing factories, and the like, and even as they jockey for political power by joining local community boards, the Hasidim see themselves as engaged in a holy mission, praying to God, singing His praises, and adhering to His laws. It is that which undergirds and justifies their existence. They do not reject materialism. In fact they enjoy it. As both Weber and Poll have observed, inner-worldy asceticism was never part of Jewish religion and culture. Thus, it is in no way their ultimate goal, or their *raison d'etre*. A community that makes intellectual satisfaction and spiritual fulfillment primary goals can withstand a great deal of adversity, be it finding a way to meet the economic needs of families with ten or more children or dealing with illness, death, crippling injuries, and other problems that afflict everyone.

A centerpiece of the Hasidic community is its large system of educational institutions. The intensive schooling that its children receive there insures the long term viability of the group's religious way of life. As Poll presciently noted, however, the Hasidim continue to view secular and religious education as incompatible in the sense that the former entail the risk that foreign ideas would threaten its religious belief system. To this day, males generally receive no more than a sixth grade secular education. Women are allowed to complete secular studies through twelfth grade. This restricts the community's earning power, but has the positive benefit of making it difficult for its members to live independently of the community.

Solomon Poll's volume has the distinction of being the first full-length work to focus exclusively on Hasidic life and culture in America. George Kranzler's volume, *Williamsburg: A Jewish Community in Transition,* studied the community in general, while Jerome Mintz's work, *Legends of the Hasidim*, concentrated on their spiritual world, and there have been other works by Samuel Heilman, Israel Rubin, Egon Mayer, and William Shaffir. But Poll's book remains a major contribution for two reasons——Its ethnographic detail and its thorough grounding in classic sociological theory.

While as an academic, Poll was regarded with suspicion by the Hasidic community, his background growing up in the European Hasidic community gave him a true insider's perspective. Religiously observant and fluent in Yiddish and Hungarian, he was able to adapt to the hostility and mistrust that greeted him as he approached people with requests for interviews. He also functioned as a participant observer, attending hundreds of functions, religious services, and meetings. In all, he spent thirteen years on the project. This resulted in a wealth of information, not only interviews, but documents, leaflets, placards, bulletins, and accounts from Yiddish newspapers, many of which were reprinted in the book.

Many ethnographers are light on theory. Poll was an exception. He analyzed the community in terms of Durkheim's well known work on the functions of religion and showed how they applied to the Hasidic world. He also drew extensively upon the work of Werner Sombart, Max Weber, and Talcott Parsons with respect to the relationship between economy and society. Of all the work done on the Hasidim, his offers the best application of theory to empirical findings.

In 1962, when Poll studied the Hasidim, they were not at all active politically. Today, the opposite is the case. They are very involved in politics and because they vote as a bloc, have a disproportionately large degree of influence. Political leaders cater to their needs and make themselves available to those in the community who wish to meet with them. Once the community grew to the point where it needed support from the government participation in the system, namely voting became a matter of necessity. This same pragmatic streak is present in Israel too, where hasidic or "haredi" Jews participate in a government they had in the past condemned as godless.

Poll discussed extensively the methods by which the community exerts social control over the lives of its members. Those who failed to conform did not receive economic support from its array of social welfare organizations and their businesses were not patronized. Psychologically, those who deviated became the objects of gossip and ridicule. These responses to external threats remain effective today, but there are increasing signs that a crisis is looming on the horizon.

According to experts familiar with the Ultra and Strictly Orthodox, there are several thousand youngsters currently at risk in the community. Drug and alcohol abuse, sexual promiscuity, and rejection of religious observance have touched many families, as reported by psychologists and social workers familiar with the community. In addition, new research by the sociologist, Hella Winston, suggests that the number of adults not adhering to community norms is significantly larger than had previously been assumed. Poll presents no information on the degree of deviance that existed when he studied the community, probably, in part, because there was so little of it at the time.

Poll gave numerous examples of how the community was able to harness technology for positive purposes. The automobile, rather than being used to leave the community, became a "vehicle" for transporting people to schools, weddings, community meetings, and work. As opposed to the Amish, there are no restrictions on the use of electricity, be it washing machines or Sabbath timers that turn lights on and off automatically. The Hasidim are deliberately selective in what they allow. Television is forbidden because the life portrayed on most of the programs is inimical to community norms and values. Tape recorders are permitted and used to enhance religious life. They may be, and are, for instance, used to record lectures by rabbis and teachers, or Hasidic music.

Has this partial embrace of modern technology been successful or has it eroded the community's strength? The answer must be yes and no. On the one hand, the Hasidim remain a vibrant and strong force. They have grown in size and have continued to benefit from all the technological developments of the past four decades. Yet there is one technological advance that seems to be creating problems for them—the computer.

It is not possible for the Hasidic community to function effectively without computers and they recognize that. That is why they allow males and females to take computer programming courses and the like. They need it in their businesses, schools, and agencies, as much as they need the telephone. The issue roiling the community, however, is the internet and the access it provides to the outside world. The internet has exposed the Hasidim, particularly the young, to secular music and culture, detailed news of the outside world, and, most disturbingly perhaps, pornography.

Indeed, interviews with Hasidim substantiate the fact that the computer is a true "window" to the outside world and the "negative influences" that they see as an integral part of that world. They are, of course, not the only ones disturbed by this. Millions of people are concerned about much of what is available on the net, but for an insular community unprepared to counter its temptations, the matter is very worrisome. They cannot ban it because its use is too pervasive. Indicative of how the internet can be, not only a conduit for cultural intrusion, it the fact that it can even be used to challenge the community itself. There are now websites that advise Hasidim on how to leave the community, where to obtain a secular education, and how to find a job in the outside world. Other websites are devoted to allowing Hasidim to communicate with each other about their problems with Orthodox beliefs, even in establishing sexual and romantic liaisons with like-minded individuals. For a community that forbids dating and still practices arranged marriage, this is a direct threat to its very existence.

Will this be the downfall of the community ultimately? Much depends on its response. If the Hasidim pretend that there are no problems, then the likelihood is that defections will increase, perhaps to the point of threatening its continued existence. If, on the other hand, they respond by addressing the issues in a rational and non-coercive manner, the chances for survival are greater. The biggest challenge will be for the leadership to recognize that in a modern society control over members of a group cannot be absolute. Ensconced as it is in major urban areas, the community cannot be run as a total institution simply because it is not a total institution. Its members must literally leave its environment every day if they are to earn their daily bread. Surviving on the dole is not a realistic option. Their families are too large and the economic expense of maintaining a religious life cannot be covered by welfare payments.

It would be ironic if a community steeped in the wisdom and knowledge of its sages fails to find a way to deal with its social problems. However, doing so demands not only intellectual acumen but what the writer, Daniel Goleman, referred to as "emotional intelligence," or what most of us call "good common sense." It may even involve a strategic retreat from previously inflexible positions with respect to religious observance. Will they do so? Only time will tell.

# Preface

IN HIS ESSAY ON JUDAISM, Max Weber described the ancient Jews as a pariah people, meaning "they were a guest people who were ritually separated, formally or *de facto*, from their social surroundings."[1] He continues, saying that "all the essential traits of Jewry's attitude toward the environment can be deduced from this pariah existence—especially its voluntary ghetto, long anteceding compulsory internment, and the dualistic nature of its in-group and out-group moralities."[2]

It is not clear how this pariah existence came about. It is, however, a fact that throughout the ages the Jews maintained a social system by which they separated themselves from their neighbors. They did not allow their community to internalize the social patterns of their neighbors. Nor did they acquaint themselves with such principles as would give them strength to replace their tradition.

In recent times this separation has taken on a different dimension. In America, where society offers more or less greater integration for the Jews into the larger society, where politically and economically they enjoy freedom equal to the members of the larger society, it is inevitable that such a society also provides greater possibilities for assimilation.

American Jewish leaders and organizations have paid close attention to the problem of assimilation. As John Slawson states, "for

1. Max Weber, *Ancient Judaism*, translated by Hans H. Gerth and Don Martindale (Glencoe: The Free Press, 1952), p. 3.
2. *Ibid.*

*xvii*

more than twenty-five years, the American Jewish Committee has involved itself with questions of Jewish identity and continuity in the United States. As overt hostility against Jews declined and the society became more and more open, these issues came to loom increasingly large."[3] In consequence of this large-scale alienation and estrangement from traditional Jewish practice in America, ultra-Orthodox Jews and Hasidim tended to exclude themselves from the newly emerged American Jewish life.

The Hasidim of Williamsburg try to separate themselves not only from non-Jews and "unreligious" Jews but also from "religious" Orthodox Jews, whose religious ideology, intensity, and frequency of traditional religious behavior do not meet Hasidic requirements. These "Hasidim" create a sociological wall between themselves and other Jews, whom they do not consider traditionally "religious."

When Jews lived in physical isolation, social separation was relatively easy. But today, particularly in New York City, where various peoples of various cultures interact and where most Jews have adopted American social norms, it is more difficult to create specifically designed, institutionalized behavior to maintain isolation. Even a Hasidic Jew, as soon as he leaves the walls of his prayer house, is exposed to symbols of change and assimilation. The automobile he rides "takes him away from the community"; the posters and placards on the streets carry messages of "acts prohibited by the community"; the gadgets he buys and the facilities he uses are "products of an outside world." In this "outside world" the people are strange, the language is foreign, the "clothes are immoral," the mannerisms are shameful—all are part of a culture that is alien to the Hasidic Jew. In this "foreign surrounding" the Hasidic Jew maintains his own identity, retains his own culture, and transmits the same values to future generations.

In order to continue to preserve their culture undisturbed, therefore, the Hasidic Jews would have to develop a system by which they can ignore the existence of the outside world. But this they can no longer do, because modern technology and American civilization have reached and influenced every walk of life.

One of the ways by which Hasidim adjust to and counter American society is by sacralizing secular activities. The automobile, instead of being considered a vehicle that takes them away from the community, becomes an object that brings children to the

3. See the foreword in Marshall Sklare and Joseph Greenblum, *Jewish Identity on the Suburban Frontier: A Study of Group Survival in the Open Society* (New York: Basic Books, 1967); see also Benjamin Ringer, *The Edge of Friendliness: A Study of Jewish–Gentile Relations* (New York: Basic Books, 1967).

house of study. The refrigerator, instead of being an example of modernity, becomes an accessory facilitating religious dietary observance. An automatic timer, instead of being a symbol of modern electronics, becomes a quasi-religious object making the observance of the Sabbath more feasible. Consequently, American culture and its contents have not thus far endangered the entity of Hasidic Jews because they have been successful in establishing a system that interlocks creed and economic activities.

Unlike certain Protestant sects of withdrawal, Hasidim do not deprive themselves. Rather, they put the material world to use in order to advance and promote their religious norms. In fact, the American culture in general and New York City society in particular have been aiding Hasidic Jews in furthering the intensification of their religious behavior to a degree unequaled in the history of the Jews. *The Hasidic Community of Williamsburg* illustrates some of those techniques by which these Jews have been able to maintain and intensify their cultural entity.

Asceticism, particularly "inner-worldly asceticism" (i.e., practiced by those who live among the worldly, in the midst of plenty, without being of them or participating in their activities), is not part of the Hasidic culture. This is strongly in line with Weber's contention that "inner-worldly asceticism was absent in [ancient] Israel."[4] Weber further states that "pharisaic [i.e., rabbinic] Judaism was also far from rejecting wealth or from thinking that it be dangerous, or that its unqualified enjoyment endangers salvation. Wealth was, indeed, considered prerequisite to certain priestly functions. . . ."[5] The Hasidic Jews, too, consider wealth and secure economic resources indispensable prerequisites for the proper observance of religion. Financial needs for the maintenance of religion may be the main incentive and stimulus in the establishment of an economic system for the Hasidic community. In addition, the American value system of hard work, strong drive for achievement, and economic success has greatly influenced the Hasidic Jews of Williamsburg. The adaption of norms related to economic activities is also part of the adjustment processes. Relative economic success in America made it possible for the Hasidim to establish a great many parochial schools, in which rigid socialization reinforced community ties and norms. Economic success also helped them to afford and to pay for the maintenance of the many rituals and religious objects owned by the members of the community.

The larger Jewish community provides strong economic support

4. Weber, *op. cit.*, p. 254.
5. *Ibid.*, p. 401.

for the Hasidim of Williamsburg. Hasidic economic activities are expanding, as their rituals provide new jobs and as their religious objects and food products find an outlet in the larger Jewish community. (Even the *Wall Street Journal* [April 10, 1963] reported that the demand for kosher products has been increasing steadily in recent years.) In addition to this economic support, the larger Jewish community allows Hasidim to remain separatists by shielding them from the demands of gentile society.

Hasidic groups are many, and most of them live in Israel, New York, and in major cities of the United States. The similarities between them are manifold: for example, (1) they are externally identifiable as Jews by their garments, beards, and sidelocks; (2) they subscribe to traditional and Hasidic principles and values; (3) they maintain high intensity and frequency of religious behavior; and (4) they are followers of a specific Hasidic leader (i.e., *rebbe*).

Despite these similarities, there are many issues and viewpoints upon which Hasidic Jews are divided. In fact, there is much intrareligious conflict between the various Hasidic groups. Since each of these groups follows a specific Hasidic leader, each places strong emphasis upon the specific peculiarities of its leaders. Each overemphasizes a specific religious observance, a specific external appearance. Consequently, groups that do not subscribe to the same peculiarities with the same zeal and vehemence antagonize each other. Although there is strong homogeneity among Hasidim, there is heterogeneity in the specific peculiarities of each group.

This book deals mainly with the Hasidim of Williamsburg. The main object of this group is to maintain itself in isolation. These Hasidim are primarily concerned with their own religiosity and with retention of the religious patterns as practiced in their community. They are neither interested nor are they anxious to persuade other Jews to subscribe to their way of life through direct contact with them.

This notion is expressed in the words of a Hasidic leader: "First we must be strong in our own conviction and behavior; we must make sure that we are able to transmit this *Yiddishkeit* [i.e., "Jewish way of life"] to our own children. Only after having this assurance can we engage in activities with other Jews."[6]

Other Hasidic groups may order their purposes quite differently from the Hasidim of Williamsburg. For example, the Habad Hasidim (the followers of the Lubavitzer Rebbe) hold that they must maintain an interaction with other Jews regardless of their lack of

6. From an interview. Translated from Yiddish.

religious observance. Habad Hasidim conduct special programs by which they attempt to "rekindle the heavenly spark" in those forlorn Jews through persuading them to observe some religious act. They visit public parks in New York and approach elderly Jews sitting on the benches to recite a prayer over palm branches on a certain Jewish holiday. They plead with visitors to the Western Wall in Jerusalem to put on phylacteries and pray.

During the summer of 1962 the Habad Hasidim exhibited religious-education literature at the United States World Trade Fairs in New York and Chicago.[7] In addition they publish religious textbooks and writings on Hasidic thoughts in twelve languages. They sponsor a news service and publish monthly and quarterly journals in Yiddish, Hebrew, English, French, Italian and German.[8]

Whereas some Hasidim are strong Zionists and see in the State of Israel a sign of the coming of the Messiah, the Hasidim of Williamsburg are anti-Zionist. They reject everything and everyone that is associated with the new state. They conceive that the existence of the State of Israel is a threat to their traditional perception of the Messiah, because "all of it must emerge through holiness." Even the Hebrew language, they feel, has been defiled. Hebrew is considered by them the holy tongue with which "God revealed himself," a tongue with which "the words of God have been spoken" and with which "hymns and prayers are sung to God." They believe this language has now become secularized and adulterated through lascivious talk and other transgressions.

Although the interaction of the Hasidim of Williamsburg with nonreligious Jews is restricted, they make their views known through their own newspapers, placards, circulars, and public protests that are often reported in the city newspapers. They admonish other Jews who do not subscribe to their pattern of behavior. They create a negative image even of outstanding public figures and "religious leaders" who are outside their community. They cast aspersions upon issues and events which take place in Non-Hasidic Jewish life and which they consider deplorable, evil, and wrong. A certain pride, verging on insolence, must characterize a community which, in its public pronouncements, considers the "whole truth" on its side—mainly because they feel they alone observe traditional Jewish Law in the most authentic and nearly perfect manner.

Thus, among the Hasidim, the Hasidim of Williamsburg are the most outspoken separatists. By isolating themselves, they try to (a) re-create a traditional society that they have transplanted from

7. *American Jewish Yearbook*, 1963, p. 147.
8. *Ibid.*, 1964, p. 81.

Europe, (*b*) divert threats of assimilation by the secular world outside, and (*c*) combat internal change.

Despite all this internal isolation some Hasidim feel that the secular atmosphere of New York City will eventually have a deteriorating effect, particularly upon the children. They are not satisfied with the social seclusion created by the community; they wanted to maintain physical isolation as well. Consequently, two Hasidic groups moved away from New York City. One group, under the leadership of the late Rabbi Joseph Jacob Twersky, the Skvirer Rebbe, established a new community in Rockland County, New York. In July 1961 it was incorporated as a township under the name New Square, after the Skvirer ("Squarer") Rebbe. (Skvir is a Russian town where the Rebbe originated.) Another group moved to Mount Olive Township, near Flanders, New Jersey, to become a farm settlement. After many difficulties, neighborhood protests, and court procedures, the group won approval from the courts to establish itself on a five-hundred-acre tract as a homogeneous, self-contained community.

Yet although these two groups have attempted to establish themselves in physical isolation, the great bulk of Hasidim remain in Williamsburg and through community norms have insulated themselves into a religious subculture.

Until now the Hasidim of Williamsburg have kept aloof and have successfully achieved social isolation. They have created a well-functioning community with effective social controls. Consequently, deviations from religious norms have been held to a minimum. However, as the values of hard work, success, progress, advancement, prosperity, profit, gain, and speed become interlocked with the value system of the community, social controls, effective until now, may be considerably weakened. Whatever doubts and questions we may have about the future of the Hasidim will be answered in the further course of their history. Some of those questions can be briefly stated: Will the Hasidim be able to hold another generation within the community, or will the tremendous lures of personal advancement and profit bring the young men out fully into the secular world? As the younger generations learn the English language, will they not attempt to widen the horizons of their lives?

It seems that these questions already cause considerable concern to the leaders of the community, and they are making much effort to counteract any possible weakening of community norms. These questions, however, will be answered for us by further studies of the community.

SOLOMON POLL

# PART ONE

## The Problem

## and Its Setting

# CHAPTER 1

# An Ultrareligious Group

HIS IS A DESCRIPTIVE STUDY of an ultrareligious Jewish group called the Hasidim. The members of this group consider their goal in life to be the perpetuation of Jewish laws, practices, and observances, and their conduct is defined by extreme religious dogma and principles. The group migrated to the United States after World War II and settled in Williamsburg, a section of Brooklyn, in New York City.

In this dynamic metropolis with its many ethnic groups, the Hasidim have rigorously and so far successfully opposed acculturation to American social patterns. Resistance to Americanization is such that although there is no physical wall to isolate them, a strong "sociological wall" separates this group from activities that might encroach on its cultural stability. All the institutions, including the economic activities of the group, are such that they are conducive to a Hasidic "way of life." The family, the religious organization, the social stratification, the religious leadership, and all other phases of the group's social structure are oriented to the preservation of group norms, and only those patterns of behavior that reflect Hasidic values and attitudes are permitted.

This study is directed especially to the group's economic activities, which are so structured that even the apparently secular elements tend to hold religious significance. This transformation of what might seem superficially to be purely economic activities into religiously significant actions has two functions: (1) to make the group better able to maintain itself economically, and (2) to increase group cohesion by providing a means of constantly reaffirming group values and group behavior.

For the student of the social sciences, and particularly the sociologist, it will be of value to observe how a religious minority group operates in a major metropolis to maintain its unique identification, how this group gives religious significance to everyday secular objects by means of which it provides special occupations and goods for community consumption, and how these objects and occupations interrelate with the many aspects of community life. As Wilbert Moore points out, "In any society an economic activity or structure is only 'predominantly' so, as such activities or organizations cannot be concretely separated from other functions."[1] The Hasidim of Williamsburg provide an example of a community whose major response is not to monetary inducement but to other values important to that society.

This community is unique in many respects, although it shows some similarities to other religious minority groups in the United States. These principal similarities and differences can be briefly indicated.

There are a small number of religious minority groups in this country that try to maintain their differentiating group norms and values in a way comparable to the Hasidim of Williamsburg. But most of these are not exposed to the diversity of behavior found in such a cultural setting as the center of New York. Their members are by-and-large physically isolated from social contact with other groups. Contrast-

1. Wilbert E. Moore, *Economy and Society* (New York: Doubleday & Company, Inc., 1955), p. 6.

ing with these are those religious minority groups that are found in large cities but that have been largely assimilated into the greater society. They are especially apt to lack control over the younger generation, who cannot understand the strange viewpoint of their own parents.

The Molokans are one of these religious minority groups. The sect originated in Russian villages near the Molotchynya (Milky Stream) River in the eighteenth century as an outgrowth of the Greek Orthodox Church of Russia. Because of their deviation from the Church, they were severely persecuted and were forced into exile in Transcaucasia. Between the years 1905 and 1907 about 5,000 Molokans fled to the United States and "settled for the most part in California and the largest colony was formed in a part of Los Angeles."[2]

As of 1932, the Molokans were described as "no longer a true primary group."[3] The community had great problems in controlling its members, especially the young. The various methods the Molokans used to perpetuate their traditions were inefficient and unsuccessful. There is a tendency among some Molokans to leave the city and develop isolated agricultural communities as the best way of holding on to the members and in order to maintain internal social cohesion. In the city "questions are asked," rules are broken, and in other ways group solidarity is weakened.

The Doukhobors are another religious minority group. They originated in Russia in the eighteenth century as an outgrowth of the Orthodox Church. Their religious beliefs are based on "direct revelation and guidance," and as a result the group has consistently denied the authority of government and opposed the use of force by anyone. Because of their religious beliefs they have undergone many conflicts with state and clerical authorities. The first emigration from Russia took place in 1899. In that year 7,427 Doukhobors settled in Canada, and from 1900 to 1920 smaller groups arrived. In Canada they continued to live in segregated communities adhering to their own cultures, which differ in

2. Pauline V. Young, *The Pilgrims of Russian-Town* (Chicago: University of Chicago Press, 1932), p. 2.
3. *Ibid.*, pp. 237–251.

religion, language, economy, food, dress, social life, and recreation from the greater society in which they are set.[4]

The Canadian economic system destroyed the Doukhobors' economic self-sufficiency by exposing them to a "wider
range of careers and of capital and consumer goods—clothes,
cars, machinery, gadgets, commercialized recreation and luxuries of all kinds."[5] These attractions that Canadian society
held for the Doukhobors "weakened their community ties
and thus undermined the whole culture and the strength of
their traditions."[6] The Doukhobor society was not able to
maintain sufficient inner cohesion without creating external
conflict. Because of this, the Doukhobor community creates
issues with the government ("in order to provoke conflict and
force [the government] into oppressive roles") that serve as
an additional external pressure toward maintaining internal
social cohesion. And although external pressure has slowed
the process of disintegration, still the Doukhobor communities have become divided and disorganized.[7]

The Mormons are another religious minority group. The
sect was established by Joseph Smith in 1823. In 1830, the
Church of Latter Day Saints, as it is called, was organized in
Fayetteville, New York, and as the sect grew in membership,
Palmyra, New York, became the Mormon center. The Mormons were driven from there and settled in Kirkland, Ohio,
and later in Independence, Missouri. In 1844, in Carthage,
Illinois, they met with further hostility and a mob killed the
"prophet" Joseph Smith. After Smith's death, Brigham
Young assumed leadership. In 1847, Young led his followers
westward to avoid the continuous oppression and into the
isolation of the Great Salt Lake Valley in Utah, which a few
years later became Salt Lake City, the concentration point
for the Mormons.[8]

4. Harry B. Hawthorn (ed.), *The Doukhobors of British Columbia*
(Vancouver: University of British Columbia and J. M. Dent and Sons
[Canada], Limited, 1955), pp. 7–22.
   5. *Ibid.*, p. 48.
   6. *Idem.*
   7. *Ibid.*, p. 49.
   8. William J. McNiff, *Heaven on Earth* (Oxford, Ohio: The Mississippi Valley Press, 1940), pp. 12–24.

Many Mormons still live in small villages that are social, economic, and educational units.[9] They are farmers who have built their own towns and established their own co-operative stores, of which every member of the community is a shareholder.[10] At one time they tended to develop their own self-sufficient political organization.[11] In 1849, they even had three respresentatives in Washington.[12] However, the Mormons became a part of the gentile world in spite of all these attempts at insularity, religiously speaking.[13] Their status in Utah became that of one of the principal denominations. In moving from sect to denomination, the Mormons have acquired respectability and lost many of the characteristics of their earlier days.

The Mennonites are another religious minority group who came to America from various countries and at various times.[14] The first known members of this group were Dutch traders and colonists who came from Holland to New York in the early days when New York was still New Netherlands.[15] However, "the first permanent Mennonite colony in America was established in Germantown, Pennsylvania, in 1683 by a group of Germans of Dutch ancestry."[16] The early Mennonites were mostly mechanics and linen weavers,[17] but the later ones were small farmers and "became tillers of the soil exclusively, avoiding the towns and cities."[18] Another group of the Mennonites moved to Iowa and there, too, became attached to the land as farmers. A great part of their

9. Leland Hargrave Greer, "Mormon Towns in the Region of the Colorado," *Anthropological Papers* (Salt Lake City: University of Utah Press), Number 32, May, 1958, p. 3.

10. McNiff, *op. cit.*, pp. 25, 42.

11. Nels Anderson, *The Desert Saints: The Mormon Frontier in Utah* (Chicago: University of Chicago Press, 1942), p. xci.

12. *Ibid.*, p. 112.

13. Edward J. Allen, *The Second United Order among the Mormons* (New York: Columbia University Press, 1936), pp. 33–34.

14. C. Henry Smith, *The Story of the Mennonites* (Newton, Kansas: Mennonite Publication Office, 1950), p. 585.

15. *Ibid.*, p. 529.

16. *Ibid.*, p. 530.

17. *Ibid.*, p. 532.

18. *Ibid.*, p. 545.

religiosity is associated with agriculture in such a way that "their entire philosophy of life tends to make them thrifty and industrious and they have come to look upon agriculture as the field in which they can make a special contribution to humanity. . . . Economic success in farming has come to represent to them the mark of character, the peculiar blessing of God upon them."[19] There are about twenty variations of Mennonitism in America as a result of their diverse European backgrounds and their isolated settlements in America.[20] However, their common religious practices, their group values such as opposition to war in any form, their sense of "otherworldliness," and their use of the German language provide strong group identification. Also, conventions and conferences bring the leaders together to discuss common problems and common experiences.[21] Some of the young men leave the farm and go to the cities, where they enter business and other occupations. In these cities there are neither associations nor organized activities to help them maintain their group identity.[22] Mennonite groups have generally been unable to maintain themselves in urban settings.

The Amish are another religious minority group. This movement was an outgrowth of the Mennonite Church led by Jacob Amman, a Swiss bishop, in the seventeenth century. The main distinction between this group and the Mennonites was one of degree of strictness in interpretation of the Scriptures. There are no specific data available concerning the migration of the Amish as a group to America; however, among the early Mennonite migrants were many Amish who also made their first permanent settlement at Germantown, Pennsylvania, in 1683. Among the Amish there are many smaller sects with a diversity of religious customs. The group is heavily concentrated in southeastern Pennsylvania.[23]

19. Melvin Gingerich, *The Mennonites in Iowa* (Iowa City: The State Historical Society of Iowa, 1939), pp. 207–208.

20. Smith, *op. cit.*, p. 743.

21. *Ibid.*, p. 783.

22. *Ibid.*, p. 780.

23. Elmer Lewis Smith, *The Amish People* (New York: Exposition Press, 1958), pp. 16–23.

The Amish people, unlike the Hasidim, are almost exclusively farmers. A study shows that in 1958, 92.8 per cent of the Amish boys followed the occupation of their fathers, of whom 92.0 per cent were farmers.[24]

Still another religious minority group are the Hutterites. The group originated in Moravia[25] in 1528 and derived its name from the leader, Jacob Hutter. The group beliefs emphasize communal philanthropy and pacifism; these beliefs are based upon the literal interpretation of the community as an extended family relationship. During the period from 1528 to 1536 a communistic system emerged in which members became equal shareholders of all goods. After many hardships and persecutions, the Hutterites migrated from Moravia to Hungary and Transylvania, then to Wallachia, and finally to the Ukraine. During the years 1874 to 1879 three colonies migrated to the Dakota Territory. The Hutterites in 1931 numbered 3,731, living in thirty-three colonies in America; in 1938, forty-eight colonies were reported.[26]

The Hutterites, too, make their living wholly from agriculture. At the beginning of their development in this country they tended toward a completely insular economy. They purchased only salt and needles outside their own community. Even today a great number of products consumed by the Hutterites are produced by the group.[27]

Outside pressures threaten the cohesion of the Hutterite community. In South Dakota they have begun to adopt "machinery and other instrumental devices from the outside world. Some colonies that moved to Manitoba have come under the influence of Winnipeg."[28] The managers have commented that "one thing leads to another. First it's one thing, then it's another thing. First [the young] go to the movies and run around the streets. That leads them to other

24. *Ibid.*, p. 150.
25. Moravia is a former province in central Czechoslovakia.
26. Lee Emerson Deets, *The Hutterites: A Study in Social Cohesion*, a doctoral dissertation for the degree of Doctor of Philosophy in the Faculty of Political Science, Columbia University, 1939, pp. 3–7.
27. *Ibid.*, pp. 9–10.
28. *Ibid.*, p. 48.

city ways."[29] Despite the various restrictions, such as those
on the use of automobiles, or visiting the city, young Hutterites become critical of the group's authority. The questioning of one central belief leads to the questioning of another. Old sustaining certainties become shaken. The validity
of the whole system that makes it necessary to dress differently becomes questioned. At this stage the young Hutterite,
"pulled between two worlds . . . [too often] becomes a person
without a culture he can call his own."[30]

There are certain features common to these groups and to
the Hasidim. All of them are religious minorities. They all
attempt to isolate themselves socially from the larger community in order to maintain their own group norms and
values. Their fear of loss of group identification, of assimilation into the larger groups around them, and of the gradual
breakdown of group values makes such isolation a seeming
necessity. Some try to maintain group identification over
their members by establishing insular economies. These
methods of control are shared by most of the groups, including the Hasidim.

However, the Hasidim differ markedly from the other
groups in several respects. Most of these groups are agricultural, but the Hasidim are not. Whereas most of these
groups live in physical isolation, away from urban industrial
areas, the Hasidim live in the middle of a metropolis.
Whereas the Hutterites produce a great number of items
for their own consumption, the Hasidim produce many
items to be sold to the outside community. The Hasidim
purchase all raw materials outside the community, some of
which they process and transform into "Hasidic goods" so
that these goods can receive the sanction of the group.
Whereas the Doukhobors must create issues with the government, provoking conflict in order to create an external
pressure to contribute to their social solidarity, the Hasidim
do not need to provoke such outside pressures, since the
"undesirable" behavior patterns of the metropolis, especially
the practices of the nonobserving Jewish community, pro-

29. *Ibid.*, p. 54.
30. *Ibid.*, p. 58.

vide sufficient external pressure to mold the group into solidarity. Whereas the Amish, who are "seeking to maintain a way of life similar to that of their martyr forefathers, must consciously seek to resist the new innovations that are continually offered through science and technology,"[31] the Hasidim use such innovations in ways in which they do not necessarily become a threat to group cohesion. The Hasidim have been able to employ technology in economic activities that not only do not require violation of religious laws but that actually complement and supplement religious observance while providing an acceptable living for individual community members and economic support for the community's religious activities.

Furthermore, there is a non-Hasidic Jewish community between the Hasidim and the non-Jewish community serving as a "social wall" to deflect the values of the outside world before they can penetrate to the Hasidim. Finally, the identification with the group is much stronger among the Hasidim than among other groups. Hasidic group cohesion is much more dependent upon internal identity than upon outside pressures forcing solidarity. As a matter of fact, the Hasidim form a cohesive community in which the cultural goals and the institutionalized norms operate jointly and effectively in shaping economic practices.

Thus the Hasidic community of Williamsburg is a subculture with its own explicit and implicit characteristics. What these characteristics are, how they have come into being, how they are currently maintained, and how the cultural goals and the institutionalized norms shape the economic practices of the community will be explored in the chapters that follow.

31. E. L. Smith, *op. cit.*, p. 37.

CHAPTER 2

# The Structure of the Jewish

# Community in Hungary

I N THE 1840'S, 1850'S, AND 1860'S, THERE WAS great religious strife between Hungarian Jews representing two
elements, the Reform and the Orthodox. The Reform
groups wanted to introduce certain changes in the religious
service that the Orthodox groups opposed—for example, the
inclusion of sermons in the synagogue services instead of the
traditional interpretations of the Scriptures, with the sermons delivered in Hungarian instead of in Yiddish. The
Reform groups also wanted to remove the reading desk from
the middle of the synagogue and give clerical vestments to
the rabbi and the cantor. An Orthodox rabbinical conven-
tion held in Mihályfalva in 1866 prohibited an observant
Jew[1] from entering synagogues where these innovations were
being introduced.

The Jews in Hungary were emancipated in 1867. A decree

1. The term "observant Jew" is used throughout this work because
it is the nearest equivalent to *obgehitener Yid,* which refers to a member of the Hasidic community who strictly observes the Jewish traditional laws.

passed by both houses of the Hungarian parliament gave the Jews civil and political rights equal to those held by other Hungarians.[2] King Franz Joseph I was very anxious that the Jews settle their differences and establish autonomous Jewish communities to direct their own religious and cultural affairs. By his decree a General Jewish Congress was called at which both the Reform and Orthodox elements would have their delegations. Out of the total of 200 delegates to the Congress, the Reform element had 132 and the Orthodox element had 88. The major difference between the two groups was the question of the authority of the *Shulhan Aruch*, the *Code of Jewish Law*. The Reform group introduced a resolution stating: "If there are a number of Jews in a community who would like to establish a congregation, they must build a synagogue, a cemetery, and a school for children like any other school for children." The Orthodox delegates introduced an amendment adding that: "They must behave in accordance with the laws prescribed in the *Shulhan Aruch*." When this amendment was defeated, the leader of the Orthodox delegates stood up and declared: "Cursed be the man who remains with these sinners." All 88 Orthodox delegates rose and left the Congress hall.[3]

The Reform resolutions were introduced in the Hungarian parliament and were adopted in 1869 as the law of the land, binding all Jews to their acceptance. The Orthodox leadership did not stand still. A delegation of the outstanding rabbis sought an audience with King Franz Joseph I and asked permission to practice the Orthodox Judaism "for which our forefathers were burned."[4] The king promised them complete religious freedom, saying, "If your liberal brethren are not interested in the Torah, I will not force them to observe it, nor will they force upon you its non-observance." Thus, in 1870 the Hungarian parliament voted that the resolutions of the General Jewish Congress were not

2. Peter Ujvári (ed.), *Magyar Zsidó Lexikon* (Budapest: Pallás Irodalmi és Nyomdai Részvénytársaságy, 1929),pp. 552 ff.

3. Leopold Greenwald, *Tausent Yahr Yidish Leben in Ungarn* (New York: Paris Press, 1945), pp. 88–91. Translated from the Yiddish.

4. *Ibid.,* p. 92.

binding upon the Orthodox Jews and that they might separate and organize themselves in every community and hire rabbis and other religious functionaries according to their own standards.

The Jewish communities were divided into three organized religious bodies: (1) the Congressional Congregations, or the Reform (or *Neolog* as they were known in Hungary), (2) the Orthodox, or the traditional, and (3) the *Status Quo,* or those communities that attached themselves neither to Reform nor to Orthodox organizations.

The Orthodox and the Reform congregations constituted corporate bodies with offices in Budapest. These national corporate organizations were run by elected officers who ruled, arbitrated and directed national religious policies, and represented the congregations to the government.

A Hungarian government report[5] shows that in 1914 the structure of the Jewish communities was as follows:

1. *The Orthodox Congregations:* The number of large congregations was 318; the number of smaller congregations that could not afford a rabbi was 1,274; the number of rabbis was 260. Besides these rabbis, there were hundreds of religious functionaries taking the role of rabbi.

2. *The Congressional (Reform) Congregations:* The number of larger congregations was 182; the number of smaller congregations was 302; and the number of rabbis was 112.

3. *The* Status Quo *Congregations:* The number of larger congregations was 60; the number of smaller congregations was 132; the number of rabbis was 40.[6]

The Jews in Hungary were not only religiously and politically divided into separate organizations, but they were also divided socially. In one camp were the observant Jews, who held that the *Shulhan Aruch,* was the major guide for their lives. In the other camp were the less observant and the non-

5. Greenwald states in his book that he had personally received this report from the Hungarian government.
6. *Ibid.,* pp. 94–95.

observant Jews, who rejected or modified the *Shulhan Aruch* and its authority.

Among the less observant and nonobservant Jews were the members of the Reform temples and most of those in the *Status Quo* synagogues. They considered the observant Jews "old-fashioned," "bigoted," and "unreasonable." They had very little in common with them in their secular lives, but their religious practices were the greatest cause of the antagonism between them. The Reform adopted modern forms of worship and held part of their religious service in the Hungarian language, with the rabbis speaking from the pulpit in Hungarian only. The Reform criticized the Orthodox for speaking Yiddish in the synagogues.

With great pain we have to observe that in many synagogues . . . not the Hungarian but the German . . . or the Jewish German is spoken. . . . But the pain we have about this is mainly applicable to our Orthodox brethren because not even in one synagogue is the Hungarian language spoken, nor do they show any sign of improvement. . . . Do our Orthodox brethern wait until they will be so instructed from higher sources, from the House of Representatives [regarding the usage of Hungarian in the synagogues]? . . . We agree that it might cause some difficulties, since many Orthodox rabbis do not speak Hungarian. But it is already high time that not only the knowledge of Hungarian be required of a rabbi, but also it should be demanded of him that he preach in Hungarian.[7]

In the camp of the observant Jews were the members of the Orthodox synagogues. The Orthodox considered the Reform "almost as non-Jews," or religiously speaking, "worse than *goyim*." Intermarriage between the two groups was not only discouraged and looked down upon, but banned. Some Orthodox families disowned a son or daughter for marrying a Reform Jew, and in extreme cases and circumstances a person who married a Reform Jew was excommunicated because he had "turned away from the ways of his fathers."

The Orthodox were composed of two groups: (1) the

7. Jakab Steinhertz, "Magyar Nyelv A Zsinagogában" ("The Hungarian Language in the Synagogues"), *Magyar Zsido Szemle*, 3:6 (1886), 340–342. Translated from the Hungarian.

*Ashkenazishe Yiden,* Ashkenazic Jews, and (2) the *Hasidishe Yiden,* Hasidic Jews.

The *Ashkenazishe Yiden* were those Orthodox Jews who observed and accepted the *Shulhan Aruch* in its entirety and conducted their lives in accord with traditional Judaism. They made a good adjustment to the Hungarian national and local societal conditions. They wore the clothing of the contemporary Hungarians and spoke Hungarian. Besides attending the religious Hebrew schools, they attended schools where academic instruction was given in Hungarian. Some of the men wore trimmed beards and some were clean-shaven. The women wore wigs but dressed in the contemporary fashion. Many of the men attended rabbinical schools, and all of them were strictly observant of the rabbinic laws, customs, ceremonies, and rituals. The majority of these Jews were located in Oberland, the upper western part of Hungary, close to the Austrian border.

The *Hasidishe Yiden* were those Orthodox Jews who observed not only the required religious customs and rituals prescribed in the *Shulhan Aruch,* but also additional rituals and ceremonies which were adopted traditionally by the Hasidic leaders and masters, who were known as *rebbes.*[8] Some of these observances were associated with deep mystical interpretations and sentiments. Other traditions and observances had allegorical and miraculous interpretations, but to the Hasidim these were real. Whatever these interpretations were and whatever their source, these rituals and ceremonies played a very important and significant part in the lives of the *Hasidishe Yiden.*

The Hasidim were less adjusted to Hungarian national and local conditions. Most of them spoke broken Hungarian and only a few had Hungarian schooling. All of them had strong, rigid, and long religious training in their special schools, in their homes, and through private instruction.

The external appearance of the Hasidic Jews differed from that of the contemporary Hungarians. They wore full beards that were never cut; such Jews were known as *Yiden mit bord und payes.* Some of them wore black overcoats, the

8. The role of the *rebbe* is described on p. 63.

*kaftan;* such Jews were known as *Yiden mit a bekecher.* Some wore round black hats, *biberhet,* and were known as *Yiden mit a biberhet.* Some wore fur hats called *shtreimel* on the Sabbath and holidays and were known as *Yiden mit a shtreimel.* Some wore special low shoes with white socks over their trousers or breeches, and these were known as *Yiden mit shich und zoken.* There were many other requirements for one to become known as, or to be considered, a *Hasidisher Yid.* The many limitations that the larger society puts upon persons of different external appearance who conform to the numerous internal controls associated with Hasidic behavior made such Jews readily identifiable as *Hasidishe Yiden,* Hasidic Jews, or Hasidim. Thus, *Hasidisher Yid* and Hasid are the same terms and will be used interchangeably throughout this study.

The majority of these Jews were located in Unterland, the lower part of Hungary, and in Marmaros, the eastern part of Hungary closer to Poland, Galicia, the Ukraine, and Rumania. In this area, and particularly in Marmaros, many Jews were occupied with the cultivation of the soil. Others were shepherds, wire workers, and so forth, "going around all week and looking for work." Some repaired earthenware and other utensils with wires, cut wood, picked fruit, cracked nuts, or cut cabbages. Some sold corn, prunes, soda water, syrup water, and sugared and colored lemonades. Some inspected *tefilin,* phylacteries, and *mezuzot,* doorpost symbols. Some made *tzitzis,* fringes for the prayer shawls; some dealt in "books containing prayers for forgiveness" and prayer books for the holidays; others, in New Year greeting cards, booklets containing the grace after meals, amulets, talismans, spice boxes, *havdalah* candles (braided candles used for a religious ritual at the conclusion of the Sabbath), books about the *lamed vov tzadikim,* the thirty-six unknown righteous men whose virtues sustain the whole world. Some "went around with a diamond and cut panes into windows" some were occupied in matchmaking, some went around the towns as beggars. Some left their homes in the fall and went into the heartland of Hungary with a writ in their possession stating that their houses had burned down, or that their only breadwinner, their horse, had died. They came home for Passover and after Passover they went out again to beg. Some went to beg for a dowry for a bride; some girls went to the cities to be domestic servants. Many just went around the streets searching for "treasures" and "bargains."[9]

There were times when the Hasidic Jews held religious viewpoints different from those of the Orthodox, or *Ashkenazishe Yiden*. Some of these differences were so pronounced that in the year 1896 it was even thought that the Hasidim would separate from the central Orthodox corporate. But a compromise was reached when a Hasidic Jew became the vice-president of the Central Orthodox Bureau.[10] Moreover, the religious conceptions and the observance of the Jewish laws in the Orthodox communities had a somewhat Hasidic flair. The rabbis were great sympathizers with the Hasidic spirit and way of life. The tendency toward secularism and assimilation, especially in the divided Jewish communities, was so strong that the Orthodox rabbis feared it might seriously affect those among the Orthodox who were unlearned in religion and those Orthodox who were learned in secular studies. Therefore, the Orthodox rabbis introduced Hasidic values and Hasidic behavior into the communities to try to divert Orthodox Jews from secular tendencies.

Why do the Orthodox rabbis associate with the Hasidim? After all, they always used to detest the Hasidim. It is because in Hungary, Orthodoxy tends little by little toward conceptions that may lead them into the arms of progress and as soon as the Orthodox man adheres to worldly knowledge, he automatically becomes Reform.

There is only a formal difference between the two [the Orthodox and the Reform], the ideology is the same. The Orthodox appear to be very smart, since many times, even against the rabbi's threat, they send their children to secular schools. Almost three-fourths of the students of the reformed rabbinical seminary come from Orthodox parents.

This is the way Orthodoxy merges into Reform. And into the

9. Greenwald, *op. cit.*
10. *Ibid.*, p. 97.

place of Orthodoxy Hasidism steps. The fight becomes very bitter because the Hasidim wave the flag of fanaticism. It is hoped that they will be the defeated ones. Those Orthodox rabbis who want to keep their dignity must have the same ideology as the Hasidim. Many Orthodox rabbis associate with the Hasidim so that they should not be labeled irreligious.[11]

The Yeshivot were the major institutions transmitting traditional Judaism and the doctrines of true Orthodoxy. There were Yeshivot that were more specifically Hasidic than others, but even in those Yeshivot known as "non-Hasidic," the Hasidic pattern and Hasidic behavior played a predominant role. While secularism and reformism were identified with "progress" in the early part of the twentieth century, Orthodoxy, with the aid of Hasidism, fought against this progress.

The Hasidim have very few Yeshivot, but they do not suffer from the lack, since the Orthodox Yeshivot serve their purpose. They have a great influence upon them. They form islands that fight against the waves of the sea and so do the Yeshivot. They both associate to paralyze progress. . . .

The Yeshivah and secular knowledge do not go hand in hand, and while we cannot doubt the victory of progress, we think in joy that this victory will shed some light around itself. In this light, the Yeshivah will notice how isolated it is and how impossible is its situation. Also the students of the Yeshivot will realize how much they have wandered in the darkness. The future of this may be too far off but its arrival is certain.[12]

This is a brief account of the background of the Hasidim in Hungary. In spite of the strong secular movements and in spite of the great attraction of "progress," the Hasidim continued to lead a traditional way of religious life until the last moment of their dislocation and evacuation into the concentration camps. When the Hasidim arrived in the United States after World War II, they found that "progress"

11. Jakab Zempleni, "A jesibak állapota hazánkban" ("The Conditions of the Yeshivot in Our Land"), *Magyar Zsido Szemle*, 3:6 (June, 1886), 415–419. Translated from the Hungarian.

12. *Ibid.*,pp. 415–419.

held sway, with a marked tendency toward secularism and assimilation. Here the Hasidim resumed their battle to re-establish, or at least to establish for themselves, a place in a Jewish community where they could live a "Hasidic way of life." Here they found a Jewish community that was not as clearly divided as in Hungary, but with similar discrepancies in basic ideology. Here in this community, where the Hasidic Jew enjoyed practically unlimited freedom, where his community internalization and voluntary isolation were not based on external pressures, he established himself and re-established the Hasidic way of life.

CHAPTER 3

# The Structure of the Jewish

# Community in the United States

HERE ARE MANY SIMILARITIES in the development of the Jewish religious organizations and institutions in Hungary and in the United States. In fact, some of the outstanding advocates of the Reform movement in America have come from Hungary.[1] The first sign of Reform Judaism in the United States appeared in Charleston, South Carolina, in 1824; this, however, did not materialize to any substantial degree.[2] A few years later a group of forty-seven leaders gathered once again and advocated Reform innovations. They wanted "a shorter, more decorous service. They requested that some prayers be read in English as well as in Hebrew.

1. Great reformers such as David Einhorn (1809–1879) and Alexander Kohut (1843–1894) came from Hungary. In no way should that be considered an indication of some interdependence between the development of Reform Judaism in Hungary and in the United States.
2. Moshe Davis, "Jewish Religious Life and Institutions in America," *The Jews, Their History, Culture, and Religion,* Louis Finkelstein (ed.), (Philadelphia: The Jewish Publication Society of America), pp. 354–443.

. . ." Although this group met with opposition, they organized the Reformed Society of Israelites. Thus:

> In 1840, American Jewry entered a new stage of its development. The dynamism of American life had released powerful forces. America and its Jews were on the move. Now centrifugal forces gained sway. The older methods of fines and bans lost their punitive powers. Disaffection and spiritual corrosion could not be met with declarations and resolutions. Intermarriage, Jewish ignorance, and above all, the paralyzing indifference to the destiny of Judaism thoroughly upset Jewish religious institional life. In the Colonial period, a Jew was zealously controlled from birth to death by the synagogue. Now a Jew could live or die as a Jew without regard to that control.[3]

The more conservative element of Reform Judaism, known as the Historical School, gained support and strength with the immigration of the Russian-Polish Jews in the 1870's. In 1886 this group founded a rabbinical institution called The Jewish Theological Seminary of America, which became the core of another American-Jewish movement, Conservative Judaism. In 1913 the United Synagogue of America was established to encompass all those synagogues affiliated with the Seminary.

With the immigration of Jews from Eastern Europe, Orthodox Judaism gained numbers and strength. Smaller Orthodox congregations were established, and the members adhered in their personal lives as well as in their religious services to the more traditional beliefs and concepts of Judaism. They were in opposition to all innovations the reformers tried to institute. There were even some attempts made in 1879 to organize the Orthodox congregations into a unified central body, such as The Union of American-Hebrew Congregations (1873) of Reform Judaism and The United Synagogue of America (1913) of Conservative Judaism. Representatives of twenty-six congregations met in 1879 to found the Board of Delegates of Orthodox Hebrew Congregations. This attempt failed when the delegates were unable to establish an Orthodox chief rabbinate. In 1902, however, the East European Orthodox rabbis organized into

3. *Ibid.*

the Union of Orthodox Rabbis, which was considered the authoritative body on religious questions of Orthodoxy. Later, in 1923, the English-speaking rabbis organized themselves into the Rabbinical Council of America. There are still other Orthodox rabbinical organizations and congregational organizations. Thus, the Orthodox groups do not form in any way one central authoritative body encompassing the Orthodox groups in America.

Although there are similarities in the historical development of the Jewish religious communities of the United States and Hungary, the structure of the American-Jewish organization is different. The Orthodox Jews in Europe belonged to a central organization having authority over the conduct of its constituents. The Reform in Hungary, unlike the Reform and Conservative groups in America, also had some authority over its membership in matters of religious behavior. Membership in these organizations constituted a definite expression of religious conviction and of religious behavior. An Orthodox Jew in Hungary was "orthodox" in the fullest meaning of the word. In the United States, there are varying degrees of "orthodoxy."[4] In some synagogues the only requirement for membership is to be of the Jewish faith. There is another distinction between the religious organizations of Hungary and those of the United States, and that is that in Hungary the demarcation between the Orthodox and the non-Orthodox was very sharp. There was little or no social intercourse between the Reform and the Orthodox. Here in the United States, the demarcation between the Orthodox and the non-Orthodox groups is very faint. The various religious groups are united for charity and other welfare benefits, whereas in Hungary they were completely separated even in these activities.

In order to see the Hasidic group in its proper perspective in the religious structure of the United States, the groups may be classified in terms of *traditional religious behavior,* or the observance of the traditional Jewish law, into the following categories: (1) Reform Judaism, (2) Conservative

4. See pp. 24–26.

Judaism, and (3) Orthodox Judaism with its four subcategories.

1. *Reform Judaism* is that phase of Jewish life in America
that is highly secularized and conducive to assimilation. It
is a religious expression trying not only to conform to the
wishes of its own members of secular background but also
to be acceptable to non-Jews, especially to the "majority"
religious group, the white Protestants. Religious expressions
revolve around the temple activities. Worship stresses intel-
lectuality and a decorous service. Within the Reform organizations there are congregations that are highly sophisticated
and are "very liberal" and there are some congregations that
are "more conservative." The extent of observance of traditional religious practices in these congregations depends
upon the historical development of the community and the
religious background of the membership.

2. *Conservative Judaism* is that branch of Judaism that
ideologically claims "the maintenance of Jewish tradition . . .
to assert and establish loyalty to the Torah . . . to further
the observance of the Sabbath and the dietary laws . . . to
maintain the traditional character of the liturgy . . . to foster
Jewish religious life in the home, as expressed in traditional
observances. . . ."[5] In practice, it has introduced many
changes. It has given religious status to women by allowing
them to sit with men in the synagogue and by giving them
the right to equal religious education. The services are "less
stringent with regard to 'religious attitude.' " It is "highly
commercial," with its men's and ladies' clubs. Friday evening
services are emphasized and the content includes a great
deal of English.[6] The personal religious behavior of its members depends entirely on the individual's religious values
and etiquette.

3. *Orthodox Judaism* is that branch of Judaism adhering
to a greater extent to the traditional religious practices. Or-

5. *United Synagogue of America,* Fourth Annual Report, (New York,
1917), pp. 9–10, quoted by Davis.
6. Marshall Sklare, "Aspects of Religious Worship in the Contemporary Conservative Synagogue," in Marshall Sklare (ed.), *The Jews.*
(Glencoe: The Free Press, Inc., 1958), pp. 357–376.

thodox Judaism may be classified into four subcategories
with regard to religious behavior:

*(a) Members in Orthodox synagogues* include those Orthodox Jews who would be classified as Conservative or Reform except that they hold membership and are associated
with a synagogue that calls itself Orthodox. These people
are classified by their associates and by those who belong to
Reform and Conservative synagogues as "Orthodox Jews."

*(b) Those in accord with Orthodox ideology* include those
Orthodox Jews who are members of an Orthodox synagogue
and accept Orthodox ideology, principles, and responsibilities in observing the Jewish traditional laws. They excuse
their failure to fulfill religious requirements by saying that
they "cannot help themselves," since they live in a country
where religious observances and strict religious practices are
difficult. To these Jews, the Reform movement is "already
too far gone," and the Conservative is "on the road toward
going too far." They identify themselves as, and are identified by others as, Orthodox Jews.

*(c)* Shomrei Torah U'mitzvot, *Observers of the Torah and
Commandments,* include those Orthodox Jews who adhere
in principle and in practice to the prescribed laws of the
*Shulhan Aruch.* This group may or may not be externally
identified as Jews. They do not necessarily wear beards or
side-locks by which they would be recognized as Orthodox
Jews. Their affiliation with religious bodies is part of their
way of life. They are almost exclusively associated with Jews
of similar background and convictions, but there is no limita-
tion to the extent of association with others in business
circles.

*(d)* Obgehitene Yiden, *"Guardian Jews,"* include those
so-called ultra-Orthodox Jews who not only observe the
*Shulhan Aruch* in the most minute detail but are most meticulous and zealous in their observance. They perform all
the prescribed commandments and precepts with the greatest
care. These people are overtly identifiable as Jews. They
wear beards and/or special traditional clothing for the exclusive purpose of being externally identified as Jewish:

beards so that the "image of God should be upon their faces," traditional garments so that they "may refrain from any possible sin." Their social life is exclusively concentrated on the one fact of being a Jew.

This category is made up of two types: (1) the *heimisher Yid* and (2) the *Hasidisher Yid*. The *heimisher Yid* (literally, "homey" or "indigenous" Jew) is a person who came originally from Europe and who has observed the *Shulhan Aruch* meticulously all his life. Usually, he comes from a family line of strictly observant Jews. The family or the family name is usually well known in this circle. Religiosity is not an innovation to him. He is not a person who has only recently been carried away by the religious stream of the neighborhood. He is a person who has had formal religious training in a well-known "religious" Yeshivah; thus, he is familiar with the laws concerning religious observance. He conforms to all the religious community norms as part of his life and participates in almost all of the religious activities of the community.

The *Hasidisher Yid*, the Hasidic Jew (literally, "pious" Jew), although having all the characteristics of the *heimisher Yid*, is more extroverted in his practices. He carries certain rituals to extremes in his zealousness. Besides his zealous observance of the *Shulhan Aruch*, he also practices the traditional rituals of his *rebbe*, with whom he has a close relationship. He visits his *rebbe* frequently and turns to him for guidance in all his spiritual and many of his nonspiritual activities.

The *obgehitene Yiden* live in the Lower East Side of Manhattan and in Williamsburg, Brooklyn (and recently in other parts of New York City). The old generation of the ultra-Orthodox Jews of the Lower East Side in New York did not have a strong hold on their children. As the children grew up and moved away from the community, they departed from the religious pattern of their parents. However, "in Williamsburg in Brooklyn, in a small area containing about 20,000 people, three-quarters of them Jews, an Orthodox revival took place."[7] During World War II, a large proportion of refugees from Austria, Hungary, Czechoslovakia, and Rumania, who were able to survive the Hitler atrocities, came and settled in this area. After the war, as the more ultra-Orthodox and Hasidic element arrived, the "native" Jews moved out and gave room to the new influx. "Soon, the 'natives' of Williamsburg, who had prided themselves on their Orthodoxy and considered themselves the most Orthodox element in American life, found themselves outflanked by even more Orthodox elements from Europe."[8] They felt uncomfortable, since their Jewish practices in comparison to the observances of the Hasidim amounted to very little. One informant, an observant Jew who does not observe religion according to Hasidic standards, was at the time of the interview still living in Williamsburg and was seriously thinking of leaving the community because he had been frequently called a *goy*, a non-Jew, in the neighborhood. He relates that:

One Saturday evening, for instance, I just came out of my synagogue after the evening services were over. As I walked down the stairs I met two Hasidic children. One said to the other, "Look at that Jew. He has already completed the evening service when our *rebbe* did not even start with the afternoon service." To this the other Hasidic child replied, "Oh, what do you want from him, he is surely a *goy*." Well, I do not wish to live in a community where I, an observant Jew, am considered a *goy*.[9]

Another informant, a woman who lived in Williamsburg for twenty years, said that she was called a *goyeh*, a non-

7. Nathan Glazer, *American Judaism* (Chicago: University of Chicago Press, 1957), pp. 143 ff. (Some of Glazer's information pertaining to the Williamsburg area is based upon George Kranzler, "The Jewish Community of Williamsburg, Brooklyn," an unpublished doctoral dissertation [1954] in the library of Columbia University.)

8. *Ibid.*

9. From an interview with ZLHU, 1957. This sign is the code number and date of the particular interview. Henceforth, these signs will indicate the code number and date of recorded interviews and case studies in the author's possession.

Jewish woman, because she does not wear a wig. She relates the story:

I was sweeping in front of my house in which I had lived for twenty years and two Hasidic children were playing and were in my way. I told the children in Yiddish to move away from this sidewalk because they were in my way. They looked at me and one said to the other, "She doesn't wear a wig, she must be a *goyeh*," and they remained playing. . . .[10]

After the war, some of the well-known Hasidic *rebbes* from Hungary and the area around Carpathian Mountains also came and settled in Williamsburg. The *rebbes* and the already existing ultra-Orthodox religious Jewish community of Williamsburg attracted more and more of the newcomers, and they organized themselves into a functioning, cohesive body. They re-established themselves as a community organization with most of the familiar associations and institutions and began to transplant the Hasidic culture of the old *shtetl*, village, to Williamsburg, in the midst of the New York metropolis. The transplantation of this culture is described in the following pages.

10. From an interview, LPE, 1957.

# CHAPTER 4

# The Transplantation

# of Hasidic Culture

I N 1943, THE JEWS WERE EVACUATED from the various Jewish communities in Hungary into German concentration camps. In the concentration camps they continued to adhere to traditional practices to the extent possible under the circumstances. Many suffered starvation and extreme maltreatment, and many died in the camps. When the war ended, some of the religious leaders went from one concentration camp to another to reorganize the group and to encourage their continued loyalty to the "tradition of their fathers." The younger element among the survivors of Nazi atrocities sought to migrate to the United States. Upon their arrival in the United States they settled in Williamsburg, which was already the center of the more religious Hungarian Jews in America.[1]

1. Williamsburg began to develop as an ultrareligious community of Hungarian Jews with the establishment of the Yeshivah Torah Vodaath in the 1920's. The gradual migration of religious Jews into Williamsburg paved the way for the permanent settlement of the Hasidim.

Most of the adult members of the community were born in Hungary and were married after their liberation from the concentration camps. This Hasidic community is now a fast-growing body, and as of 1959 its population was estimated at between ten and twelve thousand.[2] Birth control is strictly prohibited, and if there are couples who have a lapse of time between the births of their children greater than two years, they are exposed to negative sanctions in the community through gossip and insults. There are some families who already have fifteen children, and the average number is estimated at six children per completed family.[3]

The adults were educated in Hungary and speak both Hungarian and Yiddish. Hebrew is used only in prayers and studies. Some speak English, but it is not an essential factor in their everyday interaction. The males speak mostly Yiddish, while the females, particularly in gossip, use Hungarian. The children generally speak Yiddish, but English is tolerated and Hungarian is considered "cute."

Citizenship is highly prized and everyone makes positive attempts to acquire it. All informants declared their intention to become citizens of the United States. They are not anxious to be identified as Hungarians, but only as "Hungarian Jews."[4] Consequently, the group is identified by many other Jews as the *Ungarishe Yiden*.

The community is socially isolated from the metropolis. Males do not associate on a social level with anyone except other group members. If they come in contact with others,

2. Since the community has grown very rapidly, proper estimates are difficult to obtain from the census data. This estimate is based on: (1) reports from the leaders, (2) membership affiliation with various religious organizations multiplied by the average number of families, (3) religious school affiliation. Care was taken, however, to avoid duplication.

3. This estimate is based on: (1) reports from the leaders, (2) a poll taken among the children, as they came out of Hebrew school, who were asked, "How many sisters and brothers do you have?" The lowest response was four, and the highest thirteen.

4. "Hungarian Jewishness" as it is used among the group distinguishes them from non-Hungarian Jews whose patterns of customs and ceremonies based upon the same religious laws are observed with less zeal.

it is only in business associations in which no intimacy is involved. The women are even more isolated than the men, since they do not have business associates, and most of them do not work outside the community. If on rare occasions they go outside the community to shop, the ensuing relationships do not materialize into informal social intimacy. The children are constantly kept within the community and have no opportunity to associate with other children, even those who live in the neighborhood.

All members are completely sex-segregated. There are no associations whatever in which males and females participate equally. Children as young as three years of age already are segregated from the opposite sex, and even brothers and sisters are discouraged from establishing intimate social contact.

The residence of the Hasidic group is limited to a few neighborhoods, some of which are changing in ethnic composition. (See map, inside cover.) The "old" Jewish element moves out of the neighborhood, and the Puerto Ricans move in. Their existence is completely ignored. The Hasidic children know that, whatever they see on the streets, the conduct of the Puerto Ricans is not for them to follow or to imitate.

The group does not participate in any public recreation. The men gather in the houses of prayer for prayer, learning, gossip, and "politicking." The women organize themselves into ladies' auxiliaries to support their religious schools and other charitable activities. They also meet in stores and on the streets for casual talk and gossip. The children do not have any kind of facilities for even the basic needs of physical exercise. Children are brought to the religious schools in the morning and stay there until the evening, and even in the schools, games and play that could be utilized for physical exercise are prohibited. The members of the group are forbidden to attend movies and theaters or publicly sponsored activities like lectures or other educational programs, nor do they sponsor any activities of their own for their artistic expression or entertainment.

The group maintains its own culture and its own cultural values. The members are almost uniform in the way they express their thoughts and the way in which they interpret the world around them. Although the Hasidim are part of the larger Jewish community of this country, their habits are far removed from it. Their attitudes and behavior show strong conformity. This conformity is constantly enforced and reinforced by the strong group control that is prevalent in almost all their activities.

The members of the group are not allowed to have television sets in their homes. Even radio is taboo, since "it brings into the house those sounds and voices which are not conducive to the worship of God." Reading the Yiddish newspapers is strongly objected to in the community because "the editors are unsympathetic towards the Hasidic Jews and spread lies about them," and because "the Yiddish papers are published on the Sabbath, too, and what can a religious Jew expect from desecrators of the holy Sabbath?"[5] The English papers are read only casually and not with any appreciable frequency by those who can read English and happen to come in contact with such papers. No English literature is read, since it may contain heresy or take away valuable time that could be spent on "holy literature." Thus, all news that comes into the Hasidic community is that which has been sifted and interpreted by those who have read it or heard it second- or third-hand.

The major sources of communication are the Hasidic newspapers. The group maintains two weekly newspapers, *Der Yid* (The Jew), which calls itself the organ for religious Judaism in America, and *Die Yiddishe Woch* (Religious Weekly), which calls itself an organ for nonpartisan religious Judaism in America. The difference between the editorial policies of these two weekly newspapers is that while *Die Yiddishe Woch* recognizes the existence and the important function of Israel in the lives of every contemporary Jew, *Der Yid* opposes every innovation in Israel and considers the state sinful and irreligious. (NOTE: Since the writing of the manuscript *Yiddishe Woch* has ceased publication.)

In order that a society may survive, it must develop values and attitudes toward these values. Such values and attitudes

5. From the files of NFL 2, 1957.

make up the norms of that society. These norms and values characterize a given society and collectively distinguish it from any other. The practice of these norms creates the system of sentiments through which the society maintains itself. As has been stated by A. R. Radcliffe-Brown, ". . . a society depends for its existence on the presence in the minds of its members of a certain system of sentiments by which the conduct of the individual is regulated in conformity with the needs of the society."[6]

This is so while the group lives in its old established habitat where its members have learned to adjust to the environment and thus develop a culture of their own. When a group migrates from one place to another as individuals, especially to a place where the customary norms cannot be practiced, the old cultural values tend to break down. If in that society there are no values and sentiments similar to the norms and values of the migrants, and if the immigrants still continue to practice their established norms and display the values and attitudes of the old society through their behavior, this sets the stage for a culture conflict.

W. I. Thomas[7] pointed out that when an immigrant moves to a new place—to America—he is expected to change his values and attitudes. He strives to become Americanized and to take upon himself all the American customs until "the green has worn off," he is *ausgegrunt*. In this new place, in this new society, the immigrant loses both his status and his self-confidence, because he has had to leave behind the self-consciousness of status of his group. Thus, he loses self-respect and may meet with contempt and humiliation.[8]

W. I. Thomas further points out that in the old country the immigrant had been controlled by the community and that there had been little or no chance for the individual to

6. A. R. Radcliffe-Brown, *The Andaman Islanders* (Glencoe: The Free Press, Inc.), pp. 233–234.

7. See Edmund H. Volkart, *Social Behavior and Personality, Contributions of W. I. Thomas to Theory and Social Research* (New York: Social Science Research Council, 1951), pp. 59 and 259.

8. Robert E. Park and Herbert A. Miller, *Old World Traits Transplanted* (New York: Harper & Brothers), pp. 44 ff.

deviate from established norms. In a new country, however, he meets the challenges and influences of a new culture and he must respond by isolating himself with others who share his background and values or by reorganizing his habits and his total life orientation.

Bressler, utilizing W. I. Thomas' materials, has suggested that the typical Jewish immigrant coming to the United States was not controlled by his group and no longer had the advice of his religious leaders in social and religious matters. He was thus in need of sanctions for his behavior. He sought a substitute for the religious leaders and found it in the editor of the Yiddish newspaper. He wrote to the editor asking advice about his activities. The editor took on the same role for this individual that the religious leader had had in the old country.[9]

Other groups who came to the New World generally attempted to make a better social adjustment to the larger society. The immigrants brought with them Old World values and attitudes that were given up sometimes slowly, sometimes rapidly as individuals were integrated into the new society. The way individuals achieved adjustment to this new culture depended, to a greater or lesser extent, upon personal abilities and circumstances. "Some of the immigrants and their children were able to make the adjustment without major difficulties, but many others exhibited several forms of demoralization."[10] On the part of the individual there was a constant motivation to become accepted by and identified with the members of the larger group among whom he had settled. Thus, the goal of successful social adjustment was to become identified with assimilation into the larger society of which all the subgroups were fractional parts.

This was not so with the Hasidim. The members of this

9. Marvin Bressler, "Jewish Behavior Patterns as Exemplified in W. I. Thomas' Unfinished Study of the Bintl Brief," unpublished doctoral dissertation (1952) in the library of University of Pennsylvania.

10. George E. Simpson and J. Milton Yinger, *Racial and Cultural Minorities* (New York: Harper & Brothers, 1958), pp. 210–211, in their discussion of W. I. Thomas and Florina Znaniecki's *The Polish Peasant in Europe and America* (New York: Alfred A. Knopf, Inc., 1927).

group who came to the United States tried to transplant the entire Hasidic culture into the new setting. They did not strive to become identified with the earlier immigrants and thus to achieve assimilation. On the contrary, they transplanted most of their cultural values and tended to adhere to old traditions to an even greater extent than they had in Europe. They considered *Americanization* taboo[11] and did not try to become Americans like those Jews who had preceded them. The focus of attention in their adjustment processes was the traditional Hasidic group norms. The ideal was not to throw off these Hasidic norms, but to help in transplanting Hasidic culture by retaining and further cultivating it. To become *ausgegrunt,* to acculturate, was an idea they fully rejected. They were not concerned about the distinctive Hasidic dress they wore, because to them this was not the sign of being a "greenhorn." They considered the garments they wore "Hasidic garments," essential for group identification but not identification as "Europeans," which could have had the effect of reducing their status in the community into which they had immigrated.

Within the Hasidic community the members did not lose their status because of their habits, customs, traditions, language, dress, social ritual, sentimental ideals, interests, and other values. All of these expressed self- and group-consciousness giving them status and recognition in the group. These values, from which they gained group consciousness, were the most essential requisites for a Hasidic Jew.

For other immigrants the change in group control caused great difficulties in the New World. At home the immigrant was almost completely controlled by the community. In America this lifelong control was relaxed.[12] This was not so with the Hasidim, because their lives remained under the group control of the Hasidic community. The group recreated the situations in which the old community control remained appropriate and into which the individual Hasidic

11. Yet the group highly valued American citizenship because in America they enjoyed religious freedom unprecedented in Hasidic history.

12. Park and Miller, *op. cit.,* p. 61.

Jew could automatically fall without any difficulty. The Hasidim did not meet with any crises to which they failed to make personal and social adjustments. Consequently, their lives became a continuation of the old patterns rather than an adjustment and readjustment to the new. There was practically no necessity for the Hasidim to reorganize their lives and to adopt new habits and standards. It was not necessary to repudiate old habits and to establish new restraints because their behavior was almost a replica of the old pattern to which they had already made gradual adjustments throughout the ages and which was transmitted to the Hasidim from generation to generation under more difficult circumstances than those encountered in America.

CHAPTER 5

# The Threat of Assimilation

BEFORE THE HASIDIM CAME to the United States, they
visualized America as a *goldene medinah* (golden land)
—full of plenty and economic security—as a *frei land*
(free country), in the sense of "liberty," and also in the sense
of "unconfined, uncontrolled, and loose."

America meant liberty because the Americans were the
liberators of Jews from the various German concentration
camps in which many of the Hasidim had been confined and
tortured during the Nazi regime. America, on the other
hand, stood for unconfined, uncontrolled, and loose behavior.
This view was a carryover from the traditional religious Jews
in Hungary who held that "in America even the water is not
kosher,[1] and even the air can defile a religious man."[2]

When the Hasidim arrived in America, they found them-

1. Water is a neutral element, and the criterion of kosher or
nonkosher is not applicable to its use in the requirements of the
dietary laws.
2. From the files of LPS, 1957–58.

37

selves in a new world, which did not fully coincide with their preconceived ideas. Only the concept of *frei* in its second meaning, "unconfined, uncontrolled, and loose," was confirmed as they viewed a culture that seemed to them a very strange way of life. However, since they did not come into contact with other than Jews,[3] the general cultural patterns were not clearly understood.

Those Jews with whom the Hasidim came in contact were religious Jews who, to a certain extent, observed the prescribed religious laws. In the eyes of the Hasidim, however, they were "Americans" and many of them were regarded as *echteh Americans* (real Americans) who had strayed far from the traditional patterns of religious observance. The behavior of the American Jews, even of those Jews who observed traditional Judaism, was shocking to the Hasidim, and those Jews who did not observe were to be pitied because they were Jews only by birth. Even though their emotions and hearts were Jewish, in practice they were far removed from *Yiddishkeit*.

The Hasidic Jew was made aware of the crucial circumstances surrounding religious observance in America. The members were warned that they should "not fall into the trap" of the great process of Americanization. They could not allow even the smallest deviation from the tradition of their fathers, because this could mean the beginning of the extinction of the "entire Jewish existence."[4] To them there was no other Jewish existence except that of their own convictions and their own religious practices for which their parents and forefathers sacrificed their lives and for which they themselves had suffered during the Nazi atrocities.

The leadership tried to point out to the Hasidim all the evil practices existing in America so that they should not follow in these paths. The leadership was also careful to point out that the great negligence and irreligious practices among Jews in America were not only violations of Hasidic prac-

3. Few associations were with non-Jews and these associations had little or no significance in the general attitude of the Hasidim.

4. "Jewish existence" is used synonymously with the religious existence of the Jew.

tices and norms (required only of the more zealous) but also of the basic religious laws (obligatory for all members of the Jewish faith). The Hasidic leadership recognized that the greatest enemy of Hasidism is *change*. If the members should engage in even the most minute secular behavior, not necessarily irreligious, this would be a deviation from the norms of the group and might lead to more extensive deviant behavior endangering group cohesion. The leadership argued that if they were able to remain observant while in concentration camps, it should be much easier to remain religious under normal circumstances in America, where they enjoyed abundance and plenty. The Hasidim were urged not to believe, if a non-Hasidic person were called a "rabbi" or a "*rav*,"[5] that his decisions on religious matters could be *ipso facto* competent. The concept of a *rav* among the Hasidim (that is, of the ideal type of religious authority) is quite different from the concept of the rabbi prevalent in America. The Hasidim did not consider the rabbis' decisions competent. Even the status of an American *rav,* who is a higher religious authority, was questionable. Here in America people were indiscriminate with the various honorific titles attached to religious functionaries. Here the titles of "great," "wise," "scholar," and "*gaon*"[6] were given to those who were not worthy of such titles. The Hasidim were warned not to be deceived by these titles because they were not indicative of what a Hasidic Jew must think of a person who is a real *gaon* or really great. One whose family does not follow "the way of God," one who shaves off his beard, or who sends his children to college, or whose wife does not cut off her hair, or whose wife dresses according to the general norms of the

5. There is a distinction between "rabbi" and "*rav*" for the Hasidim. Rabbi indicates an American religious professional practitioner and a *rav* is one who is qualified to determine what is permitted and what is prohibited according to Jewish law and has received the "traditional ordination" according to religious laws. Rabbis, according to the Hasidim do not have this qualification.

6. "*Gaon*" is used in contemporary Jewish societies to indicate a well-known Talmudical scholar. It was used in earlier ages as a specific title for the Jewish authoritative scholar on all social and religious matters.

larger society, or who practices birth control, or who does not meet with other Hasidic qualifications cannot be called *gaon* or great.

In the Hasidic community the requisite for being called a "scholar" is not that one knows all about religious matters and have great familiarity with the law pertaining to every phase of behavior, but personal belief in and practice of the laws of "purity and holiness." One cannot be considered a scholar if he makes careless decisions about religious practices or if he has been exposed to higher secular education or has associated with people who do not encourage religious observance. One can be considered a scholar only if his total existence is governed by religious laws and religious practices and if, in addition to his knowledge, he is also a deeply observant person.

The Hasidim were shocked as they observed the synagogues in this country. They could not conceive that synagogues, which are the religious sanctuaries of the Jews and religious symbols, should not meet the traditional and necessary requisites. They were shocked not only by those synagogues where men and women sit together and share the pews but also by those synagogues where the sexes are separated by walls, but walls that were considered inappropriate because they were too low and the men could see into the women's section. The Hasidim thought it bad enough that the rabbi did not wear the traditional Jewish garment as all Hasidic Jews must, but what was worse was that he even put on a robe, which made him look like a gentile priest. The Hasidim pointed out that the religious services were attended mostly by old men who had nothing else to do. Children did not come to the synagogue for religious services, and when they did come, they came only for dancing and singing.

It was incredible to the Hasidim that a synagogue built for the purposes of prayer and worship, which according to them should serve as a sanctuary for the expression of deep religious convictions, should be used as a dance hall and a place for playing cards. It was equally inconceivable that a synagogue, of all places, should house boys and girls playing together and "dancing forbidden dances." The Hasidim disapproved of the American synagogues not only because of their improper activities, but also because they did not meet all the traditional Hasidic requirements. The synagogues in America were decorated with stars; the rabbis and cantors wore robes; there was little or no separation of the sexes. Into such synagogues, according to the Hasidim, no true believer would enter.

The Hasidim said that this process of assimilation could be seen when even the *shohet*, the ritual slaughterer whose livelihood was to be religious and a "God-fearing" man, wanted to imitate the *goy*.[7] He of all people, who did not have to associate with non-Jews in his occupation (since all Jewish slaughtering is performed only for Jews), should "look like a Jew," for this was part of his "calling."

The American-Jewish wedding ceremony appeared to the Hasidim laughable, and sheer imitation of that of the non-Jews. According to Hasidic custom, a wedding ceremony was a holy day, a day of religion and reconciliation with one's God. But here, in this country, the Hasidim noticed the great tendency to imitate the non-Jews. Jewish weddings had bridal processions. The groom was led in by his own parents; the rabbi also participated in the bridal procession; ushers attended the ceremony; the rabbi made a speech during the ceremony; pictures were taken—many times, movies. All these appeared to the Hasidim as mockeries and imitation of the *goyim* to which they vehemently objected.

It was shocking to the Hasidim to notice various customs of Jews that they considered to be almost idol worship. It was most disturbing to observe that "birthday parties" were held. This, too, they considered nothing but an idolatrous custom.

They saw with great disgust that even the more religious

7. In this context, *goyim* means "non-Jews." It will be seen later that this term is also applied to Jews who are not observant. Non-Jews are many times referred to as *goyishe goyim* (non-Jewish non-Jews), and Jews who are not observant are referred to as *Yiddishe goyim*.

in America may make a *bat mitzvah*[8] for a girl who becomes
twelve- or thirteen-years old. They could not conceive of
such a formal rite being conducted for a girl, whose initation
into Judaism is not required by traditional law. A male
child, at the age of twelve and one day, becomes *bar mitzvah*,
"son of the commandment" and is obligated from that day
on to observe all the prescribed laws, whereas a female child
does not become *bat mitzvah*, "daughter of the commandment," since she is not obligated to perform "positive commandments." She is obligated only to refrain from "negative
commandments," which if broken would cause her to be considered *bat onshin*, "punishable daughter."

It was very disturbing to the Hasidim that traditional
laws, customs, and rituals were being violated in America
and that the violators were not even reprimanded for their
violations. This the Hasidim interpreted to mean that the
violations had been sanctioned by the religious authorities.
If the Jews violated religious laws, they argued, and if they
were constantly reminded of this, they might return to the
"accepted path" through constant moralization. But if the
irreligious behavior was not formally and authoritatively
reproved and censured, this was a sign of severe "religious
disorganization of traditional Judaism."

One of the most shocking experiences the Hasidim had to
face in the New World had to do with their concern about
modesty and chastity. They could not reconcile themselves
to the idea that Jewish women were allowed to wear dresses
that were not "modest" and that "revealed their flesh" above
the line of appropriateness and that their legs were uncovered. They could not reconcile themselves to the idea
that religious Jews let their daughters wear short socks and
that many women did not wear wigs after marriage.

"Chastity" in America among Jewish women had been
broken down to such an extent that men and women sat
together. Modesty ceased to exist to such an extent that men
even looked at women regardless of their marital status and,

8. A *rite de passage* for female children who reach the age of
twelve or thirteen, as adopted by Conservative and Reform congregations. It is somewhat similar to the *bar mitzvah* for male children.

"God forbid," one might even touch another. Men and women were part of mixed crowds on the beaches. Such commonly accepted behavior the Hasidim considered "adultery."

The unmarried Hasidic woman is not distinguishable from members of the larger community as are Hasidic men with their beards, side-locks, and distinctive clothing and the married Hasidic women, who wear wigs. The only requirement of outward appearance that the unmarried Hasidic woman must meet (that her clothing be "modest"—that is, that dresses be high-necked and long-sleeved, and that hose be worn) is sufficiently flexible so that she may dress in current American fashion. For this reason, control over unmarried women has presented a greater problem than control over Hasidic young men. The Hasidic Jew believes that girls must be taught Hasidic modesty, chastity, and respect and that they must marry early in life so as to become God-fearing women and not be corrupted by the attractions of American culture.

The Hasidic Jew has been told by his leaders that he should see to it that all his children marry early in life while they are still "holy and pure." The sons do not have to earn a living right after marriage, but rather, their first duty is to become pious and religious according to Hasidic standards. A Hasidic Jew is told that he should support his children after their marriage so that they may start a pious life early in the marital state.

The problem of courtship is a difficult one. It has remained inconceivable to the Hasidim that marriage can be reached through American courtship patterns. How can a marriage become a symbol of "Jewish purity," they argue, if its establishment is based upon sin? They consider the courtship patterns of America a series of sins each more intensive than the preceding one in the severity of its religious violation. Among a group where the separation of the sexes is one of the most important community norms, every move toward marriage, if it followed the American pattern of courtship, would lead to "impurity" and "dissolution." In the minds of the Hasidim, who have become conditioned in their behavior and thinking to a separation of the sexes,

American customs are a violation of their most sacred values.

In fact, American courtship patterns involve a gradual intensification in the severity of religious violations step by step, with one sin inevitably leading to another. How is it possible for a young Hasidic man to (1) commit the sin of walking with a girl on the streets, (2) to repeat this sin by continuing to take a girl out, (3) to take her to a movie where obscenity is heard and seen in symbolic figures, or (4) to attend a theater where obscenity is heard and seen in live presentations? These are "dark places," which may lead to even greater sins. Men and women may even (5) touch each other and (6) meet in private. Even if they do not enter into a very intimate relationship, (7) the "thought of sin" in itself is dangerous, since it may lead to (8) physical impurity.

If only the children of nonobservant Jews engaged in this "modern courtship pattern," it would not be of great concern to the Hasidim, since the Hasidim are socially isolated both from the non-Jewish and from the nonreligious Jewish communities and consequently are not afraid that the practices of the latter will be imitated by their own children. The problem presented itself when the Hasidim discovered that these "modern courtship patterns" were practiced even among observant Jews. Members of the Hasidic community were informed that this courtship pattern, in which the young man comes to the house and "takes the girl out," is socially accepted among the "best" people in America. They were told that parents are glad when this happens because it gives them an opportunity to meet their future son-in-law. There are occasions when the young man calls on the telephone and does not meet the parents and when the couple does not even ask the parents' consent for their marriage. These situations were considered impossible in a patriarchal family system such as that of the Hasidim.

The marriage of the young presents a grave problem. This problem is particularly great for the Hasidic man because it is the male of the religious community who has the obligation to observe and adhere to all the positive commandments, because the Hasidic tradition is mainly transferred from generation to generation through the male members of the community, and because if the husband is Hasidic, the wife is automatically expected to behave according to Hasidic norms. In other words, the husband's influence must be the greater if the family is to remain Hasidic. The woman is considered "religious," but the husband gives "Hasidic status" to the family. However, it is of the utmost importance that the young Hasid find a girl who is willing to adhere to the husband's values and Hasidic norms.

The girl's pedigree presents an important problem. In European Hasidic communities, the religious Jew did not intermarry with the nonreligious. This religious demarcation was clear and distinct. The family lineages were known. Ancestry was traced back through three or four generations or even further. The people were certain that girls of families that were considered "religious" met all the requisites and requirements for a religious wife.

But here in America, because the communities are so large, the Jewish families are not necessarily known. Because Jewish families do not all observe the traditional laws, they are not necessarily *behezkat kashrut,* that is, considered to have a religiously appropriate status. Here in America the Hasidic Jew has to make certain, before a woman can be considered for marriage, that this woman is the descendant of a religious family; that there are no religious "defects" in her family;[9] that she is single, widowed, or divorced; that, if she is divorced, a rabbi had performed the procedures; and that the rabbi who had done so was recognized as an authoritative religious functionary, competent to perform such an important religious rite. If the woman is a divorcée who had witnesses at the divorce procedures, these witnesses must have been qualified witnesses according to the traditional law. The girl must have been born to her mother after the mother had attended a ritual bath.[10] All these questions have to be weighed and considered here in America. They were

9. This requirement, "not having any 'defects' in her family" means that no one in her family married a non-Jew or that no one was an outspoken heretic. "Defect" does not refer to any physical abnormalties.

10. If the girl were born to the mother before she attended the ritual bath, the child was considered the "daughter of an 'impure.' "

questions that had presented no problems in the old world, where no one would have acted differently, but here all these points became of grave concern to the Hasidim.

It must be obvious that the Hasidim have met with great difficulty in finding women in America who meet all these qualifications. But the necessity of checking on each possible bride is of greater consequence than simply meeting requirements for a Hasidic wife, since the investigation adds to the control of the group and is of tremendous significance in that it forces Hasidic young people to marry within their own group.

The Hasidim consider the practice of birth control "a sin that is connected with punishment by death." Yet birth control, they discovered, was frequently practiced in America. The "blessing of sons and daughters" does not occur with the same frequency among non-Hasidim as might have been expected had "nature" taken its normal course, nor is the number of births as high as in Europe. The practice of birth control among the Jews they felt represented a non-Jewish influence, and in consequence, it is vehemently opposed by the Hasidim, even in cases of hardship. This "idolatrous" practice is prohibited by all religious authorities. Some of the "later ones"[11] did give permission for birth control under special circumstances where the woman's life was clearly in danger, as indicated by the testimony of expert doctors to a rabbi who was himself a great teacher, famous for his knowledge, piety, and righteousness. But for no reason other than "real danger" is birth control ever permitted, and by no rabbis other than those possessing Hasidic qualifications can permission be given.

Despite this, it is considered most difficult to "stop the cart running down the slope" in a society where birth control is common practice. It is greatly feared by the Hasidim that this "common practice" may creep into the Hasidic

11. "Later ones" is a technical term used in later rabbinical literature and is applied to rabbinical authors who followed the age of the *Shulhan Aruch*—the end of the sixteenth century. (See Gotthard Deutsch *"Aharonim," the Jewish Encyclopedia* [New York: Funk & Wagnalls Co., 1906], Vol. 1, pp. 283–284.)

community, where it may cause disorganization of family values and lead to the erosion of the rigid standards for behavior.

Compulsory school attendance in Hungary was from ages six to twelve. In New York State the age limits are from seven to sixteen.[12] Thus, the children of the Hasidim are exposed to secular education for a longer period of time than were their fathers and mothers in Europe. In addition, there is a great tendency in America, even among the more religious Jews, to send their sons and daughters to colleges and universities. This is considered evil and sinful in the eyes of the Hasidim because a person who is exposed to higher secular education often becomes a heretic.

The Hasidim have found great danger in higher education, and they are concerned lest it affect them adversely. In America it is possible to be an "Orthodox rabbi" and to have a higher education, even a doctor's degree. For this combination of secular-sacred training, special schools are available. But in the eyes of the Hasidim it is improper to expose a Hasidic person to such a course of study, since it endangers his Hasidic values and, by implication, those of the community.

Educating the young presents a grave problem to the Hasidim. Even the American concept of religious education is objectionable to them. In Europe, religious education began when the child was three years old. Even before that he had already been indoctrinated in strict religious conduct. Before he began going to school he had learned to recite certain prayers by heart. When he reached the age of three, he was taught by pious, bearded men upon whose faces rested "the image of God." When the child was five or six years old, he already knew how to read Hebrew and studied the weekly portion[13] of the Pentateuch. At the age of seven or eight, he

12. *Statistical Abstract of the United States 1959* (Washington, D.C.: United States Government Printing Office, 1960), p. 113.

13. Every week a different portion is read from the Torah in the synagogues, and this is completed on the holiday of "Rejoicing of the Torah," the last day of *Shemini Atzeret*. At that time the cycle of the reading of the weekly portions starts all over again.

was exposed to the Talmud. By the time he had reached the age of thirteen he could study the Talmud by himself and generally comprehend it, and through it the child was formally introduced to Hasidism.

But here in America, education for the young religious boy is altogether different. In contrast to the old country, where studying the Bible and the Talmud was conceived of as study for study's sake and teaching for teaching's sake and learning as part of religion, in America study and teaching are not done for their own sakes but to serve specific utilitarian ends. Here, people teach for a livelihood. Thus, the people who teach Hebrew and the Talmud in America are not only those who are moved to do so through their religious piety but also those who are "light-minded" and far removed from true religion.

The religious training that the Hasidic child received in Europe was different in concept from the religious education a Jewish child receives in America. Here a child of religious parents is not introduced to religious instruction until he is six, and only then does he begin the Hebrew alphabet. Most children complete their religious and Hebrew education when they reach thirteen and with their *bar mitzvah* celebration religious education for most of them ends.

Those students in Europe who went on for higher rabbinical training studied all the commentaries and all the religious codes of law dealing with every phase of Jewish life. Besides the need for becoming great scholars, piety and the fear of God were greatly emphasized. In contrast to the rabbinical students in Europe, those who go on to higher religious studies here in America are considered by the Hasidim to be ignoramuses. These criticisms are directed at the Orthodox rabbinical students; students from the Conservative and Reform movements are not even worthy of coming within the realm of their criticism.

The Hasidim do not object to the English language per se, and many of them have tried to master it to some extent. The problem is that they do not find many appropriate books in English that can be adapted for their young. They consider most books to be full of lustful reading, and the visual aids to be simply "filthy pictures." The most shocking experience, however, has been that even the Hebrew characters are utilized in America for the cultivation of "things forbidden."

The Hasidim have difficulty in finding proper textbooks for use in their schools because in their view all books used by others, regardless of how innocently composed, contain thoughts that are religious heresy. In such books, "boys and girls" are mentioned, thus exposing Hasidic children to the idea of an intermingling of sexes. Or the concept of evolution is interwoven with the subject matter to such an extent that it becomes accepted as absolute truth. This the Hasidim find most objectionable.

The leadership is fully aware of the inappropriateness of these books for their children. There is a concerted opposition to them and, because of that, the danger of influence from these books is not very pronounced. In fact, it is not the books dealing with secular studies but with Jewish or religious material, especially if written in Yiddish, that can be most dangerous, because their heretical instructions or teachings are camouflaged.

As the Hasidim view the larger Jewish community and observe that the rabbis do not meet Hasidic standards and qualifications and that the ritual slaughterers, too, look like assimilated Jews, they conclude that most food products are nonkosher. The Hasidim prohibit any food product that needs supervision according to Jewish traditional law, if it is supervised by a person whose qualifications do not meet Hasidic requirements. If such products are used in any Jewish household, then according to Hasidic standards, even the pots and dishes of the ordinary household are prohibited for use.

The Hasidim are constantly exhorted to resist Americanization. Even though they have to come into contact with non-religious Jews and non-Jews in business situations, they are urged to maintain as much isolation as possible. When the Hasidim travel on the subways and trains or walk on the streets, they observe behavior that is not conducive to adherence to rigid Hasidic standards. Therefore, the Hasidim are warned by their leaders to avoid traveling on overcrowded trains, since these trains are "full of dissolute women who are half-naked."[14] It is much better, they are told, to change their jobs and work in close proximity to the Hasidic community so that they will not be exposed to sights that might have a deterrent effect on their prescribed Hasidic observances. It is better to earn less money than to work with nonreligious people and "listen to their idle talk and watch their manners." But since it is impossible for many Hasidim to stay within the community and earn a living, they inevitably meet people whose behavior is not acceptable and from whom they may learn the patterns of the general culture. To counteract this bad influence, these Hasidim are bidden to study every day before work and after work to confirm their faith and to strengthen their Hasidic behavior.

Because the Hasidic Jew is so involved during the week with "earthly matters" in making a living, and because he has fallen somewhat from the "expected degree" of religious devotion and dedication to Hasidism, on the Sabbath and the holidays he must gain back the "strength" that he has lost. He must study and listen to the words of the *rebbe*. He must become involved in the upbringing of his children, that through their indoctrination he may gain further strength in the Hasidic doctrine so that his very effort may be channeled toward Hasidic behavior. He must be interested in the progress of his children so that through this involvement he man continue the Hasidic weekly routine of which he has been deprived while earning a living.

Economic activities present many opportunities for integration with the larger culture. The good economic conditions existing in America support cultural diffusion. The Hasidic leadership views such conditions as dangerous not only because they open the way to American cultural influences, but also because they produce overemphasis on financial gain at the expense of strong Hasidic dedication. Also, a change of values in the Hasidic home may result as parents discuss money and jobs instead of the Torah.

14. Raphael Blum, *Tal Hashomayim* (New York: Hadar Linotyping and Publishing Co., 1958), pp. 7–37.

The Hasidim also recognize the disrupting effects of mass media in the United States. In a country where most products, and even ideas, are sold through advertising on billboards, radio, television, and newspapers, it is all too possible that some aspects of American culture may be sold to the Hasidim. Any such influence would be considered irreligious and might creep into the Hasidic camp as "fruits of modernism." The religious Jew should not be exposed to anything new that might lead him to disregard the ways of his forefathers.[15]

Resistance to Americanization and the prevention of cultural diffusion can be successfully advocated only if there is respect, awe, and reverence toward the elders and the leadership. Great care is taken by the leadership of the Hasidic community that this respect should not lessen because this might weaken the elders' influence and control. Such respect for leadership, the Hasidim have found, is sharply lacking in this new culture. In the United States freedom of speech is exercised to a greater extent than the Hasidim have ever experienced. If this should lead to disrespect for elders and leaders, the entire Hasidic community would be threatened with disintegration and ultimate assimilation into the larger Jewish group. This is the situation in which the Hasidic community of Williamsburg currently finds itself.

15. *Ibid.*

# CHAPTER 6

# The Hasidic Family

HE PATTERN OF HASIDIC FAMILY LIFE in Europe consisted of extended families with several generations of a family living in the same house or, at least, in close proximity. With the move to America, a major change occurred. Here, there were very few dependent elderly people in the family. Because of this uprooting, the Hasidim had to establish a means of making new acquaintances within the community so that persons might meet their own type of religious people who would qualify for marriage.

This problem of selecting a mate is met through the aid of community members who act in the capacity of *shadchan,* or marriage broker. Although a final decision on marriage rests with the young couple, their freedom of choice is limited to those who have been sanctioned by the family and who are qualified according to Hasidic requirements. "Dating" as a courtship pattern is unknown. If a father has a daughter eligible for marriage, the *shadchan* proposes *antragen,* a *shiduch* (a match). The young couple meets through the *shadchan* in most cases. The *shadchan* comes to the house and tells the parents about a particular prospect he has in mind for their daughter or son. The parents try to get all the information they can about this candidate, such as family background, financial standing, learning capacity, the Yeshivah he attended, and the kind of student he was. After the parents have obtained the necessary information, and found it satisfactory, they arrange for the two young people to meet. Usually this takes place in the house of the girl. A woman informant describes the procedure:

My husband and I were first introduced at a wedding, but the young couples usually meet for a short time in a house or in some other place. The following morning the *shadchan* called. He wanted to know what had happened. The young man seemed to be interested. The *shadchan* tried to arrange another meeting. My parents asked me if I wanted to meet the young man again. After we met for the second time, the *shadchan* called on my parents and told them that the young man was "definitely interested"; therefore, "Let's get down to business. . . ."[1]

The husband has the authority in making family decisions, since he is expected to be the learned man. Family norms are guided by religious convictions and religious rules, and the husband is the one who has received religious training. The Hasidic family organization shows a division of labor in which the husband and father is the breadwinner and the over-all supervisor of religious matters, whereas the wife and mother is in charge of the housekeeping and seeing to it that Hasidic family norms are strictly adhered to by her children. The freedom of the woman is limited, and she has to fulfill all those roles "expected of women." She may not take an active part in the labor force, and she is not prepared for any career. Personal attractiveness[2] in women is not highly emphasized; however, the zealous woman knows that she must appear feminine to her husband so that he may be encouraged to lead a "life of purity." The wife is not ex-

1. From the files of RGE, 1958.
2. Parsons' "glamor girl" role in Talcott Parsons, "Age and Sex in U.S. Social Structure," *American Sociological Review*, VII, October, 1942, pp. 610–613.

pected to be a good social companion,[3] since an excessive husband-wife relationship is discouraged. Only in her "domestic" role[4] is she expected to do valiantly. In this role she has the opportunity to display her virtues as a "woman of valor."

The children are expected to respect their parents and they are trained to be observant Jews. The boy is expected to become a *talmid hacham,* a learned man, and an *ehrlicher Yid,* an honest Jew. The girl is expected to be a *Yiddisher mama,* a Jewish mother, and a *Yiddisher tochter,* a Jewish daughter married to a *talmid hacham* and an *ehrlicher Yid.* Boys and girls are sexually segregated at a very early age, and they never attend any school or participate in activities in which the sexes are mixed.

Young adults are encouraged to marry at an early age, preferably at seventeen or eighteen, "before they open their eyes" to the social ills of the larger culture. Child-rearing is of great concern to the Hasidic parents, since as soon as the child steps out of his home, he is immediately exposed to "unhealthy influences." Thus, great care is taken that he should be brought up in an atmosphere conducive to the Hasidic way of life. The young mother does not face the problem of training her children alone, since the community and the community schools play active parts in child-rearing from the time the child is able to talk. The boy is taught to become a religious man observing all the laws and rituals prescribed by the Code of Jewish Law and by the Hasidic community. He is initiated into participation in the observance of the Jewish religious laws at an early age, when he is capable of walking with his father to the house of worship, and he is formally initiated at the age of thirteen when he becomes *bar mitzvah.* After his formal initiation he continues with his Talmudical studies and he becomes a recognized man in the society at eighteen when he comes of age for marriage. However, he becomes a full-fledged member only after marriage.

There is no official puberty ceremonial for girls. They do

3. Parsons' "good companion" role, *ibid.*
4. Parsons' "domestic" role, *ibid.*

not receive any social recognition while young. At the age of three they are considered females according to the law and subject to all restrictions applicable to women. As they grow and mature physically, they wear clothing that covers them, that is, stockings and long sleeves. Girls are socially recognized when they reach an age for marriage. Before marriage, they are allowed to display their femininity within the limitations of the group norms. There is no socially recognized period of adolescence; they grow from childhood into adulthood. The Hasidic community cannot afford a period of adolescence in the girl's development, since they cannot satisfy the needs and desires comparable to those of the period of adolescence in the larger society.

"Youth" does not have high status in the Hasidic community, since it is regarded as only a preliminary to adulthood. The status of a young person is low except in those respects where he shows initiative and the promise of becoming a good Hasidic Jew. In the Hasidic community the only real *rite de passage* is marriage. Boys and girls usually do not meet ambiguities and uncertainties concerning their expected behavior, since the role of youth is to obey their elders and behave in a way that is appropriate for Hasidic people.

Marriages are for life. Divorce is almost nonexistent. As of 1959, there were only two divorces of which the community had any knowledge and the individuals involved were not considered true Hasidim by the community. There was only one known case of infidelity—between a Hasidic man and a non-Hasidic woman. The infidelity of Hasidic women is inconceivable, and the thought alone caused horror in the respondents.

Young people are brought up in a small family unit, and they are emotionally dependent upon their parents. Through common interests and responsibilities emotional dependence is taken over by the mates. The community does not extend appreciable social recognition to unmarried people: "The only real person is a married one." This lack of social recognition contributes to molding the new family into a cohesive group. This is a very important function, since the mates

know very little of each other and know even less about
familial norms appropriate to man and wife. The great emphasis upon premarital chastity and marital fidelity is another determining factor molding the young couple into a
family unit. The young couple, before marriage, are separately given instructions concerning their "religious duties
in marriage." They are instructed about the holiness of the
sexual act. They are warned that the performance of the
sexual act must be in the line of duty along with other religious observances, but at no time should it serve as an
"abominable deed of passion and lust."

One of the most important functions of the Hasidic family
is procreation, which is a commandment of God. Birth control is not practiced among the majority of Hasidic women.
If birth control is practiced at all, it is only by the more
"worldly woman" without the knowledge of her husband
and even this only after the birth of the fifth or sixth child.
After the woman has an appreciable number of children
(four or five), it is conceivable to the community that she
has "ceased bearing in the course of nature." If the children
are very close together in age, this shows that there is no
intentional spacing, and saves a couple from malicious gossip
and slander.

Having children is of such great import to the Hasidic
family that lack of children is considered one of the major
grounds for divorce. It may seem contradictory, but divorce
never actually occurs on this ground, since the couple continues to live in the hope that, through faith and the *rebbe's*
prayers and by the blessing of God, they may yet have children. One couple interviewed, who had been married for ten
or twelve years, responded to the question about how many
children they had with *"Lesateh"*—for the time being, none.
Another woman, married eight years and without children,
when asked the size of her family, tried to evade the question.
She gave an answer irrelevant to the question at hand. But
when the interviewer was persistent in asking obviously and
specifically, "How many children do you have?" she became
silent for a moment, tears came to her eyes, and she reluc-
tantly admitted, "No children."

Romantic love is associated with sin and lustfulness. Any activity that would suggest romance is considered distasteful and vulgar to the Hasidim. There is no reason or purpose in an overt expression of love or in reaffirming love between the partners as part of the routine of marriage. Even before marriage, it is not necessary for the partners to express any kind of romantic feeling toward each other; the fact that they are going to be married suffices. Consent to marry merely indicates a willingness to live with one another. Some couples may not like each other well enough to be married, but it is community and family pressure that have the greatest influence upon their decision.

It is possible for the concept of romance or romantic love to come into question during the time when the negotiation for marriage is going on between future partners and their parents and the *shadchan*. It is also possible for romantic love to be conceived in the form of liking for each other after the engagement when the couple may have some opportunity to see each other, but "to love each other while married" or "to be romantically involved with one's wife" are concepts very far removed from Hasidic thought. A Hasid was asked if he was in love with his wife, to which he replied, "You mean in love while one is already married?" [Yes.] "I don't understand how one is in love while married. He is already married. I can understand that one might have some romantic feeling during the negotiation of the *shiduch* [match] or while engaged but how can one be in love while married? I don't understand any of that. . . ."[5]

Although marriage in the Hasidic community is not based on romantic love, there are many other binding ties that hold the marriage together such as:

1. Common obligations and responsibilities of the couple and their offspring.

2. Community status given to those who are married.

3. Low status ranking for the unmarried.

4. Negative community sanctions for the divorced or separated.

5. From the files of LPS, 1958.

5. Mutual affection and respect.

6. Isolation from outside social activities.

7. Lack of exposure to the romantic norms of the outside community.

Hasidic family life is religiously determined, since religion is the prime factor in all Hasidic behavior. The family economic activities are very closely related, especially in this society where most behavior is geared to religious observance. The family must observe all the Hasidic norms under every possible circumstance. Deviation from Hasidic norms is not acceptable even if one's subsistence is in question. Economic activities must be consistent with and complementary to the status the family has in the community. Hence, a member of a family will engage only in those economic activities that will reinforce the social and religious norms of the Hasidim.

CHAPTER 7

# The Social Stratification
# of the Hasidic Community

THE HASIDIC COMMUNITY is stratified into six distinct
social classes:

1. *Rebbes* (R).
2. *Shtickel Rebbes* (SR).
3. *Sheine Yiden* (SY).
4. *Talmidei Hachamim* (TH).
5. *Balebatishe Yiden* (BY).
6. *Yiden* (Y).

Social stratification in the Hasidic community is based
primarily upon frequency and intensity of religious observance. "Frequency" relates to the number of religious performances in the course of a day. For example, a religious
Jew upon awakening must rise immediately and be ready to
serve his Creator before evil inclinations can prevail. He

must wash his hands in a ritual manner, taking the vessel first in the right hand and then in the left; then he must spill the water with the left hand upon the right and then, in reverse, from his right hand upon the left, repeating this performance three times.[1] Similar ritualistic observances are performed throughont the day.

"Intensity" refers to the emotional manifestations, some of which may be observed during public ceremonies. A person who is intensely involved in his religious practices may shake his body during prayers, or he may pray longer or display during prayers certain mannerisms that are known as religious, symbolic gestures. The greater the number of rituals and the more intensely they are observed, the greater the esteem accorded a person. The rites, the rituals, and the elements necessary for these performances are prescribed by law. But the law does not indicate the mannerism, the body movement, the emotional ecstasy, the joy or sadness that accompany the performance. Since these expressions are not specifically prescribed, they are completely Hasidic in character. Social standing in the community is in direct proportion to the intensity of the performance.

Thus, the criteria by which the Hasidic community is stratified are not the same as in other American communities. Lineage, wealth, occupation, income, residence, morals and manners, and education operate differently. Such criteria do not determine status unless they are associated with ritualistic observance. For instance, if a person has wealth but the frequency and intensity of his observance is low, he will not rank high in the social order. Nor will a person who possesses the other characteristics ordinarily associated with high status rank high in the social structure if he is not also characterized by high frequency and intensity of ritualistic observance.

Social and economic characteristics are important determinants of position only if they are connected with ritualistic observances. If a person has wealth, it may be displayed only through luxuries that are Hasidic in character. A rich man

1. *Code of Jewish Law*, (*Kitzer Shulhan Aruch*) compiled by Solomon Gansfried and translated by Hyman E. Goldin (New York: Hebrew Publishing Co., 1927), pp. 2–4.

may have two sinks, two stoves, or even two separate kitchens —one for meat and one for dairy products—so that he can observe the dietary laws more intensely. Or a wealthy man may have a more beautiful *shtreimel,* which is again an intensification of Hasidic observances. If one is educated in Jewish matters, he will rank high only if his education is used to intensify his Hasidic behavior. Education in itself, without Hasidic observances, has little status value. Occupation, income, and residence, too, carry status value only if they supplement intensive Hasidic behavior.

Considerable upward and downward mobility is found in the Hasidic community. At the very top is a nucleus composed of the *Rebbes,* whose religious observances, ritualistic behavior, and entire behavior are living examples to the community. Those persons closest to the *rebbes* also enjoy high status in the community and the further one is from this core, the lower his rank in the social scale. Thus, the more a person absorbs a *rebbe's* teaching and is absorbed by that teaching, the closer he moves to the upmost level. No one, except a *rebbe,* ever reaches the highest rank, nor do many people desire to, since the frequency and intensity of religious observance demanded of them would limit their enjoyment of worldly rewards. However, the less one observes the laws and the less intensely one performs the rituals, the lower the ranking he has within the social structure.

Downward mobility is characterized by a decreasing adherence to Hasidic rituals and by less participation in Hasidic activities. Deviation from *any* Hasidic social and religious norm lowers prestige and initiates downward mobility.

At the bottom of the social structure are the *Yiden,* (literally, the "Jews"). They do not excel in wealth, in scholarliness, nor in intensive and frequent Hasidic behavior; therefore, no special adjectives accompany their category. However, if they are compared with non-Hasidic Jews, they are known as *Hasidishe Yiden.* But in the Hasidic group, the term *Hasidishe* is not applicable, since every member is a "Hasidic Jew." *Yiden* are Hasidic Jews who observe the Hasidic norms but who are not distinguished by the frequency and intensity of their religious behavior. Although they are at

the bottom of the Hasidic social order, persons in this grouping outdo everyone outside of the Hasidic community in
religious performance. In their own eyes, therefore, they are
not the lowest of the low, but rather the lowest of the exalted.
As one Hasidic Jew expressed it, "I would rather be the
worst among religious Jews than the best among sinners."

Next in rank are the *Balebatishe Yiden* (literally, the
"house-owning Jews"). They are the full-fledged community
members who participate in most of the local affairs. They
contribute generously to the Hasidic causes. They are known
to be "well-off" and the frequency and intensity of their
religious observance is higher than that of the *Yiden. Balebatishe Yiden* give more to charity and contribute more financially to Hasidic causes than anyone above them in social
status. They are also learned but not enough so to be called
scholars. Their wealth supplements their status because it is
used to intensify Hasidic behavior.

The next social class is the *Talmidei Hachamim* (literally,
the "students of the wise"), the learned men whose scholarliness complements intense Hasidic observance. Their observance is more frequent and intense than the observance of
the *balebatishe Yiden* and *Yiden. Talmidei Hachamim* do
not have professional religious positions; they are learned
laymen. They have less wealth than the people who are beneath them in the status order, but their more intense religious behavior as supplemented by scholarliness places
them in a higher rank. The mere fact that they spend much
time studying is in itself considered an index of their intense
religious observance.

Next are the *Sheine Yiden* (literally, the "beautiful Jews").
Their religious observance is more intensive and more frequent than that of those of lower rank. They become religious professionals such as teachers, instructors of Talmud,
ritual slaughterers, circumcisors, and so forth. The original
appointment as religious professionals results from their
religiosity, and the performance of their duties increases the
intensity and frequency of their observances. They cannot
fail, therefore, to be of high rank in the community.

Next to the top are the *Shtickel Rebbes* (literally, "piece of *rebbe*" or "bit of *rebbe*" or "something of a *rebbe*") who are persons who recently came into the *rebbishe* ranks through their intensive Hasidic activity. They are not usually in direct line of descent from well-known *rebbes,* and if they are members of a famous lineage, the dynasty and its followers have already been inherited by someone else, perhaps by an older brother. *Shtickel rebbes* are young persons or relatively new arrivals in the community. Their followers tend to be those of older *rebbes* with whom the *Shtickel rebbes* are identified. *Shtickel rebbes* are religious practitioners whose authority is second only to that of a *rebbe.*

The *rebbes* are the top-ranking religious leaders, and their authority is inherited from their fathers or other close relatives.[2] It is believed ultimately to come from God. They are beyond question or reproach. They are recognized as the "most high who exceed, outdo, and outrank every other person in the entire world." Their entire behavior is thought to be ritualistic. Every move and mannerism is a form of religious worship. Their ritualistic observance is the most frequent and the most intense of all worshipers. Thus, the *rebbes* are the core of the community.

Each of these six classes in the Hasidic community has supplementary characteristics as shown in Chart I. Briefly, these are:

The *Yiden* conform to the intense Hasidic religious performance that identifies and characterizes them as Hasidic Jews vis-à-vis observant non-Hasidic Jews.

The *balebatishe Yiden,* in addition, have wealth that they expend on Hasidic luxuries. These expenditures in themselves constitute religious observance.

The *Talmidei Hachamim,* though without wealth, are educated in religious matters and are considered learned laymen.

The *sheine Yiden,* besides having education, have a pro-

2. Intensity of religious observance is a consistent criterion for social rank. Sons of *rebbes* who do not follow their fathers in matters of religion do not rank high. Their lineage would only supplement their individual religious observance.

## Table 1. The Relationship of Social Rank and Supplementary Status Characteristics in the Hasidic Community

| Descending Social Rank Order | Inheritance of Dynasty | Lineage | Professional Affiliation | Education | Wealth | Conformity |
|---|---|---|---|---|---|---|
| 1. Rebbes | + | + | + | + | +− | + |
| 2. Shtickel Rebbes | − | + | + | + | +− | + |
| 3. Sheine Yiden | − | − | + | + | − | + |
| 4. Talmidei Hachamim | − | − | − | + | − | + |
| 5. Balebatishe Yiden | − | − | − | − | + | + |
| 6. Yiden | − | − | − | − | − | + |

+ = Positive    − = Negative    +− = Neutral

fessional affiliation as "religious performers." They, too, lack wealth.

The *Shtickel rebbes* have education, professional affiliation, and some degree of kinship with a famous *rebbe*. A *shtickel rebbe* may or may not have wealth, and his wealth may be associated with the organization with which he is affiliated.

The *rebbes* have education, professional affiliation, and lineage, are identified with a dynasty and have inherited its followers. A *rebbe* may or may not have wealth; if so, it is closely connected with the organization of which he is an integral part.

Social stratification among the Hasidim has one especially interesting feature. The Hasidim are not only externally identifiable from members of the larger community, but they are also recognizable as members of a particular social stratum. Especially on the Sabbath and holidays, a Hasidic Jew can identify the social class of another Hasidic Jew by his dress. He feels that by wearing garments identifying him as a Jew he will be helped to refrain from coming into contact with sin. "Looking like a Jew with the image of God upon one's face" will serve as a barrier against acculturation and assimilation. As one Hasidic Jew expressed it, "With my appearance I cannot attend a theater or movie or any other places where a religious Jew is not supposed to go. Thus, my beard and my sidelocks and my Hasidic clothing serve as a guard and shield from sin and obscenity."[3]

The garments the Hasidic Jews wear today are considered by them to be the traditional Jewish garments which were once the apparel of all Jews. But because most of today's Jews imitate non-Jews, these garments are now exclusively Hasidic. The types of Hasidic clothing and the ways of looking Hasidic change from class to class. The extent of affiliation with Hasidism determines the particular kind of garments worn. The different types of Hasidic garments serve as identifying symbols of social rank.

The Hasidic garments vary from *zehr Hasidish* (extremely Hasidic) to *modernish* (modern). The less Hasidic men, that

3. From the files of SFJ, 1956.

is, the persons whose religious performances are of less frequency and less intensity, wear *modernish* clothing. Though
still recognizable as "Hasidic," these garments resemble those
of western societies. Or these men wear western clothing that
is turned into Hasidic clothing by Hasidic overtones; for
instance, long-outmoded, double-breasted dark suits that button from right to left. The most observant wear *zehr Hasidish*
clothing, and through this they are indentified as persons
of high rank. Their clothing alone indicates that the frequency and intensity of their observances have secured them
high status. A person who wears *zehr Hasidish* clothing would
be ridiculed if his behavior were not consistent with his appearance.

Thus, the only persons who wear "extremely Hasidic"
garments are those whose behavior in frequency and intensity of religious observance coincides with the clothing they
wear.

Gaining recognition in a higher social stratum is a gradual
process effected by increasingly religious behavior. Individuals who display more intense religious observance are
asked by the community or by the *rebbe* to put on more
elaborate Hasidic garments to indicate their acceptance into
a higher class. Requests to wear more Hasidic garments are
also used to induce higher frequency and intensity of religious behavior. Once a person wears clothing symbolizing
a higher status, the frequency and intensity of his behavior
should be consistent with the type of garment he wears. It is
assumed that wearing a garment symbolizing higher status
will create a chain reaction of more and more intensified
religious observance.

There are two major aspects to the external appearance
of a Hasidic Jew. One is the Hasidic garment and the other
is the *bord und payes,* the beard and side-locks. These status
symbols vary with each social stratum as shown in Chart II.

Class 6, the *Yiden* (Y), has a minimum of the Hasidic status
symbols. Chief among these are the dark, double-breasted
suits that button from right to left.

Class 5, the *Balebatishe Yiden* (BY), has, besides some
minimal Hasidic identifying symbols, the identifying status

### Table II. The Relationship of Social Rank and Identifying Status Symbols in the Hasidic Community

| Descending Social Rank Order | IDENTIFYING STATUS SYMBOLS | | | | | |
|---|---|---|---|---|---|---|
| | (SZ) | (SB) | (K) | (BH) | (BP) | (SHI) |
| Class 1 (R) | + | + | + | + | + | + |
| Class 2 (SR) | − | + | + | + | + | + |
| Class 3 (SY) | − | − | + | + | + | + |
| Class 4 (TH) | − | − | − | + | + | + |
| Class 5 (BY) | − | − | − | − | + | + |
| Class 6 (Y) | − | − | − | − | − | + |

Identifying Status Symbols:
  (SZ) *Shich and Zocken* (slipper-like shoes and white knee socks)
  (SB) *Shtreimel and Bekecher* (fur hat made out of sable and long silk coat)
   (K) *Kapote* (long overcoat worn as a jacket)
  (BH) *Biber hat* (large-brimmed hat made out of beaver)
  (BP) *Bord und Payes* (beard and side-locks)
  (SHI) Some Hasidic identity

Social Rank:
   (R) *Rebbe*
  (SR) *Shtickel Rebbe*
  (SY) *Sheiner Yid*
  (TH) *Talmidei Hachamim*
  (BY) *Balebatisher Yid*
   (Y) *Yid*

+ = Positive    − = Negative

symbols of beard and side-locks (BP). Some beards are never cut or trimmed and some sidelocks are never cut or shaved, a symbol of still higher status.

Class 4, the *Talmidei Hachamim* (TH), besides having beard and side-locks, also wears a *Biber* hat (BH). This is a black, large-brimmed hat made out of beaver.

Class 3, the *Sheine Yiden* (SY), besides having the beard, side-locks and *biber* hat, also has the *Kapote* (K). The *kapote* is a long overcoat, usually black, worn instead of a jacket.

Class 2, the *Shtickel Rebbes* (SR), besides having the beard, side-locks, *biber* hat and *kapote,* has the *Shtreimel* and *Bekecher* (SB). The *shreimel* is a fur hat made out of sable. The *bekecher* is a long Hasidic coat made of silk or silky material in which the pockets are in the back.

Class 1, the *Rebbes* (R), besides having the beard, sidelocks, *biber* hat, *kapote, shtreimel* and *bekecher,* also has the *Shich* and *Zocken* (SZ). *shich* are slipper-like shoes, and *zocken* are white knee socks into which the breeches are folded.

As the classes ascend in the social structure, more and more status symbols are associated with that particular class. Since wearing the status symbols is in itself a performance of religiosity, it is consistent with the social stratification of the Hasidic community. The *rebbes* are the only ones who, as a class and without exception, wear the *shich* and *zocken.* They also wear the symbolic *shtreimel* and *bekecher, biber* hat and *kapote,* and *bord und payes.* The *shtickel rebbes* are next in rank order, and while some of them do wear the *shich* and *zocken,* most do not. However, all the *shtickel rebbes* wear the other symbols—*shtreimel, bekecher, biber* hat and *kapote, bord und payes.* Likewise, some of the *sheine Yiden* may wear the *shtreimel* and *bekecher,* but most do not, and none wear the *shich* and *zocken.* All the other symbolic garments are worn. Next in order are the *talmidei hachamim,* some of whom may wear *kapotes,* and all of whom wear the *biber* hat, the *bord und payes.* The *balebatishe Yiden,* while some of them may wear higher status symbols, always have, as a class, the *bord und payes.* At the very bottom of the scale are the *Yiden,* all of whom have some Hasidic status symbols by which they are identified as Hasidic Jews.

Thus, in the Hasidic community, religion is the major criterion for social stratification. The frequency and intensity of religious behavior and the frequency and intensity with which one observes the rites and rituals of Jewish law in the course of the day are a major class index. Wealth, occupation, residence, and other social and economic characteristics only supplement one's status position. The external appearance of the members of this group may be conceived as status symbols by which members are identified with their social position. These external status symbols and the frequency and intensity of religious behavior must be parallel and consistent with each other. This *consistency* is a very important form of social control by which the group maintains and furthers its religiosity. It will be shown later that the major classification of the group's economic activities also falls within the class structure as outlined here. The economic activities, too, supplement the status position which has been gained through intensive religious observance.

CHAPTER 8

# Organizations and Social Control

THE HASIDIC COMMUNITY has many religious organizations. Some of the most important ones are the religious congregations. These congregations have a synagogue or, as it is called, a "house of worship," or a "house
of study." In these houses of worship the male members of the
community gather for study, for worship, for gossip, and for
"politicking." They meet daily and discuss formally and in-
formally the community affairs by which the members are
controlled. In many of these houses of worship lectures are
given at which the members are instructed in the Talmud, in
the Scriptures, and in religious laws.

In most of the congregations, admittance to membership
is open only to those who state they have no television or
radio in their houses. Most of these organizations require that
members' wives wear wigs. These are symbols by which the
applicants are identified as members of the Hasidic community who fully adhere to community norms. If a member

belongs to a certain religious organization, he generally feels morally obligated to support those shop owners who are members of his organization. The members are obligated to support their organization and maintain all its auxiliary organizations such as schools, ritual baths, study groups, and so forth. They are expected to participate in all their activities, particularly in fund raising.

Secular communication methods such as radio, television, and English and Yiddish newspapers are prohibited to this group. The house of worship is the major center for exchanging information. Announcements concerning community affairs and community news are either verbally communicated from person to person, publicly announced, or communicated through notices that are hung on the walls of the synagogue, bulletin boards, and any other conspicuous place.

These houses of worship are the seats of community control where the deviants are harshly treated through gossip, ridicule, and other differential treatment. For example, a Hasidic Jew had an automobile accident involving another Hasidic Jew. As a result of this accident, the one whose car was damaged sued the other man in a civil court. Although the second man was insured and would not have been personally responsible for payment of damages, the act of taking another Hasidic Jew to a civil court rather than having the problem in question arbitrated within the community was considered "an informer's act." The man who "sued his brother" approached a friend in one of the houses of worship to exchange a few words and was told, "Don't talk to me. You are a *moser* [an informer or traitor]." Other Hasidic Jews, as they heard the story, also refrained from speaking to him.[1]

Another place where social control is exercised in the form of a negative sanction is the *mikveh*, the ritual bath. It is visited daily by those Hasidic Jews who are members of the two upper classes; visited on Mondays, Thursdays, Fridays, and Saturdays by members of Class 3; on Fridays and Saturdays by members of Class 4 and 5; and on Fridays

1. From the files of LPS, 1959.

only by Class 6. In these ritual baths there is gossiping,[2] which most people consider inappropriate in a house of worship. The most damaging gossip is usually initiated in these *mikvehs*.

Another important Hasidic institution is the religious school. In the many religious schools the children are indoctrinated in Hasidic principles. Very young children attend these schools six days a week and stay in them from morning until night. They are instructed in the most extensive observance of the religious laws and rituals, and each child must account in school for his religious practices at home. In certain schools children are even given a mimeographed form to take home and fill in, accounting for their religious observance in the home. The following is a translation from the Hebrew of an original "Report [of Religious Observance in the Home] for the week," showing whether or not the children have performed their "homework" — that is, religious observances.

I said the *Modeh Ani* [morning prayer].
I washed my hands [ritually].
I washed my hands [ritually] before eating bread.
My hands were clean before I washed my hands [ritually].
I always said a blessing before eating.
I said a blessing after eating, such as "Grace after Meals."
I said the blessing after returning from the bathroom.
I prayed the "Morning Prayer" with intense concentration.
I prayed the prayer of "Welcoming the Sabbath."
I prayed the "Afternoon Prayer" on the Sabbath.
I read my "Evening Prayer" before retiring to bed.
I did not answer back to my parents with arrogance.
I helped in the house and around the house.
I did not gossip.
I did not speak lies.
I did not transgress the law of "wasting."
I practiced the Five Books of Moses today.

2. Although it is part of the children's training to discourage them from gossiping, gossip is frequently used as a technique of social control. Actually, because gossip is so widely used in the community, school administrators try to discourage it among the children.

I studied and have done writing today.
I gave to charity.[3]

Children are isolated from the streets in these schools, and
they have very little or no opportunity to meet or associate
with other children except those of their own group. Boys
and girls are completely separated. Not only are they instructed in different classrooms but they are kept in different
buildings. Boys are instructed by male teachers and girls
by female teachers. The children graduate from a lower
school into schools of higher learning at certain intervals.
Many of them stay in these schools until their marriage. Some
of the boys stay after marriage for a number of years so that
they may study Torah "in purity." Girls' instruction does
not emphasize scholarliness or intellectual inquisitiveness
but is oriented toward practical application to the "life of a
Hasidic woman." Girls are taught the arts of keeping house,
the religious responsibilities of a Hasidic woman in the community, and the laws concerning the rites, rituals, and ab-
stinence from their husbands during the time of menstruation.

Most of the Hasidic religious schools have an English department which is staffed by part-time teachers of the New
York public school system and other private schools in the
New York area. These teachers teach in the Hasidic schools
after their regular full-time teaching assignments, and here
they teach only "subject matter" and not "the child."

The over-all education of the young is completely controlled by the religious instructors. Informal education begins at birth, formal education for male children as soon as
the child can speak, and for female children perhaps a year
later. Most of the Hasidim agree that their children should
have formal secular education, limited to reading, writing,
and arithmetic. But even for this minimum secular education, care is taken that it in no way be overdone. Almost
every religious organization has an elementary school for
English training associated with the religious school. Although these schools meet municipal requirements, the

3. From the original document. Translated from the Yiddish.

methods and hours of instruction are fully controlled by
the individual organization. Thus, the utmost care is taken
that no foreign concept should seep into the flexible minds
of the young.

These schools are supported by tuition paid by the parents, contributions of community members, funds gained by
solicitation of the outside community, collections from various parts of the country, and from the net profits of the
butcher stores that are under the supervision of the Hasidic
organizations.

The community assumes responsibility for the poor, the
sick, and the orphaned. There are various welfare organizations for this purpose. These organizations are conducted in
such a way that the recipient does not know where the
money comes from and the donors do not know to whom
the money goes. One Hasidic woman said:

> There were many occasions when I have gotten twenty-five
> dollars from my ladies' charity organization to give to a poor
> woman who I know was in need. The members or the officers
> did not question nor did they doubt to whom the money was
> given. I took the money and I gave it to the lady and she did
> not have to go through any embarrassing experiences.[4]

Before Passover, organizations are established to provide
the poor with Passover food. The author himself witnessed
how, when an immigrant family moved into their new apartment around Passover, the organization sent fifty pounds of
potatoes, ten dozen eggs, eight pounds of *matzah,* one basket
of apples, one can of oil, and a big carton full of vegetables
to the apartment before the family arrived. The recipients
did not know where these gifts had come from, and the
members of the organization did not know to whom they had
contributed. One of the officers of the organization was
merely told that as such-and-such an address there was a
needy family. The officer telephoned the grocery and told
the proprietor to deliver various items to that address.

There is an organization called the Anonymous Contributors Society for the purpose of giving charity to those "who

4. From the files of NFR2, 1959.

are not used to taking charity and are too shy to take a contribution from private persons." One of the letters that was sent out to the community by the society is the following:

*A Happy and Prosperous New Year*

Dear Sister:

We have founded an *Anonymous Contributors Society* whose purpose is a high ideal.

There are numerous families who have not the most needed things in their house for their children, because they are not used to taking charity and are shy about taking a contribution from private persons.

With one or two dollars, you can help them enormously.

Therefore, dear Sister, we ask you to take part in this great *mitzvah* and see to it that as the new year is approaching, your name should be among those inscribed in the "Book of Charity."

In the merit of this *mitzvah*, you will be inscribed in the "Book of Life," and you will be blessed with good Health and Prosperity.

> With Sisterly regards,

| | |
|---|---|
| Neitche Landau | Rachel Neiman |
| Malke Buksbaum | Ch. Sarah Greenwald |
| Pese Fishman | Golde Lieberman |
| Cheitche Fuchs | Rivka Katz |
| Silke Weiss | Perl Kaufman[5] |

Similar letters circulate inviting people of the community to participate in welfare activities. For example, a letter that was sent for the benefit of a sick *rebetzin* (a *rebbe's* wife) with six children and was signed by eleven *rebetzins* of the community reads:

Dear Sister:

You are cordially invited to attend a Party given for the benefit of *Rebetzin* Mertz (wife of the renowned Grand Rabbi Yechezkel Mertz of Kashau, Czechoslovakia), who had to be taken to the hospital and needs constant medical attention.

5. From the original document.

The Party will take place on June 7th, 1959 from 2 to 10 P.M., at the house of Mrs. Spitzer, 142 Hooper Street, Brooklyn, N.Y.

You are kindly requested to attend and thus ease the burden of a mother of six small children.

If you are unable to attend, please mail us your contribution in the enclosed envelope.

For this Great *Mitzvoh* [sic] you will be blessed with good health, happiness and much *naches*.

[Signed]

Satmarer *Rebetzin*

The Daughter of the *Rav,* the *Gaon,* the Righteous, the *Rav . . .*

| | |
|---|---|
| Papaner *Rebetzin* | Kassaver *Rebetzin* |
| Sopraner *Rebetzin* | Nyiregyhazer *Rebetzin* |
| Sigeter *Rebetzin* | Kraszner *Rebetzin* |
| Strizuber *Rebetzin* | Wishnitzer *Rebetzin*[6] |
| Zehlemer *Rebetzin* | |

There are many other welfare organizations such as the Vacation Fund for Poor and Orphaned Children, Inc., and *Bikur Cholim fin Der Popener Frauen Ferain* (Visiting the Sick of the Popener Women's Association). There are organizations such as the National Committee for Freedom of Religion in Israel that are "dedicated to the cause of fighting antireligious tendencies of leftist elements in *Ertez Yisrael* (the land of Israel)." There are burial societies, Talmudical societies, and organizations for almost every social and religious activity.

One of the most effective organizations from the standpoint of exercising control is the Hasidic rabbincial organization called in Hebrew, *Hitachdut Harabanim D'Artzot Habrit V'Canada* (literally, the Association of Rabbis of the United States and Canada), and in English, the Central Rabbinical Congress of the United States and Canada. This rabbinical body has approximately 160 members.[7] Most of them are immigrant rabbis from Hungary, but there are

6. From the original mailing.

7. A printed copy of a Hasidic announcement upon which the 160 signatures appear is in the possession of the author.

some rabbis from Poland as well. Some Hasidim have indicated that rabbis from Poland are invited to membership only to show to the non-Hasidic community that the rabbinical organization of the Hasidic rabbis is international in character.[8]

This body meets periodically and is headed by the outstanding *rebbe* of the community. The group makes major decisions about normative regulations, for instance, the prohibition of watching television or the proper religious observance and supervision of major food products such as salt and sugar. It communicates its decisions in circulars that are sent to all Hasidic houses of worship, and these decisions are considered as much traditional law as the "law that Moses received at Sinai." The group broadened its activities by giving legal advice on religious matters to the larger Orthodox Jewish community. It has recently established a "court of justice" for those seeking decisions on religious matters. This is advertised as follows:

With God's help, may His Name be blessed

An important announcement of

### The Central Rabbinical Congress of the United States and Canada

The Central Rabbinical Congress of the United States and Canada announces to the Orthodox Jewry of the City of New York and the Jews outside of New York that it has established a permanent Court of Justice in the office of the Central Rabbinical Congress, 134 Broadway, Brooklyn, which will function daily from 11 A.M. to 4 P.M. (except Friday), and anybody can turn to that court with all problems concerning prohibition and permission, matrimonial matters, divorce and marriage, payment on interest, etc.

The famous codifier [legal authority] the *Gaon Rav* Naftali H. Hennig, may he live long and happily, head of the Court in Sharmash, will officiate during the above-mentioned hours.

The Central Rabbinical Congress also announces that the office was reorganized and that it functions daily from

8. From the files of LPS, 1958.

10 A.M. to 4 P.M. and one may obtain any information there.

The address is: Central Rabbinical Congress, 134 Broadway, Brooklyn, N.Y.[9]

## THE OPERATION OF SOCIAL FORCES

The concept of social control as used throughout this work refers to the sum of those forces that induce individuals to conform to Hasidic standards and norms. It is generally assumed that social control has functional significance, serving to maintain group values and to uphold group survival. As LaPiere has stated, "The ability of a group to control the behavior of its individual members does, however, have profound effect upon the survival prospect of the group. The group in which the social control over individual members is weakening is a group on the way of dissolution; the group that can effectively enforce its norms has . . . high survival value.[10]

In order to induce the individual member of the Hasidic community to conform to Hasidic norms, the community employs a wide variety of techniques. Among these are:

1. Religious organizations are open only to those who promise complete conformity to Hasidic norms.

2. The indoctrination and socialization of children is geared and directed toward group conformity.

3. Hasidic indoctrination is further reinforced by encouraging the young married men to continue their religious studies within the *bet hamidrash* (literally, the house of study) for several years after marriage.

4. There is a general prohibition against communication with the "outside community" in the form of radio, television, non-Hasidic Yiddish newspapers, and so on, in order to avoid exposure to "strange" non-Hasidic culture.

5. Contact with individuals outside the community is discouraged in order to maintain social isolation.

9. *Der Yid*, April 3, 1959. Translated from the Yiddish.
10. Richard T. LaPiere, *A Theory of Social Control* (New York: McGraw-Hill Book Company, Inc., 1954), pp. 184–185.

6. Gossip and ridicule are forms of sanctions used to discourage any deviation from Hasidic norms.

7. Social status is accorded in direct proportion to one's scrupulous conformity to Hasidic norms.

8. The group assumes responsibility for its poor and sick in order to establish their greater dependency upon the group.

9. Welfare organizations[11] are established to distribute goods and services to those "needy" members who enjoy a "positive" reputation that has been obtained through complete conformity to group norms.

10. A powerful rabbinical organization has full and autonomous authority over all religious matters.

These techniques of social control involve three major categories of sanctions, physical, economic, and psychological,[12] and may take either a positive or a negative form. As an example of a negative physical sanction, admission to religious organizations is open only to those who are strict conformists; if one does not conform to community norms, he faces possible expulsion from the group. A positive physical sanction is seen in the activities of the anonymous welfare organizations which are established in order to distribute goods and services to those needy members who completely conform to group norms. Whether or not a person is "worthy" of support is not measured by his needs but rather by the degree of his social conformity.

Economic sanctions may also be positive.[13] It will be obvious that the community exercises considerable positive control by patronizing only those members who are "worthy of support." People are worthy of support in direct proportion to the extent to which they conform to Hasidic norms. Negative control is exercised when one loses his reputation through neglect of these norms, resulting in the community's withdrawal of its patronage. Thus, loss of reputation can

11. See pp. 74–76.
12. LaPiere, *op. cit.*, pp. 221–245.
13. See pp. 113–114.

signify economic suicide, particularly if one's business depends upon community trade.

Psychological sanctions, too, may be either positive or negative. Particularly in this community where one's "concept of himself is . . . in considerable measure a function of his group status,"[14] psychological sanction is most effective because "any perceived change in the level of his [a man's] symbolic treatment by a group will tend to change in the same direction [as] his self-judgment,"[15] group control operates effectively.

Negative psychological sanctions include gossip and ridicule, which are used to discourage deviation from any Hasidic norm. It is of crucial importance to the individual to maintain his dignity or his "face" with his reference groups. Positive control consists of the recognition one receives in the community when a person conforms to the Hasidic norms. This community recognition is displayed in various ways. For example, honors are distributed during public worship and the reading of the Torah. These honors are received in proportion to one's religiosity. Still another example of positive control is the *rebbe's* "meal ceremonials." During these ceremonials the *rebbe's* faithful followers receive *shirayim* (literally, "leftovers") from the *rebbe's* dish. A person who does not rank high in the community usually asks for *shirayim* by pushing his way toward the *rebbe*, extending his arm and grabbing *shirayim* from the plate after the *rebbe* moves his plate aside. But when a person is called and receives *shirayim* from the *rebbe's* own hand, he has received one of the most coveted honors in the community. An even greater honor is bestowed if a person receives unsolicited *shirayim* from the *rebbe*.

No deviation from group norms is tolerated in the Hasidic community. In larger, heterogeneous communities it is possible for individuals to live in considerable anonymity. In a complex society the group is more likely "to have various sets of norms some of which may be conflicting and con-

14. LaPiere, *op. cit.*, p. 239.
15. *Ibid.*

tradictory."[16] But in the Hasidic community the norms are
so clearly defined that there can be no individual misunder-
standing about their interpretation. In such a tightly structured community an individual cannot deviate markedly with
impunity, for the community sanctions will affect his life
in all its aspects.

The Hasidic community of Williamsburg is unlike the
larger complex communities where deviation from group
norms by certain "highly valued" members may be an actual
asset to the community. In these communities, according to
some authors, persons of high status are allowed to deviate
from group norms much more than those who do not rank
high in the social order.[17] In the Hasidic community, this
is not the case; the most highly valued persons are those who
most ardently conform to the traditional Jewish laws and
practices. Persons of high rank, such as the *rebbes*, set an example to all other members of the community in their daily
behavior. Upward social mobility is in direct relationship
to strict religious conformity. The Hasidic basis for upward
mobility is remarkably similar to that of the American
soldier, who has a better chance for promotion if he conforms to established military norms.[18]

Despite such strong group pressure for conformity the
members of the Hasidic community voluntarily choose to
conform to group norms. Hence, conformity is much more
effective than in other communities where no comparable
willingness to conform has been internalized. The Hasidim
are convinced that the most effective way to perpetuate traditional Jewish laws and practices, as well as the ultra-Orthodox Judaic philosophy, is through Hasidism. The community is convinced that the function of practicing Hasidism is

16. William F. Ogburn and Meyer F. Nimkoff, *Sociology* (Boston:
Houghton Mifflin Company, 1958), p. 234.

17. Harold H. Kelley and Martin N. Shapiro, "An Experiment on
Conformity to Group Norms Where Conformity Is Detrimental to
Group Achievement," *American Sociological Review,* December, 1954,
Vol. 19, pp. 667–672.

18. Samuel A. Stouffer *et al., The American Soldier: Adjustment
during Army Life,* Vol. I (Princeton: Princeton University Press, 1949),
p. 259.

to uphold Judaism itself. The ideology gives the individual members great psychological satisfaction in being part of such a group. Where such an ideology exists, it is obviously easier to maintain social control, since conforming attitudes are highly internalized. This is in line with Festinger's conclusion that "the more attractive a group is to the individual, the greater will be the effectiveness of pressure to conform to the group."[19]

19. Leon Festinger, "A Theory of Social Comparison Forces," *Human Relations*, 7 (May, 1954), pp. 117–140.

# PART TWO

# Economic Activities
## of the Hasidic Community

# CHAPTER 9

# The General Patterns
# of Hasidic Economic Behavior

THE PREVIOUS CHAPTERS gave some of the background of the Hasidic community. These chapters covered: (1) the uniqueness of the community, and the ways in which the Hasidim differ from other religious minority groups, (2) the background of the Hasidim in relation to the larger organization of the Jews in Hungary, (3) the role of the Hasidim in relation to the larger Jewish organization in the United States, (4) the transplantation of the Hasidic culture to the United States, (5) the fight against assimilation, (6) Hasidic family life, (7) social stratification among the Hasidim, and (8) Hasidic organizations and their role in social control.

In the following chapters the economic activities of the Hasidic community will be described. It will be seen that in their struggles for status, the types of economic activities are not only religiously oriented but explicitly determined by religion so that economic activities reinforce Hasidic norms. This reinforcement prevails to such an extent that the group prescribes who produces what, what is produced and what is consumed, from whom to purchase various items, and what is appropriate to sell. Since the Hasidic community is not physically isolated and members do come in contact with cultural aspects of the larger community, it is feared that familiarity with these aspects may cause assimilation. Although a given aspect may have no religious significance, the mere fact that it does not have religious significance may have a disturbing and disrupting effect on the religious life of the Hasidim. Therefore, almost all non-religious items sold in the Hasidic community are transformed into semireligious articles, thereby sanctioning them for use by the Hasidic community. The extent of the process whereby community control expands and turns the secular into the sacred to maintain its social cohesion and curtail assimilation will be shown in the following chapters.

One of the most important single factors determining an individual's daily activities in his occupation. A person usually resides in the community where he earns his living and will move to almost any community of his preference if the opportunities are more sound and promising. After he moves he usually adapts his own ideals and values to those of the community. He will probably strive to ensure that his children become integrated into community life so that they will be identified as full-fledged members of that community.

This is not so with the Hasidim. They are limited in the area to which they can move, since they want to be in an environment where they can practice the Hasidic way of life. They want to participate in the Hasidic group activities, which are provided only in a Hasidic community. If the Hasidic way of life is to continue from father to son, which the Hasidim set as the goal of their existence, then this life must be lived in a community where ritual practices, group ceremonials, and close contact with the *rebbes* and with other Hasidim can be maintained. Whereas a non-Hasidic person moves wherever he can make a living, the Hasidic person remains in a Hasidic community to be able to continue as a Hasidic Jew. His mobility is extremely limited, since he cannot move wherever his occupation or livelihood might take him but only into a Hasidic community, where he will then take up whatever occupation is available within or adjacent to the community.

For a Hasidic Jew, earning a livelihood presents many difficulties. He can establish himself in the Hasidic community only if he has gained some experience first in *fersheidene gesheften* (various businesses) and has enough capital to open a business. Since the beginner usually has neither the experience nor the capital, he must first go out into the larger community to look for a job. Here he lacks knowledge both of the language and of the working habits. of a highly industrialized society. His external appearance, particularly his beard and religious clothing, is not conducive to finding a job, especially in competition with others. Actually, he can find a job only where his being a Hasidic Jew is no great obstacle. The job opportunities available to a Hasidic Jew are those on the "trodden path"— jobs that have already been held by other Hasidic Jews or other religious Jews with similar characteristics. It is fundamental that the employer should be familiar with the working habits of the Hasidim and that the Hasidim should be familiar with the necessary requirements for the job. This is accomplished through those who have held jobs and acquainted the employer and the prospective employee with the requirements and expectations on either side.

Before the Williamsburg Hasidim came to the United States, a person who wore a beard for religious purposes was identified in America as a "pious rabbi," or as another type of religious functionary. A Jew with a full-grown beard and Hasidic garments was not conceived of, even by Jews, as a menial laborer. Now for the first time in the history of the United States, bearded Jews with Hasidic garments are seen driving trucks, operating machines, and carrying loads of merchandise.

The fact that a great many Hasidic Jews are engaged in

menial labor is objectionable to the religious Jews who have
lived in the neighborhood previous to the arrival of the
Hasidim. One of the informants, who considers himself a
Hasidic Jew, is a religious instructor in one of the well-
known Yeshivot in Williamsburg. He, too, wears a beard
and adheres to the Hasidic principles and is a regular visitor
of the *rebbes*. He expressed objection to the Hasidim:

*Q:* What are the things that you find objectionable about the
Hasidim?
*A:* I think these Hungarian Hasidic Jews have lowered the
prestige of the "Jew with a beard."
*Q:* What do you mean by that?
*A:* I mean that a Jew with a beard does not have the great
status he used to have before the Hasidim of Hungary came to
the United States.
*Q:* Do you mean to say that the Hasidim or that the Jews with
beards years ago were more religious, more observant than these
Hungarian Hasidim? Is that why they lowered the status of the
"Jew with a beard"?
*A:* It is not that at all. These people are very religious and
many of them are learned men. This is not the reason for lowering the status. The reason is that the American Jew, and also
the non-Jew, associates a Jew with a beard with a rabbi. Everyone thinks or, I should say, thought, that a Jew with a beard is
a rabbi. Today the picture has changed. A Jew with a beard
doesn't mean a rabbi at all, especially when one sees these Hasidic Jews engaged in all kinds of menial labor. Menial labor in
America has not been associated with a "Jew with a beard."
*Q:* Does menial labor reduce one's status?
*A:* Maybe it shouldn't, but it is the first time in America that
people have seen Jews with beards and side-locks working as
common laborers. This is lowering the status.[1]

The Hasidim themselves, however, are not surprised at all
that "Jews with beards" work at menial labor. Some of the
Hasidim of Hungary come from sections of the country
where menial labor on the part of Hasidic Jews was common
practice. Some of the informants expressed this quite explicitly:

1. From the files of Rabbi SS, 1957.

*Q:* Are you not surprised to see here in Williamsburg that many of these Jews with beard and side-locks engage in all kinds of menial labor?

*A:* No, I am not. Don't forget that many of these people come from Marmaros, where Jews were really working in the fields and did many kinds of menial labor. I even know of many Jewish girls from the Marmaros who used to go to the cities and become house servants and maids.[2]

The first occupation available to the Hasidic Jew is that of an "operator." Almost everyone who works outside the community is some kind of "operator," since everything is called "operating." If a Hasidic Jew is asked what his occupation is, he will almost likely reply that he is an "operator." It is much easier for the Hasidim to explain or pronounce "operator" than it is to go into the lengthy explanation that he is actually making a certain piece of a necktie or stuffing rag dolls, or sewing pants or mattresses. An operator, to the Hasidim, is one who works outside the community, although the word itself was probably picked up from the garment industry, where an "operator" is one who runs a machine.

As an operator, the individual will try to make enough money to be able to establish himself in some sort of business enterprise of his own in the Hasidic community. Or he will try to learn the trade so that he can apply it to similar work in order to establish himself through this in the Hasidic community.

As an operator, he is paid piecework rates in accordance with the amount of his production. He tries to become as efficient as possible because upon his skill depends the amount of wages he will earn during the week. He races with himself, for the faster he works, the more he produces; the more he produces, the more money he earns; the more money he earns, the more comfortably he can live as a Hasidic Jew. He finds this very difficult. No one forces him to work hard. No one stands over him to see that his work

2. From the files of RG, 1958.

is completed, but "in America *yogt man sich alein* [one chases oneself]; here one becomes his own slave."[3]

## INDUCEMENTS TO WORK

The great majority of the population of the Hasidic community is composed of younger persons. Most members of the Hasidic community are those who were in good enough physical condition to survive the torture of the concentration camps. The younger people who are reaching their late teens are not in the Hasidic labor force. The parents of these young adults encourage their children to study in the Yeshivot until marriage. Some parents even want them to continue their studies after marriage for a few years. They feel that it is only after marriage that one can study with real "purity of heart and thoughts."

The Hasidic man who remains in the Yeshivah after marriage begins to work or support himself during his middle or late twenties. It is very seldom that a Hasidic person works while in his teens. If he is exposed to the business world and to its many undersirable aspects, it is felt that he cannot pursue the Hasidic way of life as it is required of the "most zealous." Financial needs will drive him to do some labor and support himself because the funds of his father or his father-in-law are not adequate to support his constantly growing family, even though his father-in-law or his father still feels that it is his duty to support a God-fearing young man who dedicates his life to learning the Torah and observing the commandments.

The married young man usually learns a trade or business, or is taken into a family business if conditions permit, while he is still supported by his father or father-in-law. Once he learns that earning money offers more opportunity to buy things he could not have before, he feels a greater urgency to earn his own living. Besides, the young man finds out that those people in the community who spend more money in their respective houses of worship in support of their syna-

3. From the files of RSJ 1.

gogues and religious schools enjoy greater honor and prestige. He also finds that the respect and admiration he received while he was younger and dedicated his time and energy to study are not accorded to him to the same extent as before, because now the community expects him to participate and to take an active part in the financial responsibilities of the community. For example, in the houses of worship money is collected every day except on the Sabbath. People come, one after another, and ask the worshipers for money "for important and worthy causes." The young man does not have sufficient money when he is asked to contribute. Thus, he will feel uncomfortable when he cannot participate fully. While he was a younger man, he was not very frequently approached, but as he grows older, the collectors grow in number; they assume that he is a man who "gives." The urgency of acquiring money, and through this becoming equal in the community to any other *balebatisher Yid,* becomes more important to him as he grows older. After he has been initiated into work and working habits and to an organized routine, he assumes fully the responsibility of earning a living.

The female members of the community are usually discouraged from working outside their homes. Most of the women have many children and their services are gravely needed in their own households, which makes them unable to take outside jobs. The unmarried women are discouraged from such outside work because it may become dangerous for community cohesion if the young women are exposed to a world which is quite different from their own. In general, it is more difficult to control women, especially the unmarried, because they do not wear wigs or other external symbols by which they can be recognized as Hasidic women. Consequently, it becomes essential that they be kept within the community. But the community does not create jobs for them, because it wishes to preserve the prestige of the single woman as an eligible daughter of a reputable community member.

In one case where a girl did work outside the community, her father did not consider her job conducive to Hasidic living and found her another job at a lower salary at which she was not exposed to those conditions having a detrimental effect on Hasidism. This she revealed in the following interview:

*Q:* Can you tell me something about your occupational history? Were you ever employed?
*A:* Yes. I had three jobs.
*Q:* The first, give the name of the firm and the date?
*A:* The summer of 1948 I worked at ——— Kosher Restaurant . . . if you can call this a job. This was after I had taken college entrance examinations in New York and received a scholarship to Brandeis University. . . .

At a later interview she explained about the scholarship in the following way:

A few months before graduation from high school I was called into the principal's office and was told that I could have a scholarship to Brandeis University. The principal told me that I should bring in my parents to discuss the matter. My parents came and the principal told them about my achievement and progress in school and that I could have a scholarship to Brandeis University. My father told the principal that for cooking, baking, and making *cholent* (baked beans especially prepared for the Sabbath meal) one need not have a college education.[4]

*Q:* What was your average weekly wage?
*A:* Fifty dollars.
*Q:* What were the reasons for ending this job?
*A:* My father found me another.
*Q:* Why did your father find you another job?
*A:* Because my father didn't want me to work in a restaurant as a cashier among young people coming and going. . . . A young man even offered to take me home. Well, this job lasted only three weeks.
*Q:* Your second job?
*A:* My second job was at the ——— Jewelry Company in New York at ——— Street.
*Q:* Average weekly wage?
*A:* Twenty-five dollars. I was an assistant bookkeeper. Later I

4. From the files of RGE, 1958.

became the bookkeeper at a salary of thirty-five dollars. I worked there until the winter of 1949.[5]

The community tries to have its young women marry while in their teens so that marriage will be the great focus of their lives. Since they discourage them from participating in any other activities that would deter them from this indoctrination, marriage usually does become their major concern.

## OCCUPATIONAL PREFERENCES

The occupational mobility of the Hasidic Jew is very limited. Once he has begun to work at a certain occupation, most likely as an "operator," he will stay within that occupation. He usually changes his job, but he will not change the type of occupation with which he has familiarized himself at the beginning of his working career. On the first job as an operator he acclimates himself to the "idea of work"; that is, he begins to appreciate the value and necessity of some type of gainful employment. It is only with the second job that he actually learns the trade. He will hold the second job longer because he feels that he is constantly bettering himself. If the work he does is piecework, then, with the acquisition of greater skill, he earns more and has greater incentive to stay. If the work he does is on a weekly salary basis, he is given raises in proportion to the acquisition of his skill; hence, he feels that he is reaching greater heights occupationally. Once he receives a "fair wage" or a "living wage" his sense of security will hold him to the job. He cannot easily leave his job because to get a job in another line of work would mean to start to learn a new trade at lower wages. Thus, he will stay on and on as an operator.

The fact that one must be an operator is very much resented by many of the Hasidic Jews. They agree that there is a higher standard of living in the United States. They agree that they are enjoying many of the things they could not afford in Europe. Nevertheless, they strongly resent the fact

5. *Ibid.*

that for all of these things one must work very hard, as is indicated by the following conversation:

*Q:* Do you consider that your present financial circumstances permit a higher standard of living than what you had in Hungary?
*A:* Yes. However, my *personal* standard of living was higher in Europe.
*Q:* Why is that?
*A:* Because all my life I never worked as much as I have worked here in America in one year.[6]

Those Hasidim who have not had an opportunity to establish themselves in an independent business and who resent being operators discourage newcomers from becoming operators. They say to those who are seeking job opportunities: "You'd better struggle for a while and try to find a job which can lead you to some independent business, but don't become an operator, because you remain one for the rest of your years."[7]

The occupational mobility most desired is from dependent to independent labor situations. One starts to establish himself in business or in a shop while he is still working for others on a job. He does not want to risk the security of his job until he can be certain that the shop he is opening has strong possibilities of earning a living for him. This period of establishing himself in a business while still employed by another usually takes a long time. It is hardly adequate for the establishment of a new business undertaking to work at it only part time, after hours, and possibly on Sundays, provided that the regular job does not require working on Sundays.

Those people who are employed by non-Hasidim usually complain that the type of work is beneath their social and religious status. They express the feeling that they deserve "something better" since they evaluate themselves by their standing in the religious order. The occupational hierarchy and one's social and religious status in the community are

6. From the files of RSI, 1957.
7. From the files of LPS, 1958.

not compatible. One may have a high-ranking social position that depends upon religious behavior and practices but hold a job not consistent with his social rank.[8] On the Sabbath, when there is no work being done, the status symbols of clothing, home, and public rituals are the basis for judgment of the individual by which he will be ranked rather than by his occupation during the week.

The kind of work and the amount of money one earns are of course very important. After all, money buys religious goods and services that in turn give one prestige. However, a person who is an operator by occupation, but whose contributions to community services and finances reach beyond his estimated available time and capacities, has prestige accorded him in the community in proportion to his services and his financial contributions, regardless of the amount of time and money. His sacrifices and the willingness he displays will earn him prestige. When his contributions are equal to community expectations, but his religious conduct excels that of the community norm in zeal, in dedication, in piety, and in Hasidism, prestige is accorded him in line with his religious conduct. In Europe, the old and well-known Hasidic families had their respected occupations. These respected occupations were identified and associated with the people in them. For instance, if a well-known family had a grocery store (which in itself was not of high-ranking status), the grocery store was identified with the family and consequently gained status. But here in America, where family background has not yet been established, the individual Hasid must establish himself first in the Hasidic ranking to command this ranking of his establishment.

Social mobility is aimed toward self-employment. The individual Hasid wants to become an *eigener baal habayis* (literally, "house owner"), "one's own boss," a full-fledged, independent member of the community enjoying the rights and privileges of high social standing. Self-employment takes top priority over any other type of employment. To be occupationally independent is preferred to earning a larger

8. For example, in the case of the *talmidei hachamim*. (See pp. 62, 64.)

sum of money in a subordinate position. Although the professionals enjoy a higher status in the community, self-employment in one's own business is the most desirable to
most community members. A member of the community
may greatly respect, admire, and revere his religious leaders
and his religious functionaries; however, there is no necessary desire on his part to become one or to influence his
children to be religious functionaries. For this, one must
acquire more than skill; one must have a religious "calling"
to qualify. Thus, self-employment in other than religious
occupations is considered most desireable.

The second most desirable occupation is one that allows
a high financial return. This is considered desirable only
because it is hoped that it will ultimately lead to independence. The Hasidic Jew feels that he will in this way be able
to accumulate enough capital to open his own business.
Capital and experience are the prerequisites for an independent business establishment and working for others is
considered part of the transitional period while establishing
oneself in an independent position.

The third most desirable occupations are in the group
of so-called stable better jobs at which a person is well established and where his security at the job is fixed. He does
not intend to leave his job, nor does he have greater ambi-
tions for self-employment, because he can earn more as an
employee than as an independent businessman. This man
is well adjusted to his occupation since he can meet his
financial obligations to the Hasidic organization and the
*rebbe*. He can participate in the Hasidic activities without
hardship.

## COMMUNITY SHOPS AND STORES

Almost all shops and stores of Hasidic ownership have
been bought from people who have left Williamsburg.
There are no buildings built for business enterprises by
the Hasidim themselves. They have bought shops or rented
neglected locations which they have cleaned, renovated, and

fixed for their new business ventures. These locations are usually low-rental establishments—one of the major considerations in opening a business. Some stores are connected with an apartment in the back or upstairs. Not all storekeepers live in such a location, though most of them live within close proximity to their businesses. If the family does live in the building where the business is located, the wife usually participates in the running of the shop, especially during the time when her husband is occupied with religious duties. Her participation in the business is considered her contribution to piety because she gives her husband an opportunity to spend more time in studies and daily prayers in the house of worship. In general, however, wives cannot participate actively in the business if, as reputed, they have on the average six or seven children,[9] and simultaneously take full care of their homes in a community where the hiring of servants is unheard of.

## THE MERCHANDISE

Merchandise that needs rabbinical supervision is purchased in a store where one's preferred *rebbe* is in charge. However, not all *rebbes* supervise foodstuffs. They lend their names to merchandise, to stores, and to various commodities. The stores and commodities connected with a particular *rebbe's* name[10] are preferred by the Hasidic Jew who is a follower of that *rebbe*. There are, for instance, butcher stores called the Zehlemer Butcher Store, supervised by the Zehlemer *Rebbe;* the Szigeter Butcher Store, supervised by the Szigeter *Rebbe;* and the Wiener Butcher Store, supervised by the Wiener *Rebbe*. In addition, there are also butcher stores that carry the name of a *rebbe* but are not supervised by that *rebbe*. For example, the Satmarer Butcher Store is not supervised by the Satmarer *Rebbe*. He only lends his name. Most of the Zehlemer followers will purchase their meat pro-

9. This estimate has been made by Hasidic leaders.
10. The *rebbes'* names are identified with geographical locations from which the *rebbes* come or with the communities where they held rabbinical positions.

visions at the Zehlemer Butcher Store, and so on. Despite
lack of supervision by the *rebbe* himself, the Satmarer
followers feel that anything operated with their *rebbe's*
consent suffices for all religious requirements and that the
status name "Satmarer" expresses the ultimate in religious
observance, in quality, and in all other requisites. Furthermore, the profits of these stores support the Satmarer religious schools.

The various organizations appeal to the members and worshipers to support their own sponsored stores. The following is an advertisement in which members and worshipers
are asked to buy their meat and poultry "only" from those
butchers who are supervised by their own *rav.*

### Congregation Assembly of [God-] Fearers
### 27–31 Lee Avenue, Brooklyn

In the interest of our holy congregation, we request from
our members and worshipers that they purchase all their
needs of MEAT and POULTRY only from those butchers
who are under the supervision of Our Master, Our Teacher,
and *rebbe,* may God send him long and happy life.

Our butchers deliver also to the various country places.
The addresses of our butchers are the following:

A. Weinstock, 128 Lee Avenus, Brooklyn
UL 5–9600     Country Phone: Liberty 2559
J. D.Weiss, 145 Tomkins Avenue, Brooklyn
EV 8–1278     EV 7–0271
[Signed]

The Officers of the Congregation Assembly of
[God-] Fearers.[11]

Thus, a butcher store is fully associated with a particular
religious organization. First, the store carries the name by
which the organization is known. Second, the religious
organization draws an income from the store and considers
the store its own. The butcher is considered by the organization to be only a manager or owner of the equipment, but

11. From a pamphlet sent to all members of the congregation, undated. Translated from the Yiddish.

the real value of the store is the name, since it is a guarantee to the customers that the store is reliably kosher. Third, the *rebbe* who is affiliated with the organization sanctions supervision of the store, which gives the store its a priori recognition. There are stores that are not sponsored by religious organizations and are in no way connected with the *rebbe* In these stores, a Hasidic Jew will prefer items that have been manufactured under the supervision of his own *rebbe* if they are also manufactured by other companies under various *rebbes.*

There are other stores selling items that do not require as strict supervision as do meat products. For such stores— bakeries, for example—the name of the proprietor becomes symbolic of the store and of its merchandise. The proprietor must be above and beyond any question as to his Hasidic conformity. This supreme dependability and reliability of the proprietor must be applicable not only to his products, meaning that he uses only ingredients that are approved by the group, but also that he, himself, in his daily conduct must be beyond any doubt. As a matter of fact, unquestionable religious conformity and Hasidic performance earn him trust for his products and merchandise. He is not only a *begleibter Yid,* a "Jew who can be trusted," but also he must be an *ehrlicher Yid durch und durch,* an "honest Jew through and through." Shloimeh's Bakery is one example. This bakery is known throughout the community, and its merchandise does not need supervision, because Shloimeh himself and his name have become symbols of trust.

Shloimeh's Bakery advertised the following:

> All kinds of cakes for Passover and for the whole year you
> can get at
> > Shlomo Weis and Company
> > 435 Bedford Avenue, Brooklyn, N.Y.
> > EVergreen 4-8814
> We will bake this year also in honor of Passover all kinds
> of cakes such as:
> > > Sponge cake
> > > Nut cake
> > > Macaroons,   cookies

Our products are sold wholesale and retail.

The name Shlomo Weis is already your fullest guarantee for quality and *kashrut* [kosher] and a very joyous holiday.[12]

Customers who do their shopping in Hasidic stores, such as grocery stores, are not attracted by the quality of the merchandise or by the price. They purchase their because they find all the familiar products which are permissible for their use, they consider it their obligation to aid people "worthy of support," and they are fully convinced that the storekeepers can be trusted insofar as they will carry only those items that a Hasidic Jew is allowed to consume.

## THE CUSTOMER

Since Hasidic Williamsburg is a *gemeinschaft*-like community, members are expected to make their purchases from their own group members. These purchases express a sense of responsibility and loyalty to the group. The storekeeper expects community members to purchase locally not only items that are exclusively produced and made available by the community but also articles that do not have "group identity." However, many consumers feel that, "with some of my brethren it is good to go to *shul* [the house of worship] but not to do business."[13] This attitude, however, exists only among those who make their livelihood outside the Hasidic community. Some people expressed reasons for not buying a refrigerator, for instance, from an in-group member. They said that if an item did not give proper service, the customer could not demand his money back because he knew the storekeeper too well. He could not ask the merchant to guarantee his merchandise, because the merchant might lose money on him. The purchaser had a moral obligation not to cause property or money damage to his brother. So the purchaser may decide not to buy from one of his kin.

12. *Hamaor*, February 17, 1956, p. 35. Translated from the Hebrew.
13. From the files of NHM, 1957.

However, he is very careful that his relative not find out that he has gone elsewhere to buy an item that could have been obtained from him. The gossip among the women would be too much for his wife to endure, and the possible insult he might receive in the house of worship would not be worth the risk or the amount he would save by purchasing an item outside the community. However, these outside purchases are often made because many members of the community do not have reciprocal trade relationships with each other, and because many times, when merchandise is delivered in trucks, it is not known from whom it comes. It is thus possible to purchase items that are not foodstuffs or religious articles outside of the community. The tendency, however, is to purchase everything within the community, since almost every item now assumes a semireligious significance.

To illustrate, a refrigerator will be sold in the Hasidic community as such an item. There is no prescription in Jewish law that a religious person must use a refrigerator. If he wants to use a refrigerator, and especially on the Sabbath, it can be used only if he fully complies with Jewish law. Since the Sabbath must be observed in its strictest form, the Hasidic Jew may not turn on the light or the electricity on that day, nor may he directly cause an electric motor to go on, because this may be considered as desecrating the Sabbath. The opening of the refrigerator causes warm air to enter the unit and this may cause the thermometer to rise, which in turn starts the motor. Hence, the Jewish person who is extremely careful about the observance of the Sabbath may cause an electric motor to start. There are some who open the refrigerator door only while the motor is running so that they will not directly cause the motor to start. The use of an automatic time clock circumvents this situation. The time clock turns the motor on automatically at periodic intervals, and it has nothing to do with how often the refrigerator door is opened. Although this gadget is a simple time clock, in the Hasidic community it is called the Sabbath *zeiger,* or "Sabbath clock," and since it is attached to the refrigerator, it becomes "Frig-O-Matic Sabbath Zeiger."

One merchant has advertised these "Sabbath clocks" in the following way:

*With the aid of God*
*Great Announcement*

### A Law Concerning the Observance of the Sabbath

To all Jews who are Sabbath-observant and who have electric refrigerators: According to *Hidushei* Hagri [a well-known interpreter of religious laws] one is not allowed on the Sabbath to open the electric refrigerator according to the law of the *Shulhan Aruch* even when the motor from the refrigerator is still running.

We announce that we have now perfected the Frig-O-Matic Sabbath Zeiger through which you may open the door of the refrigerator on the Sabbath every time and it doesn't make any difference whether the motor is running or in a standstill position.

The Frig-O-Matic Zeiger is refined in every respect, it is much nicer, smaller, more practical, it is easier to regulate, and also it is cheaper, to make it possible for everyone to have one. It is completely automatic; once it is connected it is good for the Sabbath and for every day.

Come in for a demonstration daily after 6 in the evening and on Sundays all day.

We sell wholesale and retail. Frig-O-Matic, care of L. Kaufman, 291 Division Avenue, Brooklyn 11, New York. Telephone ST 2-6352[14]

Since there is a tendency to assign various degrees of religious significance to most Hasidic items and since customers for these are restricted by religious edicts, most commodities are not available outside the community. Here is further illustration of how nonreligious commodities become associated with religion. In 1957 a rumor started before the Passover holiday that the vegetables available in the community were generally washed with solutions of chemicals prohibited for Passover use. The community leaders were told that the

14. Placard NR1. Translated from the Yiddish-Hebrew.

chemicals used contain substances that are *hometz*.[15] According to the informant, "Some smart *hevreh man* [an expression used to indicate cleverness derogatorily] who wants to make a business of the situation purchased vegetables wholesale and put dirt and sand on them so that the vegetables would have an 'unwashed look.' " They sold such vegetables by advertising that they had "unwashed" vegetables for Passover. The informant said:

> I do not doubt the earnestness of the people who are willing to pay more for unwashed vegetables, because the people want to have every item in their homes, especially on Passover, above and beyond any question in the matter of *kashrut* [kosher]. But I sincerely question the integrity of the unwashed-vegetable sellers. I doubt very much that the vegetable sellers have really sold unwashed vegetables. I think that they bought regular vegetables available in the market and they just added the dirt to the vegetables.[16]

There is no proof that the informant's impressions are correct. He did not provide sufficient evidence that his assumptions were true. It is a fact, however, that in 1959 the Hasidic community was able to purchase "washed" vegetables that were not washed with prohibited chemical solutions but which had been washed properly, without the chemicals. These vegetables were advertised:

> The vegetables have been washed without mixtures of chemicals and they have also been packed under the supervision of the Central Rabbinical Congress of the United States and Canada.
>
> For Passover, 5719 [1959][17]

Since items of a nonreligious nature must meet religious qualifications, special service establishments develop to make the commodities religiously adequate. The best illustration

15. *Hometz*, literally, "leavened." In common usage, pertaining to everything that is prohibited for Passover use.
16. From the files of LPS, 1959.
17. Placard NR3. Translated from the Yiddish.

of such a "service establishment" is the *Shatnes* Laboratory. There is a Jewish law that prohibits wearing any garment that has been made of a mixture of wool and linen, called *shatnes*.[18] The reason for this law is not explained anywhere in the Jewish literature.[19] Nevertheless, this law has been observed throughout the ages by religious Jews. The *Halachic* literature which pertains to Jewish laws devotes much space to describing the observance of the *shatnes* law.[20] It is possible that for many centuries this law served the very important function of group cohesion. Throughout the ages, the garments worn by Jewish people were distinguished from those of the non-Jews. Especially among the pious Jews, garments of silk, fur, camel hair, and pure linen were popular. Thus, it is possible that the difference in the garments of the Hasidic Jew and those of the non-Jew have been perpetuated by this law.

The garments of the Hasidic Jew in Williamsburg are different not only from those of the general population of the metropolis but also from those of the non-Hasidic Jews who live in the area. This difference is not only in style, color, and tailoring but also in the great care taken that the garments contain no *shatnes*. Those members of the community who wear special Hasidic garments all the time usually do not come too close to the transgression of the law, because these Hasidic garments are usually made by tailors who know something about this law. However, people who wear special Hasidic garments only on the Sabbath wear different clothing on weekdays. These everyday garments may contain *shatnes*. These garments must be carefully examined to make sure that the garment proper, its inside

18. Leviticus 19:19 and Deuteronomy 22:11.

19. J. D. Eisenstein, *Ozar Dinim u-Minhagim (A Digest of Jewish Laws and Customs)* New York: Hebrew Publishing Co., 1938), p. 429. Some commentators on the law have tried to give *ex post facto* reasons for this Biblical prohibition; however, these explanations seem inadequate.

20. *Yoreh Deah, Code of Jewish Laws,* one of the Four Divisions of the *Shulhan Aruch*, "Laws concerning garments made of mixture of linen and wool," Chapters 298–303.

lining, and all material used in the garment are pure and do not contain *shatnes*. For testing purposes, there is a special establishment called the *Shatnes* Laboratory. This laboratory receives garments either from stores that are under contract or from individuals who have purchased their garments from stores that do not have contracts for such testing. In the laboratory the garments are opened at the seams and carefully examined to see if they contain any *shatnes*. If any is found in the garment, it is replaced with non-*shatnes* material. After the inspection, the laboratory puts a label on the garment certifying that the garment has been examined and that it contains no *shatnes*.

The *Shatnes* Laboratory calls the attention of the community to the fact that the transgression of the *shatnes* law is as grave a sin as the transgression of the dietary laws. This comparison is made because there is no question that everyone observes the dietary laws to the utmost. And since the observance of the *shatnes* law is written in the same Torah, there should be no difference in the observance. The laboratory has also made clear to the community that *shatnes* testing is a skilled performance and that a reliable test can be made only with chemicals and a miscroscope. Once people are aware of transgression of the law of *shatnes*, the availability of *shatnes* testing, and the free service offered to customers by stores under contract, it becomes a "sacred duty" for every Jew to request such service.

The *Shatness* Laboratory appeals to the community in the following way:

**"Thou shalt not wear *shatnes*, a mixture of wool and linen" (Deut. 22)**

Wearing *shatnes* is the same serious transgression of a law of the Torah as EATING *TREFA* [sic] [prohibited food]. Analysis has shown that garments frequently contain *shatnes*.

Scientists state that the surest way of identifying *shatnes* is by chemical or microscope test. We have, therefore, established a laboratory to determine reliably whether garments contain *shatnes.*

It is the sacred duty of every Jew to request from the store that the *Shatnes* Laboratory test the purchased garment and have its seal of approval attached to it.

Upon request garments will be tested in any store in N.Y.C. or in most sections of Brooklyn, at a very nominal charge. Just phone and the Laboratory will do the rest.

The garments you buy from the firms listed here will be tested by the *Shatnes* Laboratory—only if requested by the customer.

Parts found to be *shatnes* will be replaced by non-*shatnes* canvas with absolutely no harm to the garment. Entire service is given FREE OF CHARGE. Look for the seal of approval attached to the breast pocket.[21]

The *Shatnes* Laboratory warns that a person should not wear *shatnes* even by mischance. It emphasizes that everyone who arbitrates in matters of *shatnes* should be fully qualified to do so. It further states that the person who wears *shatnes* not only transgresses a law of the Torah, but that his prayers are not accepted. Here is such an advertisement:

Would you go for arbitration in a religious matter to a rabbi who does not have "religious ordination"?

Of course not. Then why do people depend, when it comes to *shatnes,* on the arbitration or permission of the businessman, in those instances where it has been proven by the religious court many a time that even the observers of the commandments have allowed *shatnes* by mischance. The directors of the Torah and Commandments organization have, therefore, established a special religious court for *shatnes,* and a *rav* has been trained for investigating *shatnes.*

The person who arbitrates in the "permission of clothing," regardless of who he is, must have a certificate from an experienced religious court that he is qualified for that. If not, he is not reliable. If a person prays while wearing clothing that contains *shatnes,* his prayers will not be heard (Zohar, *Kav Hayashar* 42).[22]

21. Published in one of the *Shatnes* Laboratory circulars, undated. Translated from the Yiddish.

22. *Hamaor,* Elul, 1958. Translated from the Hebrew.

[List of stores where examinations for *shatnes* may be requested free of charge follows.]

In one of the circulars the *Shatnes* Laboratory tried to indicate that it does not have a monopoly over *shatnes* examination, because if anyone else wants to qualify, he make take an examination. However, it wants to make certain that the community knows that the *Shatnes* Laboratory has passed this examination.

Persons who would like to take the examination should report to one of the directors of the Torah and Commandments organization. Simultaneously we wish to announce that the tester of the *Shatnes* Laboratory has passed such an examination.[23]

## ADVERTISING

Since no radio or television is utilized for the promotion of the various products manufactured in the community, the producers and the storekeepers, the butchers, and the candlemakers, advertise through the following means:

1. Hasidic newspapers.
2. Hasidic periodicals.
3. Placards.
4. Leaflets.
5. Circulars.

1. The Hasidic newspapers are published weekly and bi-weekly in the Yiddish language. They reach a great number in the community. Even though not everyone subscribes to them, they are passed from hand to hand, and since members want to be informed of the "Hasidic news," they are exposed to the advertisements that the newspapers carry.

2. The Hasidic periodicals are published monthly in the Hebrew language. Their circulation is less than that of the newspapers, since their contents deal with matters of religion

23. Circular of the *Shatnes* Laboratory, undated, 8 pp. Translated from the Yiddish.

and rabbinical discussions. They carry many advertisements, especially in the issues that appear before the holidays.

3. Placards are hung in the various houses of worship and public places where the community may be reached.

4. Leaflets are also hung in the various houses of worship and are distributed like the placards.

5. The circulars are booklets with six to eight pages that contain various "important" announcements. In these circulars stories are published to capture the attention of the community. They are not merely stories for entertainment, since this would not be admitted among people who are trying to introduce "holier" and loftier ideals in the community. The stories capture the attention of the reader because they are centered around someone who is known in the community or a person in the community who has been an eyewitness to the events described. These stories must be thought of by the community as "faith strengtheners" published as a public service. It is intended that through reading these stories one will gain faith and strength in his belief in God. The stories relate to miraculous occurrences to individuals in the community. They demonstrate that miracles are not something in the abstract, something far away, but that they actually occur to persons who are known in the community. The miracle becomes real and comprehensible, since it is told by a person whose truthfulness cannot be doubted.

Even though the readers of the circulars think that the stories are "faith strengtheners," well-planned advertising methods are employed. The stories are carefully spaced throughout the pages so that if one wants to read the story, he must come into contact with the advertisements. At the end of a column it is indicated that the story follows on the next page; on the next page, however, a reader must search for the column where the story continues. This is an attempt to insure that he will glance at the advertisements.

The stories themselves are vivid and arouse the curiosity of the readers. The following is an example of one of the experiences that happened to a "known person" in Williamsburg:

### A Wonderful Experience That Happened to a Jew of Williamsburg

With the aid of God

*We are bringing you the following story, which should serve as a strengthener of our faith.*

It happened during the bitter years of World War II, when thousands of Jews were massacred by the Nazis.

In the year 1945 there was a Hungarian Jew by the name of *Reb* David in the concentration camp of Dachau, near Vienna [sic]. Like many other Jews, Reb David too was sick with typhus, may God save us. It used to be the procedure when a sick person was taken to the hospital (it should not befall us), he did not return alive from there any more.

Therefore, his friends did not tell the Nazis that he was sick, and they rather took the responsibility upon themselves, knowing the consequences of this contagious disease, so they kept the secret amongst themselves. Unfortunately the self-sacrifice of his friends did not help. David died during the night. They called the overseers into the death chamber.

David's friend who slept in the same barracks suddenly dreamed that a Jew with a big beard came to him and said: "Go to the death chamber and tell David that he will have a complete recovery." He awoke from the dream, and the dream had a tremendous impact on him. However, he considered it nothing more than a dream and he went back to sleep. As he fell asleep the same dream repeated, and he awoke right away. Now a great fear fell upon him. He was given a definite command. On the other hand, he would have to face certain death if he were to carry out this command. Everyone who was found outside his barracks was shot by the Nazis without any question or investigation. The fear and the doubt did not let him go to the death chamber, so he went back to sleep. But now the old sage appeared to him for the third time and said to him: "I am the *Arugat Habosem* [name of a Hebrew work by Rabbi Moses Greenwald, Chief Rabbi of Hust, Hungary]. I am David's grandfather. Go and tell him that he will have a complete recovery. Nothing will happen to you, and the merit of this deed will be very great. . . ."

The friend jumped up from his sleep from the great fear of the dream, and without thinking, he took his jacket and ran to the death chamber. Actually, through great miracles, he was not seen by any of the Nazis who stood guard in the watch towers. As he arrived in the death chamber, he saw David lying on the floor, and he leaped to him and said: "Your grandfather, the *Arugat Habosem,* sends the message that you will have a complete recovery." Suddenly David grabbed him and yelled: "What did you say?" He repeated it again: "Your grandfather sends the message saying that you will have a complete recovery." But David did not let the friend go; his fingers dug into the friend's sleeves. "Tell me again what my grandfather said." And so the friend had to repeat about twenty times what the grandfather had said. Finally, the friend freed himself and returned peacefully to the barracks.

In the morning the Nazi watch came into the death chamber and saw David sitting trembling from cold and crying among the dead. A little human feeling touched the Nazis. They put him into a hospital from which he returned in good health.

David is now an honorable member of our community in Brooklyn and related the story himself. He also added that each time that the friend gave the message of the grandfather to him, that he would have a complete recovery, he felt that he was getting better and gaining more and more life. That was the reason why he did not want to let go of his friend.

The Rabbi from Szerdahely, Rabbi Neischloss, may he have good and long years, who was at the same concentration camp, said that he knows David's friend, Mr. Joshua Friedman, very well and that this friend told him at that time the exact story as it is related here.

Mr. Friedman settled in Israel and recently came to New York.

*If anyone knows similar stories that can serve as strengtheners of our faith, he should let us know—"Torah and Commandments," 203 Lee Avenue—and they will be published with the help of God.*[24]

24. From a circular of eight pages, undated. Translated from the Yiddish.

The following story is another illustration of one of the accounts published in the circulars. This story is not of a recent event, but a member who is known in the community was an eyewitness to it. Thus, it is just as vivid and "reliable" as if it had happened yesterday. The story goes:

### A True Miraculous Story

#### Contributor: *Rav* A. Stein

This happened thirty-seven years ago.

In the village of Ilya, in the neighborhood of Vilna, this miraculous story aroused the whole neighborhood.

An ox was brought to the ritual slaughterer in the slaughter house. The ox's legs were bound ready for the slaughter. Suddenly the ox freed itself from the ropes and ran into the street. The ritual slaughterer and the other people who were around ran after the ox and they captured it. They bound it again with strong ropes and prepared for the slaughter. But when the slaughtering knife came close to it, it freed itself again from the ropes, and it broke the slaughtering knife. They captured it again and brought it back to the slaughter house.

But now the ritual slaughterer declared that he would not slaughter the ox until he asked the advice of the *rav,* the spiritual leader of the community.

The *rav* heard the wonderful story and ordered that they should bind the ox with very strong ropes and slaughter it. And if it freed itself again, they should not try to catch it but should let it run and follow wherever it went and observe what it did.

They did so. The ox was bound with very strong ropes. Meanwhile, a large crowd gathered to see what was going on with the ox. Even the police came around. When they took the ox to slaughter it freed itself with tremendous strength and ran through the police and the crowd. The police ran after the ox, being careful not to disobey the *rav's* order.

The ox ran until it came into a certain village. It went into a barn. At this barn it stopped in a specific corner and started to stamp with its feet. It dug so deeply into the ground that a dead body became visible. People who were present dug still deeper and saw that it was a Jewish body.

The police took the *goy,* the owner of the barn, for inter-
rogation. He broke down and cried and admitted that he
had killed the Jew. The *goy* related what happened.

The Jew had come to him to buy this ox. Being alone in
the barn, the will to kill overtook the *goy* and he demanded
all of the Jew's money. The Jew pleaded with him in tears:
"Remember that the Creator who created the world sees
everything and this ox that stands here will be the witness. . . ."

The *goy* burst out laughing and he killed the Jew and
buried him in the barn where his body remained until the
ox exposed him.

The story appeared at that time in the various newspapers
and also in the *Voice of Israel* in the year 5,680.

*If anyone knows similar stories that can serve as strength-
eners of our faith, he should let us know—"Torah and
Commandments, 203 Lee Avenue—and they will be published with the help of God.*[25]

Such stories are "faith strengtheners," and in addition the
advertisements pretend to carry important messages. The
advertisements are so phrased that the reader will think they
are published for "community service." For instance, to
advertise utensils is no service to the community, but to remind the community that use of new utensils is prohibited
without first immersing them in a ritual bath is so considered. To tell the community where these ritual baths are
located is also a public service, even though these ritual baths
are in the stores where the utensils are sold. The following
advertisement is illustrative:

> Immersing utensils [in the ritual bath]
> It is an absolute prohibition to use utensils that have not
> been purified through immersing them in a ritual bath.
> The following firms have ritual baths in their stores, and
> for all those who request it, their purchases will be purified
> through immersion free of charge:[26]
> [A list of stores follows.]

25. From a circular of eight pages, undated. Translated from the
Yiddish.

26. From a circular of eight pages, undated. Translated from the
Yiddish.

By calling the attention of the community to the fact that new utensils cannot be used without first immersing them in a ritual bath, the advertisers have presumably made the community aware of this prohibition. After a person has been made aware of this, he cannot help but purchase utensils in stores equipped with ritual baths.

## THE STOREKEEPER

A person who considers opening a shop or business usually tries to establish himself within a higher ranking in the status order of the community prior to the opening of the business. This is done by one or more of the following means:

1. Becoming a member in good standing of a respected house of worship.

2. Having one's entire behavior and religious observance become beyond reproach.

3. Studying and spending time in community affairs and fully adhering to community norms and disciplines.

4. Having a wife whose behavior corresponds to community norms so that she meets community expectations in every respect.

5. Establishing for one's wife a reputation appropriate to the wife of a person who enjoys a higher status in the community, since it is expected that the wife's behavior will be in concert with that of her husband and that the status of the husband will be parallel to and complemented by the reputation of the wife.

6. Having one's children attend the school expected of a person of one's rank.

7. Wearing of Hasidic garments both by oneself and one's entire family.

8. In short, being identified as an integral part of the Hasidic community.

Once these qualifications are met, and when the individual has the capital and the proper business opportunities are available, then business may be begun with assurance of community support and patronage. If the proprietor reaches a higher status on the basis of his sincerity, piety, and Hasidism, the community will express its obligation by supporting him in preference to others. This preference will be given not only over merchants outside the group but also over people lower in status based on religious rank order. The members of the Hasidic group want to perform a *mitzvah* (a good deed) with every action possible, even one so simple as the purchase of a commodity. The mere fact that this has been purchased from a "person of worth" or a "person of stature" or a "person worthy of support" is *ipso facto* considered a *mitzvah*. "Which Hasidic Jew would not perform a *mitzvah* when he can do it simultaneously with other performances?" is a thought expressed many times by the members of the community.

# CHAPTER 10

# The Hasidic Occupational
# Hierarchy: Religious
# and Professional Services

THE OCCUPATIONAL HIERARCHY within the Hasidic community is clearly defined. The close connection between religious and occupational status is indicated in the following ranking of occupations in descending order:

1. *Rebbishe Gesheften* includes all occupations connected in any way with being a *rebbe, shtickel rebbe,* or *rav,* including those of their secretaries and assistants.

2. *Religious professional service* includes all occupations requiring religious training and for which Talmudical knowledge and familiarity with the Jewish law are prerequisites.

3. *Secular professional service* includes all occupations requiring secular training in an academic institution outside the Hasidic community.

4. *Manufacture and sale of religious articles* include all occupations connected with the manufacture or sale of articles of a religious nature.

5. *Manufacture and sale of Hasidic foodstuffs* include all occupations connected with the manufacture or sale of Hasidic food articles approved by Hasidic authorities and all occupations connected with the production or sale of articles leading to the observance of the dietary laws as prescribed by the Hasidim.

6. *Manufacture and sale of nonreligious articles* include all occupations connected with the manufacture or sale of articles not made or used for religious purposes.

7. *Other nonprofessional occupations* may be classified as (*a*) within the Hasidic community, that is, all occupations that are connected with servicing the Hasidic community exclusively, and (*b*) outside the Hasidic community, that is, all occupations that are connected with servicing the non-Hasidic community.

These occupational categories are arranged in descending order of valuation. Of Categories 1 and 2, Religious and Professional Services, discussed in Chapter 10, *Rebbishe Gesheften* is the highest in the rank order. Category 3, Secular Professional Service, also discussed in Chapter 10, because of its requisite for secular training, is basically not a Hasidic occupational category. It is, however, explored in a separate section. Of Categories 4 through 7, discussed in Chapter 11, nonprofessional occupations outside the Hasidic community are the lowest. This order of economic activity is consistent with the six social classes in the community.

All the occupations with the exception of those included under Secular Professional Service, which is not a "Hasidic" economic activity, fall within these six classes. Class 1, *Rebbes*, and Class 2, *Shtickel Rebbes*, make up the category of *Rebbishe Gesheften*. Class 3, the *Sheine Yiden*, is made up of those in the religious professional services. Class 4, the *Talmidei Hachamim*, includes those engaged in the manufacture and sale of religious articles. Class 5, the *Balebatishe Yiden*, includes those who engage in the manufacture and sale of Hasidic foodstuffs and of nonreligious articles. Class 6, the *Yiden*, includes those who are engaged in all the nonprofessional services within the Hasidic community and outside it.

Table III, which combines the two rankings, shows more clearly the relationship between status and occupations.

### Table III. The Relationship of Social Rank and Occupation in the Hasidic Community

| Social Rank | Type of Occupations |
| --- | --- |
| Class 1 *Rebbes* | |
| Class 2 *Shtickel Rebbes* | *Rebbishe Gesheften* |
| Class 3 *Sheine Yiden* | Religious professional service |
| Class 4 *Talmidei Hachamim* | Manufacture or sale of religious articles |
| Class 5 *Balebatishe Yiden* | Manufacture or sale of Hasidic Foodstuffs |
| | Manufacture or sale of nonreligious articles |
| Class 6 *Yiden* | Nonprofessional service within the Hasidic community |
| | Nonprofessional service outside the Hasidic community |

As has already been indicated, class stratification in the Hasidic community is based primarily upon the frequency and intensity of religious observance. This holds true for economic activities as well. A person automatically becomes more religiously active as soon as his occupation makes such increased activity appropriate. Or a person may choose a certain occupation because it gives him more time and opportunity to be religiously active. Finally, a person may have an occupation which in itself is considered a religious activity, as, for instance, that of *rebbe* or another religious functionary. Occupation complement and supplement general status in the community in several ways: they may require Talmudical knowledge and a keen comprehension of Hasidic norms; they may provide a person with more time or money to be more religiously active. Higher status is accorded to persons whose occupations are associated with religion. Consequently, the lowest occupations are those that have no connection with religion, or that, on the contrary, may have negative effects upon religiosity. Thus, all occupations fall within these criteria of evaluation. Each rank of the Hasidic occupations, their characteristics, their functions, how they have come into existence, and how they are currently maintained are explored in this chapter and in Chapter 11.

## REBBISHE GESHEFTEN

As has been indicated, the category of *Rebbishe Gesheften* includes all occupations connected with being a *rebbe, shtickel rebbe,* or a *rav,* including those of their secretaries and assistants.

The *rebbe* is not a functionary employed by any religious congregation. He is considered the *totum factum*; that is, he *is* the congregation. He does not receive a salary but instead receives *pidyan* (literally, "redemption" or "delivery") or money given periodically by his followers, usually around some specific holiday or at a time when there is a specific request to the *rebbe.* These specific requests are for such purposes as praying for one's health, successful delivery at childbirth, or success in a business venture or new job. On these occasions the *rebbe* is visited and begged to pray for the success of the undertaking. During this procedure, which is called the *gezegenen* (a Hasidic ceremonial when the *rebbe* is given the *pidyan*), the follower gives money to the *rebbe* or "puts the *pidyan* on the table."

The *shtickel rebbe* may receive a salary, and he may also perform the *gezegenen.* The *shtickel rebbe* may purchase a home, in which he may establish a house of worship, from the donations of worshipers. If the house of worship is not sufficient for his subsistence, the *shtickel rebbe* may subsidize his income by engaging in other religious activities, such as supervising religious schools, from which he draws an additional salary.

The *rav* has a congregation, not necessarily established by himself. He may be appointed by an already established congregation, in which case he draws a regular monthly or weekly salary. There are no contracts made, since it is understood that appointment to such a position is for life.

In this category also belong those people who are not *rebbes, shtickel rebbes,* and *ravs,* but whose major occupation and subsistence are closely associated with them. Such are the *gabbaim,* the personal secretaries and managers of the *rebbe's* household. They draw certain monetary benefits from the various transactions of the *rebbe,* especially from the followers' periodical visits to the *rebbe.* During these visits the special requests are usually presented to the *rebbe* in written form, and the *gabbaim* are the ones who transcribe the oral requests on paper, for which they are separately remunerated.

Certain *rebbes* have followers in various parts of the world. These followers may or may not be Hasidic in all their religious activities. They visit a *rebbe* on various occasions; sometimes a *rebbe* comes into a community where he has many followers, and at other times the followers come to see the *rebbe* when he is in a nearby community.[1] Some *rebbes* come from Israel to New York and some *rebbes* go to Israel and to various communities in the United States and Canada. The *gabbaim* are in charge of the arrangements for the *rebbes'* visits. The *rebbes'* visits are financially productive, since many Hasidim call upon the visitor to express their honor and respect and to offer financial aid, which is often the purpose of the visit.

These visits of a *rebbe* are advertised in the Hasidic newspapers and in special circulars throughout the community. The following is an example of such a communication:

### Wise Man Has Come to Town!

We announce with great pleasure the arrival of his honor, his holiness, our master and teacher, the *rav,* the *tzadik* [Righteous], *Rav* Joel Zussman-Hertz from Vienna, may he live long and happily.

1. In those communities where a *rebbe* has many followers, he usually organizes a religious congregation bearing his name or with which he is identified in some other way. There may be followers of a *rebbe* in different Jewish communities who do not adhere strictly to Hasidic norms, who are members of the Jewish congregations of their own communities, and whose relationship to their local religious leaders is similar to that of other non-Hasidic Jews.

[*Rav* Hertz is] the son-in-law of our master and teacher, *Rav* Jacob Frankfurter from Kassa, may the memory of the righteous be blessed. [*Rav* Hertz] has arrived in peace from Europe with the aid of God, blessed be He. The *Rav* is staying with his son, *Rav* Jechezkele, may he live long and happily, at 192 Hewes Street, Brooklyn, New York.

[Signed] His Hasidim and his friends, his followers and
his disciples in America[2]

The following announcement of a reception given in honor of a *rebbe* was a mimeographed form sent throughout the Hasidic community and hung in the various houses of worship:

*With God's help.*
To our honored friends,
We cordially invite you to come to the solemn, festive

### Reception

in honor of our *rebbe,* may he live long and happily, which will be held, God willing, on Sunday, the week when the portion *Beshalach* is read in the synagogue [corresponding to January 18], at 7 o'clock in the evening, in the home of our honored friend
     *Reb* David Leibovitz, may his light shine,
     194 Hewes Street, Brooklyn 11, New York
We expect you and all students.
*No appeals* will be made.[3]
     In the name of the *rebbe,* may he live long and happily,
          The Committee of the Students of Erlau.[4]

2. *Der Yid,* December 17, 1957. Translated from the Yiddish.
3. When a *rebbe* comes for a visit, money is usually needed for a religious organization or another religious cause. If it is known in advance that money will be collected at the *rebbe's* gathering, it may discourage some people from coming. Therefore, occasionally it is advertised that "no appeals will be made." This, however, does not mean that no money will be collected. It indicates only that no open solicitations will be made. However, all of those present will be privately asked to contribute to the "great cause."
4: Leaflet RG2, undated. Translated from the Yiddish.

The famous *rebbes* usually do not need any advertisement or special announcements of their arrival in a community as they are anxiously awaited by their followers. The latter are more than happy if they can have the *zechiyo,* the merit of visiting their *rebbe.* They consider it a special honor that has been accorded them to aid their "holy *rebbe,*" even financially. The *shtickel rebbes,* however, depend upon the stout-heartedness of their brethren. Those Hasidim who are helping the *shtickel rebbe* by according him the same honors, recognition, and financial aid as the *rebbe* do this because they recognize the *shtickel rebbes* as "Jews worthy of support," even if this support is in the form of charity. Since the *shtickel rebbe* usually is a descendant of a famous "*rebbe* of old," the supporting Hasidim consider him to have *zechut avot,* "the merit of his forefathers." The mere fact that this *shtickel rebbe* is the descendant of a famous *rebbe,* the son and the product of "holy seed," makes it a "holy duty" to support him. This *zechut avot* has the power of shielding and protecting one from sin and other harm. Hence, when a Hasidic Jew supports a *shtickel rebbe* who possesses this *zechut avot,* he feels that through his support he may evoke the "shielding power" of the great *rebbe* of old.

The *shtickel rebbe* is of course aware that he is the descendant of a great *rebbe.* He knows that his forefather had many, many followers and that his name was known throughout the Hasidic camp. He is aware of the fact that even today such a predecessor would enjoy the strong support of many Hasidim. He realizes that many of the Hasidim would still identify themselves with his forefather of old, even though today they are the followers of another *rebbe,* since the dynasty of the former *rebbe* has already withered away. Knowing all this, the *shtickel rebbe* will seek the support of those Hasidim who are willing to help him as they are reminded of the tradition of a "great man of blessed memory."

The *shtickel rebbe* has letterheads upon which his name, his father's name, his grandfather's name, and his great-grandfather's name are printed to indicate that he is the descendant of generations of great men. He uses these letterheads for requests for financial aid or to extend invitations to banquets, the main purpose of which is to appeal for financial aid. Or he may write to various friends, admirers, and followers of the *rebbe* of old and seek their support to establish a house of worship from which he can maintain his livelihood.

The following is a translation of a letterhead in which a *shtickel rebbe* appeals for help for his "critical economic circumstances":

> With the aid of the Holy Name, may it be blessed
> The *Rav* Juspe Friedlander,
>    The *Rav* from Liszka
> The son of the *Rav,* the Righteous, the Master, the Righteous of the generations, may the memory of the righteous be blessed, the head of the rabbinical board of the holy community of Liszka
> And the *Gaon,* the Holy, *Rav* Hershele Lisker, may the memory of the righteous and the holy be blessed
> The grandson of the Master, the *Gaon,* the Righteous, *Tal Chaim* [the author of this book], may the memory of the righteous be blessed
> And the Master, the *Gaon,* the Holy from Belz, may the memory of the righteous be blessed
> The *Maggid* [the preacher] of Lublin from Koznitz and from Barditsev
> And the *Rav,* the Holy, *Rebbe* Elimelech from Lizensk, may his guarding influence guard over us.

On this letterhead there is a Yiddish and an English text asking for help and expressing the *rebbe's* blessings. There is in addition the handwriting of the *rebbe* to make it more personal. In the Yiddish text this *shtickel rebbe* makes specific reference to the merits of his "holy forefathers." A translation of the Yiddish text of the letter follows:

> Dear Friends,
> With the coming of the season of the giving of our Torah I come to wish you and your worthy family a happy holiday of Shavuot, and a healthy summer with lots of success, health and prosperity and pleasure from the children and

all the Jews should be helped with all kinds of salvations.
*Amen.*

I beg you not to forget to help me in my critical economic
circumstances and also my many responsibilities according
to the goodness of your heart.

And for the merit of charity and for the merits of my
holy forefathers you will be surely helped with a happy
holiday with the flow of blessing and success and with
everything good. Selah.

[Signed] The *Rav* Juspe Friedlander

The son of the *Rav*, the Righteous, the Master, the Righteous of the Generations,

May the memory of the righteous be blessed, the head of
the rabbinical board of the holy community of Liszka[5]

There are also handwritten letters addressed to specific
persons who seem promising prospects for financial aid.

The following translation of a "personal" letter written
by a *shtickel rebbe* contains reference to his holy parents:

### With the aid of God

My deeply honored loyal well-wisher and religious brother
from home, Mr. and Mrs. Herman Lefkovitz and his dear
family, may you live for 120 years.

Before anything else, please accept my wishes for a pleas-
ant Passover holiday and a healthy summer in person and
good luck and in happiness. Amen.

As the famous Rabbi [*Rebbe*] of Olaszliszka who is also
the descendant of my holy grandparents I appeal to you for
the first time because of my difficult circumstances and that
of the five members of my family who need my help. If possible, you as well as my other acquaintances from home
should help me through your good soul which I hope that
through my holy parents and their holy blessing God's holy
blessing will be sent to you for goodness and every day will
be with good luck and well-being forever. Amen. I am grateful and waiting anxiously for your kind reply.

With hearty greetings and with deep honor,

[Signed] Rabbi J. Friedlander

5. From letter RG1. Translated from the Yiddish.

[Sealed with rubber stamp] Liszker Rabbi Friedlander

1449 - 50th Street
Brooklyn 19, New York
Telephone GAdney 5–8651[6]

Some *shtickel rebbes* send handwritten form letters that
are not to a specific person but to "friends" in general. Such
a letter also appears on a letterhead listing the *shtickel rebbe's*
entire lineage of *rebbes* in this way:

The Soniker *Rebbe*
The *Rav Reb* Eliezer Spiro, may he live long
and happily,
Third generation, son after son, of the holy *Gaon*, the
*Rav* of all the people of the Diaspora, the honored holi-
ness of his glorious name, our teacher the *Rebbe* Zevi
Elimelech Spiro of Dinev, may the memory of the
Righteous be blessed,
The writer of the books *B'nei Yisoschor* and *Egra DeKala*,
and more books,
Fourth generation of the holy *Gaon*, the *Rav* of all the
people of the Diaspora, the prince of the house of the
*Zohar*, the honored holiness of his glorious name,
Our teacher the *Rebbe* Zevi Hirsh of Ziditzov, may the
memory of the Righteous be blessed,
And also high in the rank of holiness of many *Gaonim*
and Righteous men, may their merits guard us and all
the people of Israel. *Amen.*
[End of letterhead]

Peace and good blessings to all the people of the community.
Please, please, have pity and mercy on me, to support me
with "money for wheat" for the holiday of Passover, that
is coming to us with good luck.
May it be God's will that you should celebrate the holiday,
with God's will, in ritual fitness and joy.
Your friend,
[Signed] The above[7]

6. From letter RG2. Translated from the Hungarian.
7. From letter RG4. Translated from the Hebrew.

It may be noted that instead of signing his name, he merely signs "the above" in order to refer not only to his name but also to the entire listing of his lineage.

This particular *shtickel rebbe* makes the greater part of his living from such form letters, so he must send them periodically. He even maintains in his letterhead that his sad circumstances are "already known." The following is a translation of a post card he sent to "friends" before Passover. After the usual identification of his lineage at the top of the post card, this text follows:

> Very honored friends:
>
> My mournful circumstance, in every respect, may it not befall you, is already known to you from my letters of appeal for help. I take the liberty to remind you and appeal to you for help, because on account of my old age circumstances have turned for the worse.
>
> For the merits of this great commandment and also for the merit of my holy parents, may their merits shield us, you will be helped with God's help with health and prosperity and with all things good.
>
> I wish you a kosher and a happy Passover.
>
> [Signed] The *Rav* Eliezer Shapiro[8]

The word "occupation" is not a precise term when associated with *rebbishe gesheften*. The *rebbes* are the charismatic leaders of the community. The term "charisma" is applied by Max Weber to "a certain quality of an individual's personality by virtue of which he is set apart from ordinary man and treated as endowed with supernatural, superhuman, or at least specifically exceptional powers or qualities."[9] Therefore, *rebbishe gesheften* in a strict sense represents more than just occupation. It implies the involvement in a "religious calling" and is not necessarily associated with the religious

8. Card RG3. Translated from the Yiddish.
9. Max Weber, *The Theory of Social and Economic Organization*, translated by A. M. Henderson and Talcott Parsons (Glencoe: The Free Press, 1957), p. 358.

leader's economic activities.[10] In the Hasidic community it is the obligation and duty of each member to support his religious leader. For this economic support the leader does not have to reciprocate in the form of a service. The mere fact that the *rebbe* is an exemplary symbol of religiosity makes it a moral duty to share "worldly goods" with the man who shares "spiritual goods" with the community. Monetary support given to the *rebbe* is not in the form of charity defined as alms-giving or money to relieve one in distress. Rather the "charity" with which the community supports its *rebbes* involves giving indicative of affection, love, benevolence, and high regard. It reflects as well the notion of *zechut,* or merit, virtue, privilege. It is a form of sacred duty and a religious obligation to share one's wealth with those "holy men," who are the "pillars of society and of the world." It must be noted, however, that the responsibility for, and the actual financial support of, the *rebbe* is directly related to his hierarchical position.

There is an additional point of significance here. The leader's influence upon the members is closely related to the economic activities of the Hasidim. The significance of the leader's role for economic affairs lies in the fact that he sanctions economic goods. As Max Weber states:

> Everywhere hierocracy has sought to monopolize the administration of religious values. They have also sought to bring and to temper the bestowal of religious goods into the form of "sacramental" or "corporate grace," which could be ritually bestowed only by the priesthood . . .[11]

In a community where behavior is guided by religion and where religion is the most important single factor in the lives

10. It is traditional with many orthodox Jews that for "holy work" and the study of the Torah one does not seek economic compensation. This is seen by the fact that "the medieval Rabbis earned a living as artisans, physicians, merchants, authors, pen-men, marriage-brokers, finance ministers, men of science, and it was not till the fourteenth century that the Rabbis became dependent on the support of their congregations." Cecil Roth, *Jewish Life in the Middle Ages* (London: Edward Goldston, 1932), p. 247.

11. Hans H. Gerth and C. Wright Mills, *From Max Weber: Essays in Sociology* (New York: Oxford University Press, Inc., 1958), p. 282.

of the members, it is inevitable that religious leaders will assume the highest social position. In the words of Weber, they are occupied with the "cure of soul" or, as it is termed in the Hasidic community, are engaged in leading and directing the members toward the "way of righteousness." Because the *rebbes* do religious counseling and because almost every aspect of Hasidic life falls within this realm, they have a monopoly over religious values. They define the Hasidic values and prescribe behavior to complement, supplement, and reinforce these values. Hence, the community, for the reinforcement of these values, must create religious goods whose appropriateness is sanctioned by the *rebbes*. For example, to observe the dietary laws, the community must provide food sanctioned by the *rebbe*, prepared and sold by "faithful" members who must also be acceptable to the *rebbe*. Thus, the religious leadership approves,[12] accepts,[13] and many times formally sanctions[14] the transformation of goods into items with religious significance. Such action strengthens the community's economic activities and contributes significantly to group isolation and maintenance.

## RELIGIOUS PROFESSIONAL SERVICE

The category of Religious Professional Service includes all occupations that require religious training and for which Talmudical knowledge and familiarity with religious laws is demanded. It includes the following occupations:

1. *Shohet*—ritual slaughterer.
2. *Shamash*—religious servant of the house of worship.
3. *Melamed*—instructor in religious matters.
4. *Hazan*—cantor.
5. *Baal Tefilah*—conductor of public worship.
6. *Mohel*—circumciser.

12. The *rebbe* consents to the use of a product.
13. The *rebbe* himself or his household uses a product.
14. A product is prepared or manufactured under his supervision.

7. *Mashgiach*—actual overseer of food products that require rabbinical supervision.

8. *Sofer*—scribe of religious letters and documents.

9. *Metargem*—translator.

10. *Batlan*—professional scholar, or idler.

11. Miscellaneous religious practitioner.

These will now be described individually.

## 1. The *Shohet*

The *Shohet,* or ritual slaughterer, is in charge of slaughtering and preparing animals whose consumption is otherwise prohibited. One of the major requirements for a ritual slaughterer is to be a *yerei shamayim,* or God-fearing man. He must observe all the laws prescribed in the Torah and all the Hasidic norms prevalent in the community. His God-fearingness and his integrity about religious observances and practices must be far beyond and above any question or doubt. He must be known and acknowledged in the community as a *ben Torah* (literally, "son of Torah"), a religious scholar, a *yerei shamayim,* and an *ehrlicher Yid,* an "honest-to-goodness honest Jew."

He must have a *kabalah* (literally, receipt), a certificate which certifies his God-fearingness, his skill in slaughtering, and his knowledge of the law of ritual slaughter. This certificate must be issued by a *rav* who enjoys the highest regard and reputation in the Hasidic community. It then conveys to the community the idea that any person sanctioned by him as a ritual slaughterer must be a person who is highly competent in all religious matters.

There are two kinds of ritual slaughterers, the *shohet-gassim* or ritual slaughterer for large animals, and the *shohet-ofot* or ritual slaughterer of poultry. The *shohet-gassim* is required to have the greater skill and competency in slaughtering. His conformity to the Hasidic norms is constantly watched through the many eyes of the Hasidim. When a Hasidic Jew eats meat, he must be sure that it has been ritually slaughtered by a man of outstanding Hasidic characteristics, that the prayer over slaughtering the animal has been recited by a man of great piety, and that the examination of the animal after slaughter, required by religious law, has been performed by a man outstanding in Hasidism.

The *shohet-ofot* must also be a man who meets all the Hasidic qualifications. However, since poultry slaughtering does not require as great skill, he does not have as high a status as does the ritual slaughterer of large animals.

The *shohet,* too, must be a Hasidic Jew. If he is not, his slaughtering is not considered kosher enough for the Hasidim. There are many ritual slaughterers in America; almost every community in the United States where there is a Jewish population that demands kosher food has one, but these ritual slaughterers are not religious enough for the Hasidim. They are considered to be "assimilated" and to have already "tasted the taste of sin," which disqualifies them for this high professional service.

The sentiment has been expressed by many Hasidic leaders that the *shohtim* in America do not even look like *shohtim.* They are shocked to see a ritual slaughterer who looks like a coachman or a tanner and in whose house there is no sign or trace of the Torah, only television and radio, and whose wife and daughter are bareheaded. They wonder how such a man can be called "one who fears God."[15] In Europe the ritual slaughterers were holy men, always praying and fearing God, who did their work in holiness and cleanliness. But the Hasidim cannot conceive of a slaughterer who looks like a manufacturer, who goes to the movies and to the theater, who prays in a synagogue where he is forbidden to enter according to the traditional law, who sends his sons and his daughters to college, whose wife does not remove her hair. According to the Hasidim, how can such a man be called *shohet?* From the time of the receiving of the Torah until today, there has never been such a violation.[16]

Thus, the religious conception and observance of the Hasidic norms determine the qualifications of the *shohet*

15. Raphael Blum, *Tal Hashomayim* (New York: published by the author, 1958). "Introduction." Translated from the Hebrew.
16. *Ibid.*

as well as the qualifications for most other occupations, especially in the category of professional service.

## 2. The *Shamash*

The *shamash* is the person who is in charge of the house of worship before, during, and after the services. He keeps record of the donations and contributions. He collects membership dues and various donations. He sees to it that the "holy objects" for the service are in order and that the Torah scrolls are properly prepared for reading.

He may draw a straight salary from the organization, but most of the time his salary is in proportion to the amount of money he collects. In this case he is working on a commission or percentage of his collection. Thus, "the larger the congregation, the bigger the *shamash*."

To qualify for this position, no ordination and no certification are necessary. The *shamash* must be a religious man, and his integrity in Hasidic matters must be above average. There is, however, a certain leniency toward him concerning his pecuniary activities. No individual with an obvious overriding interest in money can be recognized as an outstanding Hasid, since this interest may affect his religious observance negatively. But since the profession of *shamash* requires some skill and experience in monetary dealings, the *durchgeshpitzter shamash*, the foxy or the shrewd servant of a house of worship, is seen as highly desirable. As a matter of fact, the community is willing to admit that a good *shamash* must be a *geribener ying*, a shrewd fellow with experience and a touch of arrogance.

It is questionable where the loyalty of the *shamash* lies, whether it is with the organization or with the members. If his loyalty appears to lie with the organization, then his office gives him higher rank and he is not in a position subordinate to the members. If his loyalty seems to lie with the members, he becomes subordinate to the individual members of the organization, particularly to those who are powerful or arrogant. If the direction of his loyalty is not clearly understood, it creates a conflict situation. The following episode is an example of such a loyalty conflict where the *shamash* held that his loyalties were to the organization and the *rebbe,* and the members demanded that his loyalties and services be to them. One of the informants relates the story:

On the Saturday night which concurs with the festival of Hanukah, the *shamash* of the Satmarer house of worship lost three of his teeth. It so happened that after the religious service the members wanted to go home and wanted to take their winter coats from the cloakroom which was closed by the *shamash.* The *shamash* didn't want to open the door because the *rebbe* had not finished with the evening service. The *shamash* said that to show respect to the *rebbe* one must wait until the *rebbe* had finished with the prayers. The members insisted on getting their coats and the *shamash* insisted that they should wait for the *rebbe.* The members demanded that the *shamash* open the door but he did not comply with their request.

The members took a large prayer shawl and threw it over the head of the *shamash* and gave him such a beating that three of his teeth fell out.

The *shamash* called his attackers to *Din Torah* [Torah justice], rabbinic arbitration. The rabbinic court fined the attackers of the *shamash* eight hundred dollars in payment for the loss of his three teeth and his humiliation.[17]

In Europe the position of the *shamash* was a lifetime appointment. Once the congregation employed a *shamash,* it considered him entitled to hold the position until he was physically unable to continue. In the United States, in non-Hasidic congregations, the *shamash* receives a contract and stays until the contract expires. After its expiration, the congregation may renew his contract or the *shamash* may stay without a contract, but by that time he has established a favorable personal relationship with the members of the congregation, so that a contract is not necessary for either party.

However, in the more traditional congregations, if there is a segment that displays dissatisfaction with the services of

17. From the files of LPS, 1959.

the *shamash* or his extra touch of arrogance, they may successfully try to remove him from his position. This can be
accomplished through various internal maneuverings and
"politics." Although the removal of a *shamash* seldom occurs,
when it does happen, the *shamash* requests the amount of
money that would total his salary for the rest of his life. He
knows he cannot get this amount, since the entire assets of
the congregation are less than the amount, but he is prepared to turn to the second best measure, compromise. He
declares himself willing to accept a certain amount in the
form of *ausgleichen* (compromise) as his severance pay, but
this severance pay may be too much or some members may
feel that the *shamash* is not worthy of it. Therefore, they
may refuse to pay him the requested amount and offer instead an amount that is not acceptable to him. The *shamash*
now may turn to a third resource, rabbinical arbitration,
where both sides are given a chance to tell their story and
display their grievances. After all grievances are heard,
this religious court (consisting of one or three rabbinical
authorities) makes its final decision. The *shamash* has a very
strong chance of winning his case. However, the congregation may show lack of funds or inability to pay, in which case
the payment to the *shamash* may take a lifetime and be given
to him in ridiculously small installments. The congregation
cannot be declared insolvent and forced to sell its assets to
pay the *shamash*, because no congregation dissolves for the
sake of the *shamash*.[18] As a result of this rabbinic arbitration,
even though the *shamash* legally wins his case, he is still the
loser because he will never get the money he requested as
severance pay.

The *shamash* has still another course to follow, which is
his last resort. He may appeal to the general community,
from which he may draw sympathizers more readily because
he is not so well known as he is in his own congregation,
and also because there is a greater sympathy expressed toward
an individual in need than toward an organization, which

18. There are many precedents in which congregations have been
dissolved for a *rav* or a *rebbe* in similar circumstances.

cannot suffer pain and agony. The *shamash* will appeal to the public conveying the idea that an *avlah*, an injustice, has been done to him. As far as he is concerned, he is still the *shamash* of his congregation and therefore no one should "raise a hand" to hire another *shamash* until the congregation has settled with him first. By making this public appeal, the *shamash* will gain three advantages. First, he will evoke the compassion of the individual in the congregation who does the actual hiring of the *shamash*, saying that if he is a person of any moral character, he should not be part of an injustice, for he will be "reckonable" in the world-to-come if this "*avlah* stains his hands." This may prevent the hiring of another *shamash* while there are still claims associated with that position. Secondly, no *shamash* will consider taking the position because there is an *avlah* associated with it. A *shamash*-candidate understands the position of a *shamash* and would feel that whatever happened to his colleague might very well happen to him. Thirdly, the people who have found out about the *shamash* will bring pressure on the members of the congregation, telling them that "it is not worth ruining the prestige of the congregation by suffering the 'hanging-on' of a *shamash*." The sympathetic members who have been influenced by this will try to be liaisons between the *shamash* and the congregation so that the situation in which the *shamash* is *ohntzepenish* (hanging-on), which is marring the organizational structure, may be settled. This last course, which the *shamash* takes in appealing to the Hasidic community for aid and sympathy, is illustrated by the following advertisement:

**NOBODY SHALL RAISE HIS HAND, WHOEVER HE IS,**

to hire a *shamash*, a Reader of the Torah, a person who officiates at the morning service in the Great House of Study on the East Side.

60 Norfolk Street, New York

Until they settle with me in the most satisfactory manner.

Haim Natan Goldberg

Deacon, reader, performer of the morning service in the

*Bet Hamidrash Hagadol* [The Great House of Study] Downtown[19]

## 3. The *Melamed*

The *melamed,* or instructor in religious matters, is in charge of teaching children the knowledge of the Torah and religious ethics, and of indoctrinating them with Hasidic principles. He must not only be equipped with the ability to teach but must also be a person whose behavior exemplifies to the children the Hasidic way of life. The *melamed* is employed by a religious school and spends approximately ten hours every day, six days a week, and almost fifty-two weeks a year with the children. He teaches them the Torah, Scriptures, laws concerning everyday behavior, and respect for the *rebbe* and for their parents.

The melamed is called "*Rebbe*" by the Hasidic children and is addressed as such. In the miniature world of the child the *melamed* is an actual "*rebbe*," and all his mannerisms, his intonations, the way he carries his body, the way he moves around the classroom, the way he recites a prayer, the way he yells at the children, and almost everything about him is imitated by the children. This imitation is carried home, where a very vivid picture is unveiled of the personality, pedagogical ability, and Hasidic integrity of the *melamed* through the imitative behavior of the children. The *melamed's* participation in Hasidic affairs is constantly evaluated and re-evaluated in the Hasidic community. This evaluation is based on very high standards. The *melamed* cannot afford to lapse in any way or to change the mental image of himself to a less desirable form. After all, "the future of the Hasidic community and the future of the Holy Torah are in his hands." It is his responsibility to nurture the *tzon kedoshim,* the "holy herd." Thus, the *melamed* holds one of the

19. *Der Yid,* August 23, 1957. Translated from the Yiddish. This congregation is not a Hasidic house of worship, but since the Hasidic community has many potential *shamashim,* and because it may draw more sympathizers from the community who may convey this sentiment to members of the congregation, this advertisement in the leading Hasidic newspaper is most appropriate.

most functionally important positions in the Hasidic community.

The major requisites and qualifications of a *melamed* are first and foremost to be an *ehrlicher Yid.*It is also important that he know how to learn and how to teach and how to conduct himself in a classroom. It is assumed in the community that if he is a real *ehrlicher Yid,* the other qualifications will automatically follow. A real *ehrlicher Yid* has full awareness of the holy responsibilities accorded to him. He will study for study's sake, he will try to teach to the best of his ability, and he will give all of himself to this most sacred calling.

There are two types of *melamdim.* One type teaches children up to the age where they can read, translate, and study the Talmud by themselves. The second type of *melamed* is the one who teaches young men who are advanced in Talmudical studies. The latter may be in the category of *rav* or *shtickel rebbe.* The former is remunerated by an actual weekly salary from the religious school. In Europe, those in charge of the more advanced Talmudical studies were not financially rewarded, since they were usually heads of congregations or other religious organizations, but in the United States they are remunerated. The money they receive for their Talmudical teaching is not merely an additional income but is the major source of their earnings. If they are affiliated with a religious organization, this affiliation is only for purposes of status.

Another occupation that is classed as *melamed* does not include instructing classes. Such a *melamed* is usually a *rav* or *shtickel rebbe* who is appointed by one or more religious schools at which he is the *ferherer,* the examiner. It is the examiner's duty to go from class to class or from school to school and examine the children's weekly accomplishments. This examination gives an incentive to the children to be well prepared and also to the *melamed,* since this examination is a check on his performance.

It is paramount for the *melamed* to be an *ehrlicher Yid;* scholarship is only secondary. A *melamed* who teaches small children need not be a scholar; however, the one who teaches

Talmud and the method of Talmudical and rabbinical studies must also be a real scholar besides being an *ehrlicher Yid*. Since scholarship is necessary for the teaching of Talmudic rabbinical studies, such a *melamed* is recruited from the class of *talmidei Hachamim* in the community. The religious school proposes and offers him a position matching or exceeding his previous earnings.

A *melamed* for small children is also recruited from the community on the basis of teaching ability, but these positions are usually publicly advertised. The following is a typical advertisement for a *melamed:*

> A *melamed* for Small Children Wanted
> Good conditions.
> Nyitra Yeshivah.
> Mount Kisco.
> Call EVergreen 7–0422[20]

Most *melamdim* are employed by religious organizations from which they draw a regular salary, and instructing is their only occupation. However, there are also *melamdim* who teach on a free-lance basis in addition to their other occupation. They supplement their other income by giving private lessons in Talmudical studies to children. The free-lance *melamed* advertises in the following way:

> Private lessons for children!
> I give private lessons for children who learn Talmud with commentators each day from 3 o'clock in the afternoon until 6 in the evening.
> Interested persons can find me during the public worship in the synagogue of Sziget.
> Moshe Heller, 152 Hewes Street, Brooklyn, New York[21]

## 4. The *Hazan*

The *hazan,* or cantor with singing ability, is the person who conducts the religious services on the Sabbath, holidays,

20. *Der Yid,* January 31, 1958. Translated from the Yiddish.
21. *Der Yid,* November 15, 1957. Translated from the Yiddish.

and special occasions. The Hasidic houses of worship do not engage a *hazan* because: (1) "there is no need to attract worshipers with semimusical entertainment," and (2) the houses of worship will not engage a person whose singing and quality of worship is not taken seriously by religious people. There are, however, *hazanim* who are engaged by non-Hasidic congregations. There are also *hazanim* who do cantorial free lancing on various occasions such as weddings, engagement parties, and other religious gatherings.

Although the *hazan* is a member of the Hasidic community, he does not enjoy the high status accorded to riligious professional functionaries in other Jewish communities in the United States. His trills and mannerisms displayed during prayers are sometimes ridiculed in the Hasidic community. His performances as a *hazan* are associated with acting, which has no place in the Hasidic community. According to the Hasidim, religious ecstasy and religious thrill must have spontaneity; it must come from within. A person must be inspired to do whatever come naturally to him during prayers. Prayers cannot be rehearsed, premeditated, displayed with prepared body movements and facial expressions. Thus, the *hazan* is considered a person who has already "tasted the flavor of sin and whose heart has been tainted with deceiving applause." His songs and melodies are considered only entertainment and are not taken seriously in formal public worship.

## 5. The *Baal Tefilah*

The *baal tefilah* (literally, "master of prayers") is the conductor of prayers during public worship. This person too must be recognized in the community as a real *ehrlicher Yid*. According to the *Code of Jewish Law*, it is required that the *baal tefilah* be a person of excellent moral and religious character, as it is stated:

It is proper that the Reader who recites the Propitiatory Prayers and who conducts the services on the awe-inspiring days [Rosh Hashanah and Yom Kippur] should be a man of eminent respectability, greatly learned in the Torah and excelling in goodness, as good a man as can be found. He should be at least thirty years old, for then the blood of his youth has already stopped boiling and his heart has become humble, and he should be married and have children so that he make supplication with a full heart.[22]

If there is a question of choosing between two persons, one of whom possesses superior ability in singing and conducting the service and the other, a superior moral and religious character, in the Hasidic community the person with the greater religious and moral qualifications is given preference for the following reasons: the *baal tefilah* is interchangeably called *sheliach tzibur,* an emissary of the congregation; he is expected to pray for the community and devotion, display of zeal, and "flaming enthusiasm" must be part of prayers.

There are *baalei tefilah* who are engaged as the conductors of prayers during the Jewish High Holy Days in religious congregations outside the Hasidic community. For this service a contractual remuneration is arranged. Since the Hasidic Jew leaves his community and his *rebbe* for the High Holy Days and consequently cannot be an actual beneficiary of the "holy man's grace," but instead must bestow grace upon others with his prayers, the amount of his remuneration must be substantial. Therefore, he expects to be compensated not only for the service he renders but also for his inability to attend his *rebbe's* service on such a holy day.

The *baal tefilah* in the Hasidic community, in addition to being a conductor of prayers, has another occupation. This occupation must be complementary to being a *baal tefilah;* he may be a *melamed* or a *shohet.* But he will not be a *baal tefilah* alone, because in a Hasidic community almost everyone knows how to conduct services and it is considered an honor for a person to be given that privilege, so that compensation is considered improper. When a *baal telfilah* does receive remuneration, it is usually for other activities he performs and not for conducting prayers.

22. *Code of Jewish Law (Kitzur Shulhan Aruch),* compiled by Solomon Gansfried and translated by Hyman E. Goldin (New York: Hebrew Publishing Co., 1927), 128:7.

Persons who engage in nonreligious activities during the week and become *baalei tefilah* for any of the holidays are not considered to be practicing an occupation, but only enjoying an honor and a privilege that the congregation grants them in recognition of their high status in the community.

### 6. The *Mohel*

The *mohel,* or circumciser, in the non-Hasidic Jewish communities, is a full-time circumciser whose major occupation is to circumcise infant male Jewish children ritually. For this service he is compensated, and he draws his livelihood solely from this service.

In the Hasidic community, however, being a *mohel* is not a full-time occupation, but is usually connected with some other religious activity. There are many circumcisers in the Hasidic community, since it is considered a great religious performance to circumcise a child and to become an "initiator into the covenant of Abraham." Thus, many circumcisers are not remunerated at all. When one is, it is reciprocally understood that the remuneration is not given for the actual circumcision, because for this honorific performance one should not receive any payment. It is understood that the father of the child is giving money to the *mohel* because he is a person "worthy of support," and the circumcision gives him an opportunity to express this support.

There are many *rabanim* and *shtickel rebbes* who are circumcisers. There are also some lay people who perform circumcision. These laymen perform circumcision mainly because of the prestige connected with it. Seldom is economics a major consideration. The circumciser used will depend on the religious status in the community of the infant's father. If he is a high-ranking member of the Hasidic community, he will choose a circumciser of higher rank, since the ceremonial of this higher-ranking *mohel* will be executed with greater ceremonial and preparation.

The *mohel* must have skill in the actual performance of circumcision. He must also be a "righteous man." This is stated in the *Code of Jewish Law:*

It is essential that the circumciser should be versed in the laws concerning circumcision.

One should be particular in his choice of a circumciser . . . who should be the best and most righteous man possible to select.[23]

Besides the requirements prescribed by the *Code of Jewish Law,* there are additional requirements for a *mohel* that are Hasidic in nature. He must be such an *ehrlicher Yid* that the father will consider it a good omen in the religious development of his son for him to be circumcised by a man of such high caliber. The father feels that if the circumcision of his son is done by a pious, religious, zealous, and dedicated man, the spiritual strength of the latter will influence his son to become a man of similar virtues.

### 7. The *Mashgiach*

The *mashgiach* is the actual supervisor of those foodstuffs whose production and preparation need supervision. He is the agent who does the actual overseeing on the premises rather than the person who lends his name to or who underwrites a certain product.

*Mashgichim* supervising at places where foods are produced see to it that these foods are prepared according to the religious law. They make sure that no foreign food or material is brought into the premises, that only raw materials acceptable to the Hasidim are used. They are employed in sausage factories, matzah bakeries, candy factories, dairies, butcher stores, salt works, sugar refineries, hotels, restaurants, catering establishments, and other places where the preparation of food requires supervision according to Hasidic authorities.

There are certain owners of food establishments who enjoy the reputation and the trust of the community who do not employ professional *mashgichim.* In these cases the owner of the establishment is the actual *mashigiach.* He will use nothing but those raw materials and ingredients that

23. *Ibid.,* 163:1-3.

are accepted in the Hasidic community by the "most zealous of the zealous." For example, there are bakery owners who enjoy this high reputation in the community who will use only those ingredients — flour, salt, sugar — acceptable to the community. They will bake on those days that are required by the community and will pack their goods in packages produced by the community. They are above and beyond any question or doubt. Therefore, these proprietors will not only be personally identified as meeting Hasidic requirements, but also everything with which they come into contact, in personal life as well as in business, in the shop as well as at home, will be completely Hasidic.

## 8. The *Sofer*

The *sofer* is the scribe of religious letters and documents. He is the person who is in charge of writing the Hebrew inscription on parchment for the *tefilin,* or phylacteries, which are worn by the religious Jew every weekday morning during the Morning Prayers. He writes the *mezuzah,* a religious symbol that is permanently placed on the right doorpost of the Jewish home. He writes and repairs the *Sefer Torah,* the Torah scroll. He is in charge of writing those Jewish documents that require a religious scribe, such as the document of divorce, or divorce letter. Religious articles need periodical examination to see whether the parchment, the writing, and the ink are still in good condition, and it is the *sofer* who keeps these articles usable in accordance with the law.

The *sofer* may have a store or a shop where he works and sells religious articles such as prayer books, prayer shawls, and other items.

The qualifications of the scribe are that he be a God-fearing man above and beyond any question. He must be completely familiar with the law of "Scripture writing" and the laws concerning holy articles. The requirements of piety of a Hasidic scribe are actually limitless. Numerous scribes, whenever they write the Torah scroll, go to the ritual bath before each time they write the name of God. The quality of the scribe's product is measured less by the authenticity of the religious article than by the quality and character of the man himself. The scribe's religiosity is an actual product that accompanies the religious object.

Since the quality of the man becomes part of his product and since it is necessary for him to have a most favorable reputation, a scribe will try to be identified as a scribe who was already known in Europe. If he has not been well known, he identifies himself with a scribe who enjoyed fame in Europe. He wants the community to view him as a person of professional competence and a person of status by saying that he is the son of a well-known religious figure of Europe.

A *sofer* advertises in the leading Hasidic newspaper the following:

> *Sofer S'tam,* Scribe of Torah Scrolls, *Tefilin* and *Mezuzot*
> The famous Scribe of Hust announces that he buys and sells, repairs and examines *tefilin, mezuzot,* Torah scrolls and *megilot* [scrolls of the Book of Esther]. He has also a large selection of ox-leather receptacles for the phylacteries and with excellent inscriptions of parchment.
> Lipe Hacohen Friedman
> Son of the famous *Gaon* and Righteous *Rav* Shmuel David, may the memory of the righteous be blessed, head of the court of justice in the holy community of Hust, 1936
> Rabbi L. Friedman
> 70 Lee Avenue, Brooklyn, New York
> Telephone: EVergreen 8–3145
> Residence: 145 Hewes Street
> Telephone: ULster 8–5814[24]

## 9. The *Metargem*

The *metargem* is the person who translates Talmudical laws and legends into English or Yiddish. This occupation is adapted to American society, since there are many instances in which English translations are required. The self-employed translator will combine this work with mimeo-

24. *Der Yid,* March 21, 1958. Translated from the Yiddish.

graphing and typing letters and articles, since translation alone is not a full-time occupation.

One translator advertises in the leading Hasidic newspaper the following:

## SPECIALIST

in Talmudical laws and legends, typing, mimeographing, and translation.

M. Frankenthal
4417 Thirteenth Avenue, Brooklyn
Telephone: GAdney 8–8544[25]

### 10. The *Batlan*

The *batlan* (literally, "idler") is a professional scholar whose occupation is to "sit and study." *Batalnim* are people who have nothing else to do but to sit in the houses of worship and study. They are married with many children and are supported by the *rebbe*. Their selection by the *rebbe* is based upon their scholarship, studiousness, inability to work, and inability to adjust themselves to some work situation in the community. Although they do not provide any practical service to the community, their behavior and high moral standards set the example for an exemplary life. They are the uplifters of Hasidic morals, the "learners" in the house of worship. They see to it that the "light of Torah is continuously burning." They are the participators in the *rebbe's* weekday religious services when the Hasidic community members are away in their shops and stores and cannot join in the *rebbe's* elaborate worship.

### 11. Miscellaneous Religious Practitioners

Miscellaneous religious practitioners include those who may be composites of some or all of the various religious professionals. One may be concurrently a *melamed*, a *shohet*, a *hazan*, and a *shamash*. An individual who follows a variety of these callings advertises:

25. *Der Yid*, February 28, 19958. Translated from the Yiddish.

Religious teacher, organizer, cantor, religious slaughterer, and sexton seeks a position; any salary.
Write Post Office Box 9, Brooklyn 13, New York[26]

A miscellaneous religious practitioner may also write
speeches for a *bar-mitzvah* boy. One advertises:

If you need a *bar-mitzvah* speech in the
old familiar style, call ULster 5–6028.[27]

Such miscellaneous religious practitioners may also be
professional *kadish* sayers, saying the Mourner's Prayers for
a deceased person. These prayers are supposed to be said by
a member of the deceased person's family. The following is
an advertisement of such a professional *kadish* sayer:

Saying *kadish* and studying the Mishnah [in memory of
a deceased one], $20.00 a year
Do not leave even one day without *kadish* for your dear
and beloved, who departed from you into the "world of
truth." . . . In the Congregation Beth Halevi where the
members pray and study every morning and evening, the
saying of *kadish* and the study of the Mishnah by Jewish
scholars, are very honestly observed, all for only 20 dollars
a year. Come or call by phone. Rabbis order *kadishes* here.
Congregation Beth Halevi
1704 Nelson Avenue, Bronx, New York[28]

Also in the category of miscellaneous religious practitioners is the so-called *moleh zoger,* "*moleh-sayer.*" *Moleh-
sayers* are those who go to the various Jewish cemeteries of
greater New York before the High Holy Days or on special
occasions like Father's Day, Mother's Day, and Decoration
Day. On these days, the family of a deceased person visits the
graves and acquires the services of this man to recite the
Hebrew prayer, the *El moleh rahamim,* hence the name
*Moleh-sayers. Moleh-sayers* may have other religious or non-

26. *Der Yid,* November 16, 1956. Translated from the Yiddish.
27. *Der Yid,* February 8, 1957. Translated from the Yiddish.
28. It should be pointed out that this service is not a service for the
Hasidic community; however, there are Hasidic participants in this
kind of service.

religious occupations, so that their religious prayer-saying serves as a source of additional income.

In the Hasidic community religious professionals rank higher in status than businessmen, despite the fact that the latter's economic reward is greater than that of the former. Although a society sometimes rewards its members for their performance of specially valued or difficult tasks, above the reward for other tasks, in the Hasidic community highly valued tasks are not rewarded economically. Thus, professions in which incomes are relatively low rank higher than some vocations in which the incomes are high. Hasidic professional occupations confer high prestige despite their low economic reward. This has been found in the larger American society, where professionals may have higher status and greater prestige than those people whose income is considerably higher. This contention is borne out in the United States by Cecil C. North and the late Paul K. Hatt of the National Opinion Research Center in their study of popular evaluations of jobs and occupations. They show that:

Highly specialized training and a considerable degree of responsibility for the public welfare appeared to be the chief factors making for job prestige. When people were asked to evaluate ninety different jobs at all occupational levels, they gave the best ratings to positions involving these two factors.[29]

Religious professionals have been rigidly trained to understand that even in their economic activities they must have a strong religious orientation. The community accords them high status for their highly specialized training and for their responsibility in religious matters. At the same time the community expects the religious professionals to perform their duties because of religious convictions and dedication rather than for economic rewards. Businessmen have no restrictions on pursuing economic gain as long as they operate within the prescribed Jewish laws.

The difference in the institutional patterns between pro-

29. Cecil C. North and Paul K. Hatt, "Jobs and Occupations: A Popular Evaluation," *Public Opinion News*, 9 (1947), pp. 3–13; reprinted in Reinhard Bendix and Seymour Martin Lipset (eds.), *Class Status and Power* (Glencoe: The Free Press, Inc., 1953), p. 411.

fessionals and business people is also present in American society. Talcott Parsons recognizes the differences between "professionalism" and "commercialism."[30] He points out that the professionals have numerous limitations inasmuch as they cannot show an "aggressive pursuit of self-interest." Parsons offers the following illustration:

> Medical men are forbidden, in the codes of medical ethics, to advertise their services. They are expected, in any case, to treat a patient regardless of the probability that he will pay, that he is a good "credit risk." They are forbidden to enter into direct and explicit price competition with other physicians, to urge patients to come to them on the ground that they will provide the same service at a cheaper rate.[31]

In the Hasidic community there is another aspect involved with regard to the religious professionals. Not only technical competence determines one's ability to perform in his professional capacity, but also the *ferleslichkeit,* or "trustworthiness," qualifies an individual for religious professional services. Involved in this community judgment is the individual's personal conduct in every aspect of life. He is under constant surveillance and community examination. Thus, the religious professional must reinforce his standing in the community through extensive and intensive religious behavior in order to hold his position and maintain public trust. The trust and prestige that a religious professional enjoys are so highly valued in the community that they compensate for the lack of material reward.

In the Hasidic community the authority of the religious professional is based upon religious behavior and not on his more technical competence. In this respect Hasidic professionals differ a great deal from professionals elsewhere in the United States. In America, the authority of a professional man is not based upon personal attributes that he displays outside of his professional affiliation. His authority is based purely upon his technical competence in his own field as

30. Talcott Parsons, *Essays in Sociological Theory* (Glencoe: The Free Press, Inc., 1958), pp. 62–63.
31. *Ibid.*

evaluated by his peers and by laymen. This has been stated by Parsons:

This is a very important sense in which the professional practitioner in our society exercises authority. . . . This professional authority has a peculiar sociological structure. It is not as such based on a generally superior status, as is the authority a Southern white man tends to assume over any Negro, nor is it a manifestation of superior "wisdom" in general or of higher moral character. It is rather based on the superior "technical competence" of the professional man. He often exercises his authority over people who are, or are reputed to be, his superiors in social status, in intellectual attainments or in moral character.[32]

In the Hasidic community, where religion is the basic concern, religious professionals exercise their authority not so much because they are reputed to have technical competence as because their religious behavior and moral character cause them to be held in esteem. Only when personal conduct demonstrates extreme religiosity can they assume superior positions.

## SECULAR PROFESSIONAL SERVICE

The category of secular professional service includes all professions requiring secular academic training outside of the Hasidic community. Hasidic people are excluded from these, since Hasidim are not allowed to have higher secular training. Therefore, these professional people have obviously not become professionals while members of the group. They may have become professionals first and joined the Hasidim later on, or they may have become identified with the group, although they themselves are not Hasidic, through servicing that community almost exclusively. In this category are the following professionals:

1. The Physician.
2. The Dentist.
3. The Lawyer.

32. *Ibid.*, p. 38.

4. The Teacher.
5. The Accountant.
6. The Pharmacist.

## 1. The Physician

The physician who practices in the Hasidic community is an observant Jew. He observes the Sabbath and all major laws and ceremonials. All physicians practicing in the Hasidic community originally came from Europe and received their academic training in European universities. Some of these participate in certain Hasidic activities beyond the "mere requirements of a religious Jew." To practice and to participate in such activities is not as important as to understand the Hasidic way of life, however. If a Hasidic man or woman discusses his health or ailments with the doctor, his major concern is always interrelated with his Hasidism. For instance, questions arise about whether an individual is allowed to act in a certain way on the Sabbath or whether he can take certain pills or drugs which may not be kosher. The physician must be able to display familiarity with these Hasidic matters, and he must also show that he is personally involved and that the matter is of great concern to him.

Once the physician does so, he enjoys the confidence of the community and becomes identified as a *frumer* doctor, a pious doctor, or a *frumer Yid,* a pious Jew. But the community is aware that he cannot be as *frum* as anyone else in the community, because the mere fact that he is a doctor means, according to the Talmud, that "he goes to Hell." Doctors go to Hell because they cure people and "create a certain doubt in the powers of God." God is the Healer, and the doctor thinks he is doing the healing. Nevertheless, members of the Hasidic community go to physicians for treatment because with the help of God and the prayer of the *rebbe* and the knowledge of the physician, they have a better chance of being cured. The community is also aware that in special cases, with the aid of God and the prayer of the *rebbe* and the help of a well-known physician *outside the Hasidic community,* there is an even greater chance of being cured. Thus, the help of God and the *rebbe's* prayers and the knowledge of a famous specialist in a certain field are sought in critical situations.

Everyday ailments, house calls, and child deliveries are performed by the physicians in the Hasidic community. Critical ailments that require operations are performed by physicians outside, specialists in certain fields, again with the aid of God and the prayer and advice of the *rebbe*.

When outside medical aid is sought, only the male physician is utilized. Female physicians are not allowed to treat male Hasidim; however, male physicians are allowed to treat Hasidic women. Regardless of the role of a woman, physician or not, she is still considered a woman by the Hasidim and required to conform to traditional conceptions of her position.

When the District Health Committee of the Brooklyn Tuberculosis and Health Association, in cooperation with the Brooklyn Department of Health, ran tuberculosis and diabetes tests in Williamsburg, the Hasidic community was asked to participate. The community cooperated, but it requested that the religious norms of the community not be disturbed. The nurse in charge explained that the diabetes test consisted of a blood test and urinalysis, which must be made immediately after receiving a specimen. A question was raised about male and female doctors and male and female patients. It was said that a male doctor could take blood from a woman patient but that a female doctor could not take it from a man. Nothing was said about urinalyses.[33]

## 2. The Dentist

The dentist serving the Hasidic community is usually a Sabbath-observant Jew who came from Hungary. He is not accepted as part of the community; however, since he is a Sabbath-observant man, he is patronized by the Hasidim. The services of the dentist are not as frequently sought as

33. From an interview with Miss Morgan of the District Health Committee of the Brooklyn Tuberculosis and Health Association, December, 1958.

those of a physician. Many members of the community have poor teeth and neglected dentures and show lack of dental care.

### 3. The Lawyer

The lawyer is considered a somewhat despicable person. His services are not sought if it can be at all prevented. Only necessity forces a Hasidic man to engage a lawyer for services he feels he would obtain free of charge in the community. Such necessary transactions would be representations before the civil law or important immigration cases, for which the services of a lawyer *is* required. These lawyers usually observe the Sabbath and other religious laws. There are no lawyers who are identified with the Hasidic community. Most settlements, disputes, civil cases, and other matters requiring arbitration within the community are usually arbitrated by the *rebbe,* or *rav,* or a court consisting of three *ravs.*

### 4. The Teacher

The teacher is in a different position from the physician, the dentist, and the attorney. He is employed by various religious schools to teach secular studies in the so-called English departments. Since teachers come in very close contact with the children, it is of utmost importance that they be imbued with Hasidism, or at least with an understanding of Jewish religion and religious behavior. There are many teachers who are full-fledged members of the Hasidic community. Some of them even wear full-grown beards. Teachers usually have attended non-Hasidic Yeshivot that were semi-Hasidic in their approach toward religious behavior. Some teachers have also attended universities where they obtained academic degrees and certification for teaching. After they had completed their courses of study at a university, they continued their studies in the Yeshivot and became members of the community. Their excuse for not wearing beards before this time is that they were engaged in activities in which wearing of beards was not desirable, but in their hearts and in their everyday practices they considered themselves "bearded." Now that they are engaged in teaching in an environment where the wearing of a beard is not only desirable but advantageous, they wear beards and are identified as members of the Hasidic community. However, not all teachers wear beards, nor are they all Hasidic, but most of them are observant Jews.

Some of these teachers are employed in the public school system and in the afternoons, after regular teaching hours, they teach in the Hasidic Yeshivot in the English department. The children do not consider these teachers equal to the *melamdim,* since there is a tremendous contrast between the *melamed* and the teacher. The children recognize that the *melamed* is the one from whom they should learn Torah, commandments, and behavior; they know that the *melamed* is the person who should be imitated, respected, and feared. They also know that the teacher is a "necessary evil" about whose presence they cannot help themselves. The teacher is the person who teaches English, and if his material or presentation becomes cumbersome, his role will not be taken seriously but he will be considered a person who *fardreit a kopf* (twists the head). The child knows that academically he is going nowhere, that academic studies are not emphasized in the home or by the directors of the schools. He will soon find that he already knows as much or more English than either or both of his parents. Thus, the role of the teacher is not very significant in the Hasidic community.

## 5. The Accountant

The accountant is in almost the same position in the Hasidic community as the teacher. He also attended a Yeshivah, and after that he received academic training in some university. Some accountants are religious and adhere fully to Hasidic patterns. They are regarded by some Hasidim as part of the community.

The accountant serves the Hasidic community by filing income tax returns and by doing general bookkeeping. He is not employed by the bigger Hasidic firms, since it is far more advantageous for them to use more experienced non-Hasidic accountants.

### 6. The Pharmacist

There is no pharmacist who is a member of the Hasidic community. Consequently, if a pharmacist is a Sabbath-observant Jew, or at least closes his pharmacy on the Sabbath, he is patronized by the Hasidim. Some of the Hasidim even question the pharmacist's sympathy with Hasidic causes. The only overt criterion used in judging the pharmacist, however, is whether or not he is closed on the Sabbath.

There are some Sabbath-observant pharmacists outside the Hasidic community who produce pharmaceutical products such as baby powder, make-up, lipstick, toothpowder, soap, aspirin, and saccharin that are permissible for Passover use. These articles are marketed in the non-Hasidic Jewish community.

In general, the Hasidic community utilizes the services of these professionals, some of whom are members of the community and some of whom are only casually identified with it. But the Hasidic community has not produced a single member of a profession requiring academic training and is not likely to do so soon. Thus far, the strict attitudes against secularization and secular training prohibit the acquisition of these professional skills. It is unlikely that the Hasidim, under prevailing conditions, will allow their members to prepare for professional occupations requiring secular training.

CHAPTER **11**

# The Hasidic
# Occupational Hierarchy:
# Nonprofessional Occupations

## THE MANUFACTURE AND SALE
## OF RELIGIOUS ARTICLES

HE MANUFACTURE AND SALE of religious articles provide occupations for many persons. These articles are used in the houses of worship for religious purposes or as religious symbols in the home. Since the Hasidic community is deeply imbued with religiosity, many articles that are not obviously religious to an outsider belong in this category.

The more obvious religious articles include the *parochet,* curtain for the Holy Ark, *matzah* (unleavened bread) covers; *hallah* (Sabbath bread) covers; *yarmelkas,* skullcaps; *tachrichim,* shrouds or eternal cloths; *sidurim,* prayer books; *sefarim,* books of religious content; *tefilin,* phylacteries; and *tzitzis,* fringes for prayer shawls. These religious articles are used by Jewish communities everywhere. In the Hasidic community they are not considered "fit for religious use" unless they are made to Hasidic specifications, which embody the strictest fulfillment of the religious law concerning their manufacture.

For example, phylacteries are used by every religious Jew

during the weekday morning prayers. The phylacteries that the Hasidic Jew uses must, however, be manufactured and sold by Hasidic people who are "reliable and trustworthy." Ordinary phylacteries, which cost 10 to 15 dollars, are not permissible for use. The phylacteries that Hasidic Jews must use cost at least 30 to 35 dollars. Some even sell for 100 to 125 dollars. These are made with great care by highly qualified scribes with superior materials.

The following is a public "announcement and warning" through which the "Supporters of Religion" appealed to merchants and the community not to sell or use the cheaper phylacteries and thus cause religious men to use "unfit" articles, which would mean a "grave sin."

### Announcement, Warning, and Request

Every Jew who puts on phylacteries surely wants to put on kosher phylacteries; therefore we consider it our duty to announce that the cheap or inexpensive phylacteries around the neighborhood of $15 to $17 are definitely *pasul*, ineligible for ritual usage. Examinations were made of these phylacteries for a few weeks, and it was found that all of them are unfit for ritual usage and every Jew is responsible that God forbid, he should not be considered as having *a skull that does not put on tefilin* [phylacteries] [since unfit *tefilin* would be considered equivalent to wearing none; and wearing none is equivalent to not having the benefit of the religious performance]. Simultaneously, we are appealing and warning all booksellers and scribes who have until today permitted the wearing of these phylacteries, through which they have brought a great many people to sin, that they should stop these activities because it is already going too far, since they are bringing religious Jews to sin. They are causing religious Jews to commit very grave sins when they put on these nonkosher phylacteries, and they say the prayers in vain, and also they neglect the commandments of putting on the phylacteries. And if, God forbid, you will not stop your activities, *we will publicize openly your names, with grave voices,* and we will take away your opportunity to sell unfit phylacteries to kosher Jews.

And all those who listen will be blessed with all kinds of blessings.

[Signed] Supporters of Religion[1]

A firm manufacturing *hallah* covers, *yarmelkas,* and *tachrichim* also sells "earth from Israel," which the religious Jew uses at burial rites.

### Miriam Art Embroidery

Manufacturers of *parochet,* matzah, and *hallah* covers, *yarmelkas,* and *tachrichim.*

With a limited amount of earth from the Land of Israel from *Har Hazetim* [Mount of Olives]

Funeral attendants, undertakers, societies and synagogues —assure your members with our eternal cloths when they reach 120 years, of pure linen, hand made. Made by Sabbath observers, according to the law, by Miriam, 47 Norfolk Street, New York, Telephone GRe–1462[2]

Another firm sells knives for ritual slaughterers, whetstones for sharpening ritual knives, and all instruments for circumcision. This is the proclamation of the well-known book shop:

Rabbi Haim Natan Goldberg, also known by the name of Lomzer, a bookseller for forty years, 60 Suffolk Street, New York

My brothers, the slaughterers, I am begging: Look and see a new thing! "If not now, then when?" Slaughter knives 3 dollars. Slaughter knives from Israel, in all sizes: for large cattle, small cattle, poultry, stainless, a bargain buy! Used slaughter knives, all sorts and all sizes: black whetstones, green polish stones, white Belgian stones.

Miller's slaughter knives, all sizes, new and used. Instruments for circumcisers, circumcision knives, protectors, "removing scissors," scissors. We receive for repair old slaughter knives, and we make them like new, at a low price. We buy new and old slaughter knives of all firms and pay the highest prices.

Open every day from 9 A.M. to 9 P.M. except Saturday and Holy Days.

1. From circular RA5. Translated from the Yiddish. Italics added.
2. *Der Yid,* January 31, 1958. Translated from the Yiddish.

During the winter we are open Saturday evenings.

Orders from the four corners of the world delivered quickly and at low prices. Wholesale and retail at wholesale prices—stock for the synagogue, home, Hebrew school, Yeshivot, centers, temples, sisterhoods, auxiliaries. Ready for shipping. Satisfaction guaranteed.[3]

There are various religious articles manufactured and sold in the Hasidic community that are unique. These articles are not known to exist outside the community, and some have never been sold for commercial purposes. Their manufacture was an outgrowth of conditions that existed in America and of the ingenuity of a people who were able to take advantage of the circumstances. One person, for example, is engaged in manufacturing "Leaven-Searching Sets." The *Code of Jewish Law* requires of every religious person that:

On the night preceding the eve of Passover, a search for leaven should be made. It must be made immediately after dark, and it is forbidden to begin eating or doing any manner of work an hour before nightfall.

The search should be made only with a single wax candle and not several woven together, for then it is a torch, but in any emergency, if one has no wax candle he may search with a candle of tallow.

All the rooms wherein it is surmised leaven was brought should be searched; even the wine cellars, garrets, stores, and woodsheds, all those vessels in which leaven was kept should also be searched. Before the search all these places should be carefully swept and cleansed from leaven in order to facilitate the search thereafter.[4]

To fulfill this law, on the eve before Passover the religious Jew takes a candle, a couple of feathers to serve as a small broom, and a wooden spoon that has been used for cooking.[5]

3. *Der Yid*, September 6, 1957. Translated from the Yiddish.

4. *Code of Jewish Law (Kitzur Shulchan Aruch)*, compiled by Solomon Gansfried and translated by Hyman E. Goldin (New York: Hebrew Publishing Co., 1927) 61:1–3.

5. The wooden spoon is used because it is so stained with leavened substances that it has to be burned before Passover.

With these and a little bag the religious Jew goes from room to room searching for leaven, sweeping the little bread crumbs into the bag. The next day—the day before Passover—he burns this little bag with its contents.

In Europe, the items for the leaven-searching ceremonial were prepared by the individual performing the ceremony. In America, people are usually busy with their various pursuits of a livelihood. Here, cooking with a wooden spoon is somewhat unusual. Here, the access to feathers is difficult unless one goes into the slaughter houses to obtain them from fowl. Thus, to collect all the items necessary for the ritual would be difficult and time consuming. Hasidic ingenuity has taken advantage of these new circumstances where the necessary items for the fulfillment of the law are not accessible. A Hasidic man is engaged in manufacturing Leaven-Searching Sets and puts them on the local market. In this way he enables the members of the community to perform the ancient rite of searching for leaven. In this set he provides all the necessary items: the candle, made of pure beeswax to meet all requirements of a real kosher candle, which is never made of animal fat; two feathers to serve as a broom for sweeping the bread crumbs; and the wooden spoon. These spoons are unused; in fact, the manufacturer imports them from Sweden. In this set there is also a leaflet containing twenty-six paragraphs concerning the law of searching for leaven. All these items are put into a paper bag labeled *Bedikat Hometz Set* (Leaven-Searching Set). These are sold throughout the community to religious bookstores, groceries, and other places where they are easily accessible to the Hasidic Jew and to other religious Jews who follow this ritual.

The manufacturer advertises as follows in circulars and in the Hasidic newspapers:

**And a Word in Due Season, How Good is it! [Proverbs, 15:23]**

Leaven-Searching Set can be obtained here.
According to this Biblical sentence I prepare for every season the proper articles, for instance,

For Succot—nice tabernacles

For Purim—masks with beards

For Passover—a set for searching for leaven

*Talit-Katan* [small prayer shawl which is worn at all times] with reliable fringes. Top summer wear, it is made of porous material.

Each grocer will order Leaven-Searching Sets. The customers will be thankful.

Prompt delivery in New York and Brooklyn.

For orders call J. P.

EV 8–5141    EV 7–8788[6]

On the bag which contains this Leaven-Searching Set, the following inscription is also printed: *isur hasagat gevul Yadua,* "Beware of the prohibition against trespassing the property of another." This is a community copyright in which the manufacturer warns the people that this set was his idea and that no one has the right to imitate it. He also advertises in other circulars and newspapers that he has obtained rabbinical authority from *rabanim* confirming the prohibition against imitating or reproducing this set.

He sends circulars to those stores where his Leaven-Searching Sets are being sold, enclosing a copy of the Prohibition of Encroachment (the Hasidic copyright) with its authoritative signature of the *rabanim* who have authorized it.

The following is the translation of this Prohibition of Encroachment:

### With the Help of God
### The Prohibition of Encroachment

We the undersigned come to warn and to contest our Jewish brethren that they should not reproduce this package put together which is called Leaven-Searching Set without the permission of Mr. Israel Fogel, may his light shine, because he labored [troubled] and toiled until he assembled the above mentioned. Through this he obtained privilege [that no one should] trespass his territory.

Signed on the first day of the week of [when the weekly portion] *Terumah* [is read in the synagogues], 5719 [corresponding

6. *Der Yid,* April 5, 1957. Translated from the Yiddish.

to February 8, 1959] in Brooklyn, may Zion and Jerusalem be rebuilt.

Simon Posen      Jacob Lebowitz
*Rav* from Sopron      *Rav* from Kapos[7]

Candles are frequently used in Hasidic homes for religious ceremonials. The candles used on Friday evening are called the *shabbos lecht,* at the outgoing of the Sabbath on Saturday evening, the *havdalah lecht,* on the anniversary of a death, *yahrzeit lecht,* on the holiday of Hanukah, *Hanukah lecht,* and on the night before Passover, the *bedikas hometz lecht.* According to some religious authorities,[8] candles made of pure beeswax are more appropriate for religious purposes than candles made of any other substance. Candles that are made of animal fats are considered inappropriate for religious purposes. Even candles that are made of paraffin raise doubts for religious ceremonial usage. In line with the belief that candles made of pure beeswax are most appropriate, there is a Hasidic candle company that produces such candles for the various religious ceremonials. The following is a label from a *yahrzeit lecht:*

**With the Help of God**

**Commandment Candles**

Candle of Wax

Pure beeswax candles for the High Holy Days and for death anniversaries

Guaranteed for 25 hours' burning

Also available from us are *havdalah* candles, candles for *Hanukah,* and candles for searching for leaven.

All of pure wax

Produced by Candles from Wax Company
Brooklyn, New York
Through Mr. Leib Glick—EVergreen 7–9707
See *Mateh Ephraim,* Chapter 603[9]

7. From the original document. Translated from the Hebrew.

8. *Mateh Ephraim,* Chapter 603, as it appears on the label of the Candles from Wax Company.

9. From the label appearing on a *yahrzeit* candle. Translated from the Yiddish-Hebrew.

The same company manufactures *havdalah* candles, also produced from pure beeswax. The inscription on this label is much more elaborate. It gives the sources of all the religious authorities who specify the use of beeswax and also tells that if one "smells the candle of *havdalah* made of wax, he will be saved from bad spirits during the whole week."

### With the Aid of God
### Commandment Candles
#### *Havdalah* of Wax

Produced from 100% guaranteed pure beeswax and also beautifully woven. The great importance of the *havdalah* of wax can be seen in the *Shulhan Aruch, Orach Hayim,* Chapter 297, in the *Magen Avraham,* subchapter 3 and subchapter 4, and also in *Baer Hetev,* in subchapter 2 and subchapter 3, that one must perform the benediction at the conclusion of the Sabbath and festival with the *havdalah* candle that is made purely of wax. See also the *Shulhan Aruch* of the *Rav* in Chapter 298, subchapter 4, and in the *Kitzur Shulhan Aruch,* Chapter 96, subchapter 9. Also in the *Mishnah Berurah,* Chapter 298, subchapter 5, and also in many other books of law and mysticism. See in the *Sidur Yeshuot Yisrael* in the law concerning the *havdalah,* that if one smells the candle of the *havdalah* made of wax, he will be saved from bad spirits during the whole week. There are also available from us lamps for a death anniversary and for the High Holy Days, candles for *Hanukah,* and also for searching for leaven, all these being made of pure wax. All of these are produced by the Nerot Shel Shavah Company [Candles from Wax Company], Brooklyn, by *Reb* Leib Glick.

It does not drip on the floor.

It burns beautifully. It lasts a long time.

Telephone EVergreen 7-9707[10]

Jewish law requires that during the Holiday of Tabernacles (Succot) the religious Jew must make his living quarters in a *succah,* a temporary booth built for this holiday.[11] Although

---

10. From the label appearing on the box containing *havdalah* candle. Translated from the Hebrew.

11. *Code of Jewish Law, loc. cit.,* 134:1–5 and 134:1–22.

not all of the Hasidim sleep in a *succah,* it is essential that
every male person have all his meals in one during the seven
days of Tabernacles. In the metropolis of New York, especially Williamsburg, where space is a problem, some members
of the community sell a portable *succah.* This can be erected
in backyards, on fire escapes, roofs, or any space under the
open sky, as required by the law. A person in the portable
*succah* business will advertise in the following way:

### A New Model of Ready-Made Tabernacles

Water- and fireproof. Can be erected in 15 minutes. You
can put the whole tabernacle together yourself—ready-
made. Tools are not needed; hammer, nails, or screws are
not needed. If you have complained about our last year's
tabernacles, we are ready to help you.

Zeiger and Farkas Corp., 181 Marcy Avenue, Corner
Broadway, Brooklyn.[12]

There is another firm producing prefabricated tabernacles.[13]

The firm's name is *Succat Shalom,* Shelter of Peace, or Perfect
Shelter. This firm advertises:

Ready-made tabernacles
The most beautifully detailed craftsmanship
Easy to erect
Come in all sizes—with bamboo tops
Ask for price list with pictures

Succat Shalom Woodworking
175 Lee Avenue, Brooklyn
Telephone: EVergreen 4-4446
Home: MA 5-5640[14]

12. *Der Yid,* September 25, 1957. Translated from the Yiddish.
13. Persons in the portable *succah* business do not apply for "copyright" because the idea is an old one. In Europe many Jews who lived
in urban communities had *succahs* which they put away from year to
year. The new fact about the portable *succahs* is that they are commercially produced.
14. *Der Yid,* September 25, 1957. Translated from the Yiddish.

According to the Code of Jewish Law,[15] the tabernacles must be covered with "branches of trees, or with reeds, which are a product of the soil and severed therefrom." Since these tabernacle tops must have special qualifications according to Jewish law, they are sold in the Hasidic community as religious articles.

The tabernacle top is called *s'chach*. There are special dealers who sell *s'chach* throughout the community and who advertise before the holiday in the Hasidic newspapers and on placards posted in the various houses of worship. One dealer advertises on a placard in Yiddish and English:

> Order your *s'chach*
> Big bundles from the Yeshivah Farm Settlement
> We have beautiful evergreen *s'chach* at reasonable prices.
> Please call EVergreen 7–0422.[16]

There is much competition in the *s'chach* business within the Hasidic community. Another dealer sends out placards to various houses of worship with the following advertisement:

> With the aid of God
> Do you want to have a beautiful *succah?*
> Buy beautiful green fresh *s'chach*
> Special large bundles
> Moderate prices
> Free delivery
> Order it on time so that we can satisfy your needs.
> First come, first served.
>
> Call EVergreen 7–8849
> A. J. Weinberger, 94 Morton Street, Brooklyn, New York[17]

The competition in the *s'chach* business is so great that there is even a business establishment selling *s'chach* that calls itself *S'chach* Incorporated. *S'chach* Incorporated advertises with the following circulars:

15. *Code of Jewish Law, loc. cit.,* 134:3.
16. From the original placard. Translated from the Yiddish.
17. From the original placard. Translated from the Yiddish.

**With the Aid of God**

A good advice
Listen to me and order your *s'chach* right away from

**S'chach Incorporated**

Fresh, cheap, punctual, and free delivery
Call all day long EVergreen 7-4213[18]

Not only are the ready-made tabernacle and the *s'chach* merchants concerned with the building of a tabernacle, but the linoleum merchant as well has gone into the tabernacle business. He, too, sells merchandise that beautifies the tabernacle. He advertises that for a really beautiful *succah,* there should be a linoleum rug on the floor. Linoleum has nothing to do with the *succah,* nor is there any requirement of having a floor covering in the *succah;* nevertheless, he appeals to the members of the community in terms of having a "beautified *succah.*" He also calls to the attention of the community that if one does not have a linoleum rug in his *succah,* he may transgress a prohibition of the *Code of Jewish Law.* According to this law, one is not allowed to sweep the uneven dirt floor on the Sabbath and holidays. Since the dirt floor is not even, there may be some small holes in the ground, and by sweeping the floor one may cover the holes. Such "covering of holes" is considered "working on the holiday." But if one has a smooth linoleum rug on the floor, he cannot "cover holes" on the Sabbath and holidays.

There is still another latent implication: by converting the linoleum to a semireligious item, the merchant is identified in the community as a "person who cares" about precise religious observance. Thus, a person buying from him not only can be sure to get a serviceable linoleum but, in addition, will be aiding a "person who is worthy of support," since it is obvious from his display of concern about religious matters that he is an *obgehitener Yid,* a fastidious Jew, who is extremely conscientious in his observance of religion.

One linoleum merchant's leaflet reads as follows:

18. Circular SI6. Translated from the Yiddish.

Almost free—the most beautiful *succah* ornament
A beautiful fine linoleum
For the floor in the *succah*
On which you can, on the Sabbath and holiday,
Sweep easier without any doubt [of transgressing the law]
Is available at
  Aron Fischer, 318 Roebling Street, Brooklyn, New York,
          EV 4-4208
    Bring the measurement.[19]

Jewish law requires that for the Holiday of Tabernacles a
Jew must have *arba minim*, "four kinds of plants." This is
stated in Leviticus: "And ye shall take to you on the first day
[of the Feast of Tabernacles] the fruit of goodly trees [*esrog*],
branches of palm trees [*lulav*], boughs of thick trees [*hadassim*], and willows of the brook [*hoshanos*] . . ."[20]

The most important of these "four kinds" is the *esrog*,
"the fruit of a goodly tree."[21] Among its other requirements,
the *esrog* must not be dry, round, joined with another,
smaller than an egg, rotten, bad smelling, smooth, or without the stem. It must be complete, yellowish in color, and,
above all, beautiful.[22]

The most zealous religious Jew is very careful that even
the most minute blemish shall not mar his *esrog*. Before he
buys an *esrog*, he gives it a microscopic examination. During
the *esrog* season, Hasidic Jews are seen in front of the *esrog*
stores with magnifying glasses in their right hands and
*esrogrim* in their left hands, turning them, twisting them,
looking for the tiniest blemish. The price of an average *esrog*
is approximately 10 to 15 dollars, but the price of an *esrog*
that stands this microscopic examination may be as much as
50 to 75 dollars. A Hasidic man whose major concern is his
religion will pay such a price if he can afford it. And if he
cannot afford it, he will pick a low-priced *esrog* but he will
be sure that it is one that is positively kosher.

19. From the original leaflet. Translated from the Yiddish.
20. Leviticus 23:40.
21. A yellowish citrus fruit grown mainly in Israel, Greece, and
Yanev. It is also grown in Arizona and California.
22. *Code of Jewish Law, loc. cit.*, 648:1-22.

The dealer knows exactly how to take advantage of the detailed and complicated interpretations of the religious laws concerning *esrogim*. For example, many Hasidic Jews will not use Israeli *esrogim*. The laws "concerning the land" are applicable only in the "Land of Israel." Hasidic Jews believe that these laws are not being observed in Israel today, and consequently, they buy *esrogim* imported from Yanev, Greece, or Arizona, where the Biblical law does not apply. The Hasidic *esrog* dealer must have all kinds of *esrogim* to satisfy differing views.

Because almost all Hasidic adult males will have an *esrog* for the holiday, this becomes a "big business" in Hasidic circles. Merchants hang their circulars on the walls and doors of the houses of worship far in advance, telling the community about their "beautiful *esrogim*." The following is an example of such a circular:

*With the aid of God*

**Announcement**

I make it known to the honored community that you can buy from me
*Esrogim* that are beautiful and selected [which are] not the product of grafting
Also palm branches and three-leaved myrtles for cheap prices
208 Division Avenue (near Marcy Avenue)
Res. Phone: EV 4–4639
Business Phone: EV 7–0158
With respect
[Signed] Eliezer Abbe (Cohen) Herman[23]

The *esrogim* are usually sold in stores carrying religious articles. This is the most appropriate place, one where the customer will automatically look for *esrogim*. However, there are people who are not in the religious-article business but who enter the *esrog* business just before the holiday because of the profitable economic return and because of the short duration of the season. These dealers sublet a store or part

23. Circular ES9. Translated from the Hebrew-Yiddish.

of a store in a "good" neighborhood for two weeks until the season ends. The following translation of a placard exemplifies such an *esrog* dealer's advertising. He has moved into a clothing store for the duration of the *esrog* season.

### Esrogim

From Israel and from Yanev, beautiful, the most selected
   of the selected
         Palm branches from Arizona and Italy
         Three-leaved myrtles
   Royal service
   In the clothing store of *Reb* Moshe Grossman
   42 Hester (Corner Essex Street)
   New York      Telephone OR 4–1639
         [Signed] Chayim Nachman Marmelstein and
            his partner, the *Rav,* the Master, Y. Klein
      Wholesale—Big Selection—Retail[24]

The *esrog* business also attracts those people who rank higher in the status system of the community. One may even be a *rav* and engage in selling *esrogim* during the season. There was no precedent in Europe for a *rav* himself actively to engage in commercial enterprises, even to sell such a holy article as an *esrog*. Selling *esrogim* by a *rav* is a purely American development. But since a *rav* who sells *esrogim* must be careful not to hurt his prestige, he will use a "dignified" approach in this business venture. He does not hang placards or circulars in the various houses of worship, because this may be considered "too commercial," which may not be becoming to a *rav*. In any event, every *esrog* dealer does that. The *rav* in the *esrog* business applies the "exclusive and personal touch" among those prospective customers whom he knows personally. He sends out printed post cards with a text that is "really and truly becoming for a *rav*." He assures his customers that he has all kinds of *esrogim,* which are "the most select of the select," which were picked "in the presence of a God-fearing man," and that the *esrogim* "are not grafted," that the Israeli *esrogim* came "from trustworthy

24. Placard ES10. Translated from the Hebrew-Yiddish.

orchard owners," and that the Greek *esrogim* have been "approved by our forefathers." The following is a translation of such a text:

### With God's help

Brooklyn, end of *Elul* 5718 [August–September 1958]

Peace and good wishes, Amen, to his honor,[25] my friend the *Rav*, the righteous *Gaon*, the noble and pious scholar, may he live long and happily. Amen.

After greeting him and wishing him well, it is my great honor to inform his highness that, with the help of God, I have bought several hundreds of *"Esrogim* from Yanev," the most selected of the selected, which were picked in the citrus orchards in the presence of one of my faithful men, a scholar and God-fearing man, who knows very well all the details about the growing of *esrogim* and his eyes and his heart were in the orchard since the beginning of the picking and until its delivery, in such a way that, with God's blessing, it is certain, beyond any doubt, that my *esrogim* are not grafted. I will also have *esrogim* from the Land of Israel from trustworthy orchard owners and also Greek *esrogim,* which are approved by our forefathers, may their memory be blessed, and perfect palm branches and three-leaved myrtles; all of these are extremely beautiful. I am ready, with God's help, to be at his service, to serve him with respect and with a reasonable price according to the current price in the market, in a way that he will be satisfied in all matters, with God's help.

Therefore, I hope that his honor will come to the place of business, 35 Lee Avenue, near the house of worship, the Wiener Synagogue, Congregation of [God-]fearers. May he please come as soon as possible, for on this matter it is said, "the first has the best choice." This year, particularly, one has to be early and not late, because the time between [the holidays] Yom Kippur and Succot is very short, on account of the Holy Sabbath that falls in between. Thus, time is very short.

His respectful friend who inquires about his well-being,

SHLOMO DOV WIEDER

The *Rav* from Nyirbator

25. This is addressed in the third person singular to accord honor and respect to the recipient.

Directions: By B.M.T. to Marcy Avenue Station, or by
Nostrand bus to the door.

P.S. Please be careful not to miss my store, which is at 35
Lee Avenue.[26]

In the category of religious articles also belong the manufacture and sale of all silver ornaments, such as spice boxes,
candelabra, and knives for the Sabbath. Because the life of
the Hasidic Jew is completely surrounded with religious
practices, the merchant takes advantage of certain holidays
to sell his religious articles. On the holiday of Purim it is
customary to give gifts to one's friends. The merchant selling
religious articles tells the community that by giving religious
ornaments or presents one can fulfill the commandment of
"sending presents."

Silver is the answer to all.
All sorts of ornaments for prayer shawls
Silvered spice boxes
Knives for the holy Sabbath
And all sorts of silver gifts
In order to fulfill the commandment of sending presents at Purim
God Willing, you can obtain them at the lowest prices at

Nataniel Farkas

184 Marcy Avenue, Brooklyn 11, New York

Telephone ST 2-0522[27]

Another activity that falls in this category is the private
publishing of old manuscripts with religious content, prayer
books, and responsa of European Hasidic *rebbes*. Some of
these private publishers advertise in the Hasidic newspapers
and by letters. Publishers of Hasidic *rebbes'* manuscripts obtain the addresses of religious functionaries in the larger
Jewish community and send them the published books. A
letter is enclosed indicating that they are looking forward to
the recipient's "generous response." If the person sends
money, the transaction is closed. If the publisher does not

26. From a postcard sent out to select members of the community.
Translated from the Hebrew.

27. *Der Yid*, February 28, 1958. Translated from the Yiddish.

receive any "generous response," or any response at all, reminders are sent out in which the recipient is informed that the publishing of the book has forced the publisher into a "colossal debt," and that, since this is his "only means of livelihood," he will be grateful for the recipient's immediate attention. If the recipient responds to this "friendly reminder," the deal is closed; if not, then the same letter or similar ones follow one after another. There are even reminders sent to a recipient noting that holding on to an object that does not belong to him may be considered stealing, unless he sends his "generous response" immediately. The following are samples of such letters:

> Esteemed Friend:
> We are taking the liberty of sending you the enclosed volume, *Jashroth Jacob,* the author of which is the famous *Gaon Rabbi Jacob Zwijolish* of Dinow, author of the famous book *Melo Horoim.*
> Being aware of the great interest and deepest appreciation on your part of all works on our Holy Torah, we feel sure that you will accept this worthy book, which is now printed for the first time from an old manuscript. We trust then that you will help defray the cost of this outstanding work. Your participation means that you too will have a share in the important field of Jewish Scholarship and in the *mitzvah* of spreading Torah. And with this privilege may you be blessed by the Torah for long life, good standing, health and general comfort. With thanks in advance.
> > Yours very respectfully,
> > RABBI BENZION COHEN
> > 72 Wilson Street
> > Post Office Box 67
> > Brooklyn 11, New York[28]

Again:

> Esteemed Friend:
> Some time ago, I took the liberty of sending you a volume *Jashroth Jacob,* the author of which is the famous *Gaon, Rabbi Jacob Zwijolish* of Dinow, author of the famous book

28. From the original letter, printed in English and Yiddish. Transcription of the English letter.

*Melo Horoim.* I hope you have received the book and accept it with favor.

As yet I have not been compensated. I genuinely hope that you will be kind enough to send me as the price of the book any amount you feel it is worth or which you can afford in order to defray the expense of printing this book the first time from an old manuscript and of binding it.

With this privilege may you be blessed by the Torah for long life, good standing, health and general comfort. With thanks in advance.

Yours very respectfully,
Rabbi Benzion Cohen
72 Wilson Street
Post Office Box 67
Brooklyn 11, New York[29]

One individual reprints prayer books with which Hasidic Jews in Europe were familiar. He advertises that he has prayer books for *heimishe Yiden,* homey Jews. He appeals to those Jews who identify themselves with traditional values and standards. *"Heimishe Yiden"* also signifies that one is still a Jew of the "old fold" and that he does not show any sign of assimilation. The advertisement also states that this prayer book has been printed by Sabbath-observant Jews. Thus, it is "suitable for religious Jews."

### Good Tidings

To all *Heimishe* Jews, it has appeared in print again, a prayer book with the various additions, as for instance, the prayer of the holy *Rav* R. Elimelech, of blessed memory, and *Petach Eliahu;* printed by Sabbath observers, suitable for pious Jews.

All prayers are complete and separate, so that you do not have to turn the pages; afternoon and evening services, the four chapters and "prayers for forgiveness" and the familiar prayer of *Shema* before retiring, printed—with special big letters—suitable also for children.

Everyone who buys this prayer book will convince himself that not in vain is the name of the prayer book —

29. From the original letter, printed in English and Yiddish. Transcription of the English letter.

## "The Full Complete Beauty"

It is really beautiful and it is complete, with all the qualities a prayer book must have. It can be obtained from the editor, Yosef Weiss.

Yosef Weiss 623 Bedford Avenue
Brooklyn, New York Telephone MA 4–1403[30]

Another example of publishing activity is shown by the announcement from E. Grossman's publishing house, which published the manuscript of the responsa of the famous Rabbi Moshe Sofer. The publication is advertised in the Hasidic newspapers as follows:

### Important

Already in press—it will appear very shortly—
the Responsa of Rabbi Moshe Sofer—*Hatam Sofer.*
In seven parts, with addition of a detailed index and sources of quotations from the Babylonian and Jerusalem Talmud, Maimonides, and the four sections of the *Shulhan Aruch.*
Arranged by the *Rav, Gaon* R. Moshe Stern, head of the religious court of Debrecen the grandson of the author.
E. Grossman's Publishing House[31]

The publication of religious books in the Hasidic community is more extensive than just publishing old manuscripts and lithographing out-of-print books. There are many new publications available such as the *rebbes'* weekly speeches and addresses. These speeches appear in leaflet form and then are published collectively in book form. There are books dealing with material concerning Jewish law, chastisement, discipline, reproof, and instruction in ethics and morals. There are some publications that describe the behavior of a *rebbe* who has passed away. These books are memorials and living symbols among the Hasidim. The customs of the *rebbe* are perpetuated through these publications. There are also publications that list the names of

30. *Der Yid,* January 3, 1958. Translated from the Yiddish. Also placard SID2. Translated from the Yiddish.
31. *Der Yid,* November 29, 1957. Translated from the Yiddish.

some of the outstanding Hasidic Jews "who died martyrs' deaths in Hitler's gas chambers." The authors of these books try to compile their materials with the aid of letters and questionnaires sent out to members of the community. The following is a translation from the Hebrew of a letter that was sent out to collect materials about "deceased holy men."

> The *Rav* Yechiel Zevi Halevi Klein
> Son of my master and father, our teacher, Rabbi Simon (may his blood be avenged), the offspring of the holy Rabbi, the *Sh'loh Hakodesh* [Yeshayah Horwitz], who has published many books, formerly in Grosswardein and now publisher of *Shem Hagdolim Hechodosh* and *Sidura Shel Shabbos.*
>
> Now he is in the process of publishing, God willing, the book, *Kovod Hachamim,* a great collection of the names and the lives and detailed histories of our *gaonim,* our righteous and our holy, who were killed for the sake of the sanctification of the name of God (may their blood be avenged).
>
> [End of letterhead]
> Peace and all goodness to his honored highness, the *Rav* and *Gaon.* Several years have passed since we began to arouse, to beg and to remind in newspapers [In the footnote to the letter: "Also in the columns of the monthly magazine *Hamaor,* Tishri 5713 (corresponding to September, 1953) may be found a long and complete comment on this book, which will be named *Deshochvei V'dechayeh"*] and in letters to the relatives and students of the *Gaonim* and the righteous rabbis and of the heads of Yeshivot, who were killed, due to our many sins, for the sanctification of the name of God—*the holy people killed by the Nazis;* (may their names be erased)—that they should be kind enough to send us the details of their lives (similar to the enclosed questionnaire). Please do whatever is in your power to "give us strength" to establish at least a memory of their holy souls.
>
> From many we did not receive any answer at all, and others only answered part of the questionnaire, although they possess much more information. . . . Why? The reason is not known. . . .
>
> It is not necessary to speak at length and to arouse you

about the *importance of the matter and the book,* which is known and understood by any reasonable person; here we want duly to emphasize that the book is already in proof, and anyone who wants to make an eternal memorial to his relatives or his teachers should hurry and answer us within the coming two weeks, may they come to us with goodness.

The price of the book which has approximately 300 pages and some 3,000 names of the great men of this generation is only five dollars.

[Signed] The *Rav* Yechiel Zevi Halevi Klein,
   son of my master and father, our teacher Rabbi Simon (may his blood be avenged), the offspring of the holy Rabbi, the *Sh'loh Hakodesh* [Yeshayah Horwitz], publisher of the book, *Shem Hagdolim Hechodosh.*[32]

The following is the translation from the Hebrew of another letter and the enclosed questionnaire.

**Yechiel Zevi Klein**
**Son of my master and father, our teacher, Rabbi Simon (may his blood be avenged), the offspring of the holy Rabbi, the *Sh'loh Hakodesh* [Yeshayah Horwitz], publisher of many books in Europe, and presently of the book, *Shem Hagdolim Hechodosh.***
[End of letterhead]
With God's help, may His Name be blessed.

Peace and good wishes, Amen, to his honored highness, the *Rav* and *Gaon* [space for insertion of name]

After inquiring about his well-being, [space for insertion of name]

Many of my friends who have received and seen the book, *Shem Hagdolim Hechodosh,* which I have newly published, called my attention to the booklet, *Bet Shalom,* in which I have added only the names and names of the cities of 1,000 of our *Gaonim,* our righteous and our holy, may their blood be avenged.

According to their right opinion, it is proper to establish an *eternal memorial* to our holy men, the holy of this valley of weeping, with a more suitable honor, and to describe more extensively the history of their lives and their lineages, and also something about the way of their life and their

32. From the original letter, JK. Translated from the Hebrew.

behavior, the place and the way of their passing away, may God have mercy on us; also who were their teachers and their famous students, their writings and occurrences—and I have answered their request.

And now I turn to his honor requesting kindly to let me know, all known and required details about those of his relatives who were mentioned in the booklet *Bet Shalom,* and about those who were omitted and will be included in the new book, and to fill out the following questionnaire in clear and legible writing, and to send it back to me by the first day of the month of Kislev, may it come to us with goodness and, God willing, I will publish it compiled in a prayer book for eternal memory, that will be honorable for the dead and honorable for the living.

The questionnaire:[33]

*a.* The name of the holy man, his father, his father-in-law and their lineage.

*b.* The title: *Rav,* Righteous Master, Director of a Yeshivah, Sitting in the Tent of Torah.

*c.* The names of his teachers.

*d.* How many years he served in the holy service; the names of the communities.

*e.* If he was a teacher in a Yeshivah, what approximately was the number of students in one year?

*f.* What was his age? Where did he pass away, and how?

*g.* The date of the death anniversary (*yahrzeit*) if known.

*h.* The names of his sons and sons-in-law who passed away, and their titles.

*i.* The names of his sons and sons-in-law who are alive, and their titles.

*j.* The names of his published works, the year of publication and their nature: Responsa, Law, Legend.

*k.* A short survey of the important events in his life, his actions for the welfare of the congregation.

Please give accurate answers in clear writing as soon as possible.[34]

Religious articles are sold both inside and outside the Hasidic community. It is the conviction of the non-Hasidic

33. Space is provided after each question for the reply.
34. From the original documents, JK2. Translated from the Hebrew.

religious Jews that one does not have to be Hasidic in order to observe all the religious laws, that one can be a strict observer without becoming involved in extremes of external appearance and behavior. Understandably, the non-Hasidic religious Jews who observe Judaism in strictly orthodox manner prefer to use those religious articles that facilitate the strictest possible observance. Therefore, non-Hasidic religious Jews purchase religious articles that have been produced by the Hasidim because they are more appropriate for religious use than the same items available elsewhere.

Thus, Hasidic economic activities, particularly the manufacture and sale of those items that require religious sanction, are not limited to the Hasidic community alone. The market for Hasidic goods is extended to a larger orthodox Jewish group within and beyond the New York metropolitan area. Such outside purchase of Hasidic items expands production and creates additional jobs for Hasidic Jews. Some of the articles that are now sold to other than Hasidim were not commercially produced earlier. The demand did not justify their production in volume. It is interesting to see how the Hasidic advocacy of more intensive religious observance has promoted the production of religious articles and enhanced Hasidic economic activities.

## THE MANUFACTURE OR SALE
## OF HASIDIC FOODSTUFFS

In this category belong the occupations of all those persons who are engaged in manufacturing, preparing, handling, or selling food products. Before this category is described, a short explanation of the Jewish dietary practices is presented as a help in understanding Hasidic behavior.

According to Jewish dietary practices all foods can be grouped as either prohibited (nonkosher) or permitted (kosher). Prohibited foods may not be consumed in any form whatsoever. In this category belong all those animals (and the by-products of those animals) that have been enumerated and prohibited in the Mosaic Law. These are animals that do not chew the cud and do not have cloven hoofs, for example, the pig and the horse. In addition, fish that do not have fins and scales and all other seafood such as clams, oysters, shrimp, crabs, and any other living creatures that creep, as well as those fowls that are enumerated in the Bible as not permitted, belong to the prohibited-food category. Such foods may not be eaten regardless of the way in which they are prepared.

Permitted foods are all those the usage and consumption of which are not proscribed by religious law. Some of these foods need special or ritual preparation to make them permissible, such as meat and meat products, while others do not require any preparation at all, such as fruits and vegetables (unless they contain foreign properties such as worms or mildew, which are prohibited). The food that a Jew is permitted to eat is called kosher. Kosher foods are subdivided into three categories:

1. *Fleishig*—meat and meat products.
2. *Milchig*—dairy and milk products.
3. *Parve*—neutral foods that contain no meat or milk.

The *fleishig* foods are those that have been prepared or manufactured from animals that Jews are permitted to eat according to religious law. These products are permitted only if they have been slaughtered and examined according to the prescribed law of slaughtering. An animal must be slaughtered and examined by professional ritual slaughterers who have full familiarity with the law concerning the preparation of animals. Meat products need strict supervision not only because the skill of the slaughtering and the examination of the slaughtered animal are required, but also because only those people can be trusted with the slaughtering who are "truly religious Jews."

*Milchig* foods must be the extract of permitted animals such as cows, sheep, and goats. Supervision is required to make certain that the milk is indeed the milk of a permitted (kosher) animal, and that the ingredients of dairy products contain nothing but substances that are permitted.

*Parve* foodstuffs can be used with either meat or dairy products. To this category belong all vegetables, fruits, and honey (although it is an insect extract). These foods do not need any supervision so long as they are in their raw, natural form. Wine, although it is a "neutral" food, must be produced by observant Jews. It should be noted, too, that fish are considered *parve*.[35] During the holiday of Passover, the "neutral" foodstuffs must meet special requirements because on that holiday anything leavened is prohibited.

These, in general, are the Jewish dietary requirements. In the Hasidic community, however, there are more strict requirements. For instance, only those meats are permitted that have been ritually prepared by another Hasidic Jew, on the assumption that only Hasidic Jews can be trusted with the preparation of animals. According to the Hasidic Jew, the only person trusted with kosher food is a "person who cares," that is, one who observes all the Jewish rituals as required by Jewish law. It is believed that such a person would not sell any food that has not been prepared in full compliance with the religious laws.

In the Hasidic community, the requirements for kosher food are more extensive than in other Jewish groups. A Hasidic Jew is concerned not only with those food products that everywhere require strict supervision, but also with neutral foods to which the terms kosher and nonkosher are hardly applicable. The Hasidic community is organized in such a way that all foods consumed in the community are prepared and produced by Hasidic Jews and fulfill all Hasidic requirements for being kosher. The Hasidim consider their own products the only real kosher food.

In the Hasidic community there is no food product that is not carefully considered in terms of its permissibility for use. The only way a given food can become kosher is for it to be prepared by a Hasidic Jew with the consent of Hasidic authorities. Even such food as canned fruit, which does not raise the question of kosher or nonkosher, may cause a *hash-ash*—apprehension, fear, or distrust—that it has been pre-

35. Religious law does not require ritual slaughter in their preparation.

pared with some substance that is not permissible, or that it has come into contact with substances that are not permissible, or that somebody who is not trusted has handled the product and may have mixed in something that is not permissible. Such apprehension can be limitless. If any food product is not accepted in the Hasidic community, it is because some *hashash* is present.

"Kosher," as has been stated, means that the foodstuffs is ritually permitted or fit for consumption. An animal must be ritually slaughtered by a ritual slaughterer. After the slaughtering it must be examined internally to see whether or not it was healthy and could have continued living on its own. If this internal examination reveals any signs of sickness or disease indicating that the animal would not have been able to live, this animal is declared prohibited or *trefah* (literally, "torn"), showing organic defect. Thus it becomes forbidden for eating. If this internal examination shows some other blemish that makes the animal not *trefah*, but only questionable, whether the animal is kosher or *trefah* is decided by the ritual slaughterer. He makes this decision in accordance with the prescribed law that fully describes how to decide cases of this sort. However, the Hasidic Jew in Williamsburg does not use the meat of any animal that has been examined and found questionable. The meat he uses must be from an animal that is unquestionably kosher—beyond any shadow of doubt. This unquestionableness, this assurance that the meat of the animal can be used without hesitancy, without reluctance and without any skepticism, the Hasidic Jew calls *glat* kosher. *Glat* means "smooth," and it expresses the fact that the meat is kosher without any suspicion whatsoever. If the meat is *glat* kosher, it can be used by those who are most careful in their observance of the dietary laws.

There are *glat* kosher butcher stores that carry nothing but *glat* kosher meat that has been slaughtered and examined by Hasidic slaughterers whose trustworthiness is above and beyond any question or doubt. These butcher stores are directly supervised by Hasidic Jews whose religious integrity and proficiency are certain. They are under the over-all supervision of a *rebbe* or *rav* whose good reputation, high esteem, and God-fearingness are well known and whose characteristics and behavior are symbolic of the very essence of religion.

The *glat* kosher butcher store carries the name of the sponsoring *rebbe* or of the *rebbe's* organization. It maintains that its net profit goes for the maintenance of the religious school. The advertising of such a butcher store is handled by the organization itself. An example of such advertising shows this:

### The Yeshivah Torah Veyirah of Satmar
### In Boro Park

Makes known that we have opened a butcher store in Boro Park where you can obtain at moderate prices fresh chicken and all sorts of meat which are *"glat* kosher *in the perfection of Kashrut* [kosher] *requirements.*
*The whole profit from the butcher store belongs to the Yeshivah in Boro Park.* By buying meat from us, you help support a Yeshivah in Boro Park, which has, in a short time, made itself a good name in all circles of Boro Park.
We deliver orders in all parts of Brooklyn. Call us by phone, and the order will be delivered to your house. Come and convince yourself.

[Signed] The management of the Yeshivah
The address of the store is 5120 12th Avenue, Brooklyn[36]

There are also sausage factories that make sausage out of *glat* kosher meat. One such factory advertises:

### Yitzhak Levy's special *Mechadrin Glat* Kosher Company

In the heart of Williamsburg
A *glat* kosher sausage factory
Where every day new delicatessen items are produced:
    Salami, Frankfurters, Pastrami, Corned Beef, Tongue
All kinds of smoked meats in cans
Everything only *glat* kosher and at moderate prices

36. *Der Yid,* November 29, 1952. Translated from the Yiddish. Italics the author's.

In the following butcher stores in Williamsburg: You can obtain our products
Kahal Yetav Lev Desatmar
   174 Rudny Street, Brooklyn, New York
Kahal Arugat Habosem (Zehlimer Butcher Store)
   61 Lee Avenue
Kahal Torat Haim (Wisnitzer Butcher Store)
   Ross Street

You can also obtain our products in all parts of the mountains [Catskills]. Please demand from your butcher or grocery man only Yitzhak Levy's *glat* kosher products. You are sure that you receiver kosher and fresh pure meat products.
        Respectfully,
        Yitzhak Levy's *Mehadrin Glat* Kosher Company
        Brooklyn, New York
        ST 2–2600[37]

There are *glat* kosher catering places that serve only *glat* kosher meat. An establishment that has only *glat* kosher meat is automatically identified as a place that is associated with the Hasidic community. The proprietor is usually a member of the community or a Jew who strictly observes Jewish law. Although the very fact that he sells only *glat* kosher meat indicates that he is a "person who cares," the strictness of Hasidic dietary regulations demands that he be especially known, in addition, as a trustworthy Jew.

The Hasidic catering establishment that caters for all occasions does not identify itself with Hasidic Jews through its *glat* kosher meats alone, but also through maintaining other facilities that meet Hasidic requirements. For instance, a traditional wedding ceremony is held in the open, out of doors, "under the skies." Under-the-sky wedding ceremonies are not practical in Brooklyn, where there is little room and weather conditions may be prohibitive. Catering establishments serving observant Jews have a room for wedding ceremonies indoors, where a skylight can be opened above the canopy during the ceremony. Thus, the catering establishment advertises that it has *"glat* kosher food" that is

37. *Der Yid,* August 9, 1957. Translated from the Yiddish.

"kosher for the most zealous of the zealous" and also that it has a "canopy-hall under the vault of heaven."

One of these advertisements reads:

**Weddings!**
**Bar Mitzvahs!**
**Banquets!**
**Happy Occasions!**

With true peace of mind and happiness of soul and *kashrut* for the most zealous of the zealous

*Prave* [is served for those who do not eat meat products even in a *glat* kosher establishment] in the beautiful, elegant, modern halls of the famous

**Grand Paradise**

under the management of the well-known kosher caterer *Rav* A. D. Shajowitz

The halls excel in rare beauty and elegance

Special newly redecorated

Canopy-hall under the vault of heaven for 1000 persons

Accommodates from 50 to 1,000 guests

The name—*Rav Shajowitz*—is a guarantee of the best *glat* kosher foods at reasonable prices with the most cordial service

Grand Paradise
320 Grand Street (Corner Havemeyer Street)
Brooklyn 11, New York
Telephone EVergreen 7–1123 – 8470[38]

Similarly, *glat* kosher restaurants in the Hasidic community serve only *glat* kosher food products. Like the catering establishments, these restaurants serve the general neighborhood and not simply those who require such foods. In these restaurants not only is the meat *glat* kosher, but all food ingredients meet the requirements of the Hasidic community. Thus, *glat* kosher has become a symbol showing full compliance with all Hasidic requirements for food.

These restaurants are not usually under the supervision of a *rav*, since the restaurant owner himself is a Hasidic Jew who is above and beyond any question or doubt. Even before

38. *Hamaor*, August, 1958. Translated from Yiddish-Hebrew.

he considers opening a restaurant, he must establish himself
in the community as a reliable, full-fledged Hasidic Jew who
adheres to the Hasidic principles and can be fully trusted to
meet dietary requirements. He must command the confidence of the Hasidic community if he expects to be patronized.

A Hasidic Jew eats only in those places where *glat* kosher
meats are served. Only those hotels, country places, and vacation resorts that are identified as "Hasidic places" can be
patronized. Usually the two terms, *"glat* kosher meat" and
"Hasidic place," go together. A hotel will buy *glat* kosher
meat because the owner is a Hasidic Jew, and because he is a
Hasidic Jew he will buy only *glat* kosher meat. Such hotels
and resorts advertise typically as follows:

> Friedman's *Glat* Kosher Hotel in the Mountains
> Woodridge, New York, Lew Street and Hessen-Hill
> Formerly Kleinberg Hotel
> > With the aid of God
> We announce to the dear community that, thank God,
> > there is under our management during this summer, this
> > beautiful and elegant hotel
> Airy single and double rooms
> Beautiful grounds
> A room [school] for small children
> A baby sitter for small children
> Filtered swimming pool
> One mile from Woodridge
> *Glat* Kosher for the most zealous of the zealous
> Jewish milk
> Single guests and families will be accepted
> Special rates for families
> > With honor,
> > [Signed] Ephraim Moshe Friedman
> As it happened last year that many did not get accommoda-
> > tions with us, we beg that reservations be made im-
> > mediately.
> For information and reservations call:
> New York City: UL 8–4352
> Woodridge: 765–766[39]

39. Placard FR5. Translated from the Yiddish.

*Glat* kosher products are produced by the Hasidim and are known as Hasidic foodstuffs. There are some religious Jews who observe the dietary laws but who resent what they consider the over-zealousness of the Hasidim and do not care to purchase *glat* kosher meat products. Therefore, when a *glat* kosher meat market opens in the Catskill Mountain area of New York, where many observant Jews spend their summers, this meat market does not advertise itself as *glat* kosher, even though it carries nothing but *glat* kosher products. To do so would identify it as a Hasidic store, which might lead to a loss of business. An example of this is the notice of the Yeshivah & Mesivta Torah Veyirah. It reads:

### Notice

We have opened a butcher store in *Swan Lake, N.Y.*
Under our supervision, where you can acquire fresh meats and poultry of best quality and at low prices.
We deliver to all bungalows in all parts of the mountains:
Call LIberty 2559 and we will deliver your order.
The proceeds of this butcher store go to the Yeshivah and Mesivta Torah Veyirah of Satmar.
With your assistance you are helping us to carry on our Yeshivah with its 1600 pupils.
Bring us customers from among your friends and neighbors. In return for your kind-hearted support, the Almighty will bless you with a happy and healthy summer.

| Yeshivah and Mesivta | Congregation Yetev Lev |
| Torah Veyirah | Butcher Store[40] |

*Glat* kosher meat products in New York City are a comparatively new phenomenon. They are handled by restaurants other than Hasidic ones. Delicatessen stores that close on the Sabbath are patronized by Sabbath-observant Jews. Some of these Sabbath-observant Jews also prefer to use *glat* kosher products. In these delicatessen stores, the customer who has ordered sandwiches is asked, "Do you want *glat* or non-*glat?*"

*Glat* kosher meat production is one of the largest indus-

40. Placard TV2. Printed in English and Yiddish.

tries of the Hasidim. This type of meat is consumed not only in the Hasidic community but also in various parts of the country. Yet even within the Hasidic community most of those who are on the margin between "very religious" and Hasidic have expressed the sentiment that *a priori* they would not require *glat* kosher meat, but that, since it is available and since it is the kind of meat "religious" Jews use, they too will use only *glat* kosher meat. Some of this feeling is expressed in the following excerpts from an interview.

*A.* I'm sorry, I don't use that product.

*Q.* Well, it is kosher.

*A.* Yes, I know it is kosher, but it isn't *glat* kosher.

*Q.* Do you use only *glat* kosher?

*A.* Yes, I use only *glat* kosher products.

*Q.* You were here in America when *glat* kosher meat was not even known. Then you must have been using non-*glat* kosher products.

*A.* Yes, I know, I had been using that product. But since *glat* kosher meat is abundant and is available everywhere in New York . . . I can obtain it without any difficulty at all, and since it is produced by religious Jews and all religious Jews use it, there is no reason why I should not use *glat* kosher meat. I don't claim to be extremely religious, but all religious Jews use it, and I think it is even better in quality than other meats. You practically know the people who handle the *glat* kosher meat, so you can trust them better.

*Q.* Isn't *glat* kosher meat too expensive?

*A.* The difference in price between *glat* kosher meat and just kosher meat is so little that it is worth the difference.[41]

Use of *glat* kosher meat by religious Jews has gained popularity in the United States, where, for the first time, it is consumed on a large scale. In a small European Jewish community, for instance, only one or two large animals were

41. From the files of RGE, 1958.

slaughtered for kosher consumption during any week. If the ritual internal examination of the slaughtered animals raised some question of blemish, but if after proper consultation with the *rav* of the community (if the question required consultation with a higher religious authority), the animals were declared kosher, their meat was used by the most pious Jews throughout the most religious European Jewish communities. It is true, however, that there were even then some extremely religious Jews (not necessarily Hasidim) who would eat the meat of an animal only if it happened to be *glat*. In the United States, where there is a great abundance of animals and a large slaughtering industry, people can afford to produce and to purchase *glat* kosher meat. All these factors have greatly contributed to the popularity of *glat* kosher meat. It may be noted that the favorable economic organization contributes to religiosity in spite of the tremendous secularization in the United States.

Since *"glat* kosher" signifies strict observance of the dietary laws, many non-Hasidic butcher stores and delicatessens carry and advertise *glat* kosher products. The Hasidic community vehemently opposes all identification of such stores with *glat* kosher products, since they fear that such stores may also carry non-*glat* kosher products. Thus, a customer who intends to buy only *glat* kosher products may be deceived into thinking that all the merchandise is of the same caliber. The Hasidic rabbinical authority, the Central Rabbinical Congress of the United States and Canada, sends out large placards printed in three languages—English, Yiddish, and Hebrew—to be posted in all Hasidic houses of worship, warning the "observant public" about these fraudulent conditions. The English text of such an announcement follows:

Central Rabbinical Congress of the U.S.A. and Canada
134 Broadway—Brooklyn, N. Y.—EVergreen 4-1547

**Important Announcement**

All observant Jews are fully aware of the importance of the laws of Kashruth, on which the sanctity of the Jewish people depends.

Unfortunately, however, many people are either too careless or too much absorbed by their business, and therefore
often fail to take the necessary precautions in the matter
of Kashruth.

We therefore wish to call the attention of the broad
observant public to the following matters:

1. Many meat retailers who have no supervision by a
reliable Rabbi claim to sell "Glatt Kosher"[42] merchandise.
In some cases they actually do keep some "Glatt Kosher"
items, but only as a camouflage, to cover up all other sorts
of meat which they also sell.

2. Various frauds or grave errors are frequent in many
chicken markets where the proprietors are not themselves
trustworthy. Even where the Shochet is reliable, a permanent Mashgiach [supervisor] must be present, having no
other occupation but the supervision of the entire process
from the slaughtering until the chickens are sealed in sacks.
Experience has proved that otherwise frauds or grave mis-
takes are practically inevitable.

We therefore earnestly admonish all observant Jews:

1. To buy chickens only from such places where there
is a full-time Mashgiach supervising the entire process from
the slaughtering until the packing into sacks.

2. To buy meat only from exclusively Glatt Kosher butchers.

3. To see to it that also the retailer be under reliable
Rabbinical supervision, not only the wholesaler from whom
the retailer buys.

We are not in a position as yet to improve the situation
further,[43] since we are not able to appoint supervisors for
every individual place where meat or poultry is sold. We
have therefore considered it our duty to make the situation
known, so that every individual Jew should take the necessary precaution as to where and what he buys.

May the Almighty save us from every fault.

Central Rabbinical Congress of the U.S.A. and Canada[44]

42. The spelling of the word "*Glatt*" with two *t*'s is inconsistent. In
other places, as well as in Yiddish, it is spelled with one *t*.

43. Note the language, "We are not in a position as yet . . ." indicating an intention to broaden the Hasidic authority over *kashrut*
outside the Hasidic community.

44. Placard GK2.

*Milchig* products used in the Hasidic community must be made from the milk of a kosher animal that a Jew is permitted to eat. The milk of a nonkosher animal is called *halav tameh*, unclean milk. Since there is an apprehension that milk products may contain *halav tameh*, the milking and processing of dairy products must be supervised by a *ferleslicher Yid*, a trustworthy Jew. Milk that has been milked under the supervision of a *ferleslicher Yid* is called in Hebrew, *halav Yisrael*, "Jewish milk," or in Yiddish, *koshere milach*. Although there are state and government agencies that supervise milk production, and various testing facilities through which it is determined that milk is pure cow's milk with no foreign agents added, and although milk and milk products are graded according to standards that are strictly enforced, this does not make the milk *halav Yisrael*. The Hasidic Jew must have milk that is supervised in fact by a *ferleslicher Yid*, and this person must be under the supervision of a Hasidic *rav*.

One of the first Hasidic dairy companies was the *Kahal* Dairy Company, Incorporated. A few years ago (1950–51), before *koshere milach* gained the popularity it has today, many dairy restaurants in New York served two kinds of milk, the "regular" and "*Kahal.*" When a customer ordered milk, or coffee with milk, he was asked: "*Kahal* or regular?" *Kahal* was known to be the *koshere milach*. Today this question is no longer asked, because *koshere milach* companies have become numerous, and it is not a wise business tactic for a restaurant catering to people who demand *koshere milach* to carry the "regular" milk also.

Today there are many Hasidic dairy companies and even more dairy products. The names of these companies indicate their affiliation with the Hasidic community and that they are "truly kosher." The *Machmirim* ("the ones who are strict") Dairy Corporation produces light sour cream. On the top of their sour cream bottle the following is printed:

> This is made under supervision from the beginning of the milking until the product is completed.
> Under the supervision of the *Rav*, the head of the religious court in the holy community of Papa, may his light shine.

> Presently [the *rav* is] in Brooklyn, may Zion and Jerusalem be rebuilt.
>
> *Machmirim* Dairy Corporation
> 1907 Strauss Street, Brooklyn[45]

The *Mehadrin* ("zealous") Dairy Corporation also produces light sour cream, creamed cottage cheese, and sweet kosher butter. On the package of butter the following is printed:

> Kosher for Passover
> *Mehadrin*'s Kosher Sweet Butter
> Made from Jewish milk
> under the supervision of Chananyah Yom Tov
> Lipa Teitelbaum, the head of the religious court
> of the holy community of Nyirbator
> *Mehadrin* Dairy Corporation, 441–3 White Avenue
> Brooklyn, New York[46]

Some of the fancier cheeses which these Hasidic companies cannot produce are imported from Switzerland and from Denmark. These imported cheeses are made under the strict supervision of a *rav* whose religious authority is accepted by the Hasidic leaders of Williamsburg.

For *parve* foods the Jewish dietary laws do not prescribe any type of ritual performance in their preparation, such as is required for animals, which, for instance, must be ritually slaughtered. But in the Hasidic community, even this type of food must meet with Hasidic requirements. The question can be asked: If there is no religious requirements concerning *parve* foodstuff, than what makes such food Hasidic? The answer to this is the concept of *hashash*, apprehension.

The Hasidic community doubts any foodstuff that has been prepared by a non-*ferleslicher Yid* lest it contain some substances that are not permissible for a Hasidic Jew to eat. *Hashash* is the most vital and decisive phenomenon through which the Hasidic community tries to control its own food consumption and establish its own economics. Every con-

---

45. From the bottle top. Translated from the Hebrew.
46. From the package. Translated from the Hebrew.

ceivable food that needs some kind of preparation can present a certain *hashash* concerning its use, but if it is prepared by a *ferleslicher Yid* or by a Hasidic Jew, who is, of course, beyond doubt a *ferleslicher Yid*, the *hashash* is removed and it may be used by a Hasidic Jew. Thus any foodstuff that has been prepared, manufactured, produced, handled, and packed by Hasidic Jews has no *hashash* connected with it.

To make the phenomenon of *hashash* clearer, an additional explanation is necessary. The only general necessary requirement for food that Jews are allowed to eat is that it be kosher—permissible according to the religious dietary laws. There are four ways in which *kashrut* is fully assured.

1. The food substance and its ingredients must themselves be reliably kosher.

2. The person preparing the food must be reliable.

3. The person under whose supervision food is prepared must be a well-known religious authority.

4. The food preparation must be done in accordance with the interpretations of well-known religious authorities.

It should be noted that while basic dietary requirements are quite specific in the law, the question of "reliability" is very subjective. "Reliable" for what and for whom? "Well known" by whom? To the Hasidim, the answer is that everything must be acceptable in the Hasidic community. It is the community that determines whether one is or is not a religious authority; it is the community that determines who is "well known" and for what.

Of all these four criteria of *kashrut, hashash* is the most important element. The food substance and its ingredients must be reliably kosher in such a way that they are beyond any *hashash*, any apprehension or doubt. The only way this *hashash* can be removed is for the Hasidic community to decree something "reliable," and it is reliable only if it has been prepared in the community.

Secondly, the person preparing the food must be reliable. He must be a religious man who conforms to community norms and who is well known to religious authorities. But a person who is not known in the Hasidic community is of doubtful reliability, and since his qualifications are in doubt by the Hasidic community, anything he prepares is *ipso facto* doubtful and questionable and has a *hashash*. Therefore, the Hasidic community itself provides foodstuffs that have been prepared by those people who are above and beyond any *hashash*.

Furthermore, the person under whose supervision food is prepared must be a well-known religious authority. The authority of such persons is fully accepted by the community. But if food has been produced under the supervision of persons who are not known in the community, whose behavior is questionable, whose religiosity may not coincide with the requirements of Hasidism, there is a *hashash* whether or not it can be used by Hasidic Jews. Thus, the Hasidic community demands foodstuff that has been supervised by those whose religious authority and Hasidic behavior are above and beyond any question or doubt, that is, primarily by members of the community itself.

Finally, the food must be prepared in accordance with the interpretations of well-known Hasidic authorities. There are certain conditions concerning kosher food that are not specifically described in the dietary laws. Therefore, an interpretation is necessary. There are some religious authorities who are lenient (*mekel*) and some who are strict (*mahmir*) in their interpretations. The Hasidim are strict in the interpretation of the law, since leniency may reflect upon one's "leniency in other religious matters." The Hasidic community will refer to religious authorities known to be strict in their determination. Again, the concept of *hashash* is applied if a lenient interpretation is followed. Since the Hasidic community accepts the most rigid form of interpretation of the law, the community will advertise and call to the attention of its members that the Hasidic community is producing foodstuff which is far above and beyond any question or doubt. It complies with all aspects of religious requirements.

It can be seen how almost all food products are controlled in the Hasidic community and how the economy tends to be internalized:

1. *Hashash* is applicable to all conceivable food products.

2. If a certain food has been labeled or stigmatized with *hashash,* it is no longer permissible for use in the Hasidic community.

3. Stigmatized products are replaced by Hasidic products that are beyond question or doubt.

4. Since this food can be obtained without *hashash,* it is the duty of every Hasid to purchase these items.

Thus, only the Hasidic community produces foods without any *hashash* whatever. These food products having no *hashashim* whatever are called "kosher *alibe d'chol hadeut,*" kosher according to all (authoritative) opinions. Once these foodstuffs are kosher according to all religious authorities because they have no *hashashim* whatever, they become kosher even for the *mehadrin min hamehadrin,* the "most zealous of the zealous" in religious observance. The terms *mehadrin* (zealous) and *mehadrin min hamehadrin* have become identifying symbols of Hasidic products and of strict observance of religious law. Consequently, there are food companies which have taken the word *mehadrin* as part of their names, such as the *Mehadrin* Dairy Corporation or the *Mehadrin* Food Corporation. These considerations control the food market in the Hasidic community.

The illustrations that follow show that everything produced outside the community is stigmatized by a *hashash* and that these items have been replaced by Hasidic foodstuffs without *hashash.*

**Egg Noodles**

According to religious law, a Jew is not allowed to eat blood. If an egg contains even a drop of blood, it is prohibited. Egg noodles are obviously made from eggs, but the *hashash* is whether they have been made from eggs that contain blood drops. Another *hashash* is whether the person who states that the egg noodles are made of bloodless eggs is reliable. The noodle with *hashashim* have been replaced by the products of the Chuster Noodle Company. This company produces double egg noodles made from bloodless eggs under the supervision of *Rav* Naphtali Landau, the former *Rav* of Chust.[47]

## Mayonnaise

This product is also made from eggs. Again the *hashash* is present, since it may have been made from eggs with blood droplets in them. Another *hashash* is whether the person who produces it can be trusted to use bloodless eggs. This *hashash* has been replaced by the Schischa Brothers'

Real kosher mayonnaise [which is]
kosher for the most zealous of the zealous
under the supervision of
the *Rav*, the *Gaon, Rav* Jonathan Steif,
may he live long and happily.[48]

## Potato Chips

There is a *hashash* that potato chips may have been fried in oils that are not pure vegetable oils. Again, the second *hashash* is whether the person who states that they are fried in pure vegetable oil can be trusted. These *hashashim* have been removed by the *"Madanim"* potato chips, which

. . . are kosher for *parve*, neutral use, made under the supervision of the *Rav* and *Gaon* S. L. Friedman, the head of the rabbinical court of the holy community of Tenka, may he be blessed with long years.[49]

## Peanuts

Even peanuts have a *hashash* that they may have been roasted in impure vegetable oil. This *hashash* has been removed by the Carlton Nut and Chocolate Company, which manufacturers

One hundred per cent *parve* freshly roated Virginia peanuts that have been fried in pure vegetable oil without additives and stabilizers.[50]

47. From the package. Translated from the Yiddish.
48. From the package. Translated from the Yiddish.
49. From the label on the package. Translated from the Yiddish.
50. From the label on the package. Translated from the Yiddish.

According to Jewish law, a Jew is not permitted to eat any kind of worm, and he must examine any fruit that may contain worms or maggots before eating it. Cherries, for example, may contain maggots, especially if they are overripe. Thus, cherries that have been commercially prepared have the *hashash* that they have not been strictly examined before canning and that they may contain maggots. The *Mehadrin* Food Corporation cans red cherries that have no worms and therefore no *hashash*. Their label states that:

> These cherries do not possess worms, and they were cooked under the supervision of the *Rabbanim, Gaonim*
> [signed] Jonathan Steif
> The *Rav* of the religious court of the holy community of Budapest, head of the rabbinical court of Congregation Adath Yereim, Brooklyn
> Chananiah Yom Tov Lipa Teitelbaum
> The head of the religious court of Nyirbátor at present in Brooklyn[51]

Everything that comes in contact with food during Passover has a *hashash,* apprehension. Passover is different from all other holidays because the dietary requirements are much more strict than those at any other time. *Hometz* is prohibited on Passover not only to eat but even to have in one's possession. Whenever Jewish law prohibits eating a certain food substance, the law specifies the minimum forbidden amount as "the size of an olive." A priori, a person may not eat any amount of forbidden foods; however, *ex post facto* a person is not punishable according to the law unless he has eaten an amount the size of an average olive or more. If he has eaten an amount less than the size of an olive, he is not punishable. The amount of *hometz* eaten on Passover for which a person is punishable, however, is not the minimal amount specified in the law; it is instead "the smallest infinitesimal amount." Because of this, great care and special supervision are required for all kinds of food products so that even the minutest amount of *hometz* will not come in contact with Passover food. This is the reason why religious Jews will not eat anything with the smallest

51. From the label on the can. Translated from the Hebrew.

*hashash* that it may contain *hometz*. This *hashash* is applicable to all kinds of food for Passover.

The *hashash* may be that a certain food contains *hometz*. If this condition does not exist, the *hashash* may be that the food has come in contact with *hometz*, that its preparation or the production of one of its ingredients has not been supervised properly, on that the person who supervised its preparation is not trustworthy. This can go on and on; the *hashashim* for Passover are actually unlimited.

Since for Passover there are so many *hashashim*, even about foodstuffs that usually do not need any supervision, almost every foodstuff used in the Hasidic community during Passover must be produced by the Hasidim themselves under the supervision of Hasidic authority. This is why Appel's egg market advertises that it is selling unwashed eggs for Passover. There is a *hashash* that eggs may have been washed in solutions containing *hometz*, leaven. But eggs from Appel's egg market have no *hashash* whatever. It advertises:

### Visit Appel's Egg Market

All year you can get fresh eggs at cheap prices.
We have special reduced prices for Passover.
Also every day we have fresh cracked eggs.
Also, we have unwashed eggs available.

Come in and prove it for yourself. Free delivery

Appel's Egg Market, 50 Lee Avenue
EVergreen 7–5756     Residence: BR 5–8881[52]

There are basic food ingredients such as sugar and salt that need supervision in order to remove the *hashash*. Sugar has the *hashash* that it may have been processed with chemicals or with the aid of chemicals that contain *hometz*. Thus, according to the Hasidic community, commercial sugar may not be used on Passover. For this reason the Central Rabbinical Congress of the United States and Canada, the authoritative Hasidic rabbinical body, supervises production

52. Leaflets hung in the various Hasidic houses of worship. Translated from the Yiddish.

of sugar. The print on the sugar bags, sold at two pounds for fifty cents in the Hasidic community, reads as follows:

**This sugar**

from the beginning of the bringing in of the raw material until the very end of packaging is produced under the strict supervision of the Central Rabbinical Congress of the United States and Canada and is thus kosher for Passover for the most zealous of the zealous in religious matters.

Sugar—Kosher for Passover
Net weight 2 lbs.

Packed and distributed by:
Spitzer and Lefkovits
68 Lee Avenue, Brooklyn 11, N.Y.,—EV 7–7490

These bags have been pasted with paste that is permitted for Passover under the supervision of the Central Rabbinical Congress of the United States and Canada.[53]

As a result of this, the Lipschutz Kosher Wines firm advertises that for sweetening its wine it uses sugar that has been supervised by the Central Rabbinical Congress of the United States and Canada. The advertisement reads in part:

Also we announce that this year, as well as every other year, we have natural sweet wine without sugar and also sweet wines that have been produced and sweetened with the sugar of the Central Rabbinical Congress of the United States and Canada.[54]

Another basic food ingredient is salt. Kosher salt for Passover produced outside the community is available, but it is not kosher enough for the Hasidim. Salt has the *hashash* that it was not properly supervised, that it has come in contact with substances not permissible for Passover use, or that it contains chemicals that are *hometz*. The rabbis who supervise so-called kosher-for-Passover salt are not "religious enough" or "authoritative enough." Therefore, the Hasidic

53. From the imprint on a paper sugar bag. Translated from the Yiddish.
54. *Der Yid*, February 28, 1958. Translated from the Yiddish.

community provides salt for Passover with "absolutely no *hashash* whatever." This salt is supervised by the Central Rabbinical Congress of the United States and Canada. The label on the bags of salt reads as follows:

**This salt**

was dug, ground and packed under the supervision of the Central Rabbinical Congress of the United States and Canada and is kosher for Passover, for the most zealous of the zealous

Packed and distributed by:
Spitzer and Lefkovits
68 Lee Avenue, Brooklyn, N.Y.—EV 7-7490[55]

Once the Hasidic community knows that there is Hasidic supervision over salt and sugar, especially by such an authoritative rabbinical organization as the Central Rabbinical Congress of the United States and Canada, all other salt and sugar become automatically unfit for use in the community. Hence, all commercial establishments that process foods requiring salt or sugar must use Hasidic salt and sugar. Many companies like bakeries, where the use of sugar and salt is taken for granted, do not even make special mention in their advertising of their use of Hasidic sugar and salt, since it is "self-evident" that the proprietors, who are fully trusted and enjoys a fine reputation in the community, would use nothing but sugar and salt that has been supervised by Hasidic rabbinical authority.

The following is an advertisement of a chocolate- and candymaker who uses only sugar supervised by the Central Rabbinical Congress of the United States and Canada. The candymaker tries to convey to the community that these products are kosher for Passover use and that they can also be used by the "most zealous of the zealous."

**In honor of twenty-five years in the chocolate business**

Paskesz' products
Twenty-five kinds of new chocolates

55. From the imprint on a salt bag. Translated from the Yiddish.

Finest quality of all kosher and *parve* are available under the supervision of the *Rav* Moshe Stern, head of the Jewish court of the holy community of Debrecen.

Demand from your grocer and at your bakery exclusive Paskesz' chocolates, finger biscuits, chocolate syrup, hazel nuts, potato chips packed in fancy boxes.

For gift-giving for Purim, the firm Paskesz' is the only one that also produces Passover chocolates, candies, and chocolate syrup under the supervision of the *Rav* of Debrecen and *uses only sugar that is produced under the supervision of the Central Rabbinical Congress of the United States and Canada.*

All grocery men are requested to make their orders as soon as possible so that we can fill their demands.

Attention, Jews of Brownsville, Paskesz' has opened a new store in the heart of Brownsville.

Paskesz'  418 Saratoga Avenue  Telephone EVergreen 5-2559 and SL 6-8248[56]

Another example is the Spritzer and Lefkovitz food store's advertisement of Passover products:

### Announcement of the firm Spritzer and Lefkovitz

We have this year, as well as in other years, Passover products—for instance, *sugar and salt under strict supervision of the Central Rabbinical Congress of the United States and Canada.*

We have also strictly Passover products: Winn's chocolate, chocolate syrup, jams, tea, potato starch, coffee, made under strict supervision.

Also we have made this year our own small and large jars of *Mehadrin instant coffee* which is usable for the most zealous of the zealous.

Also ground coffee in cans under the strict supervision of the *Rav, Gaon Shlomo* Friedman, head of the Jewish court of Tenke. *Our sugar is under the supervision of the Central Rabbinical Congress and does not contain any chemical material including ultra-marine.*

Attention grocery men, butcher stores, and so on.

56. *Der Yid,* February 28, 1958. Translated from the Yiddish. Italics the author's.

*Special Passover paper bags glued with Passover glues under strict supervision of the Central Rabbinical Congress, are available to wrap groceries, meats, fruits, and so on.*[57]

The most important food for Passover is matzah. Matzah, "unleavened bread," is a flat, crackerlike, baked product made of flour and water. The preparation and baking of matzah for Passover must be done with great care. The following are some excerpts from the law concerning kneading and baking matzah.

The unleavened bread should be kneaded and made only in a room that has a roof and not opposite an open window, even if the sun does not shine through. If the windows are shut and there are panes in them, it is permissible if the sun does not shine through. But if the sun shines through, the glass window-panes are of no avail, but it is necessary to spread a curtain to shut out the sun's rays. Care should also be taken that the room should not be heated or warm.

No greater quantity of dough should be kneaded at one time than what is necessary for the separation of the dough-cake. And it is best to make it small, for our rabbis, of blessed memory, surmised that if the dough is larger than the above prescribed limit, it cannot be worked at one and the same time, thus leaving some part of it unworked, and there is apprehension that it may become leavened in the meantime. If the dough was made soft, it should not be made thicker by adding some flour.

When the flour is measured, it should not be stuffed into the measure lest some flour be left in the *matzoth* unkneaded and when put in soup become leavened. One should be careful not to place the flour near water so that the flour dust should not fall therein. One who measures the flour should likewise not go near the dough or the water. It is well to take care not to needlessly handle the flour, as it might warm it slightly.

Care should be taken that there should be neither crack nor crevice in the vessel used for kneading wherein any particle of dough might remain and turn into leaven. Nor should the vessel be placed upon cushioned articles while in the act of kneading lest it become warm, the vessel must be thoroughly cleansed every eighteen minutes, when the hands, too, must be carefully

57. *Der Yid*, February 28, 1958. Translated from the Yiddish. Italics the author's.

washed. The boards and rollers should also be free from cracks or crevices, and should be thoroughly cleansed at least every eighteen minutes. The instruments with which the perforations are made should be kept clean without any dough on them. The peel with which the unleavened bread is thrust into the oven should be critically examined that there be no crack therein, where a particle of food might be entered and become leavened.

If anything colorific fell into the dough, such as salt, spices, or quicklime, even a particle thereof, and was kneaded therein, the use of the entire dough is forbidden, inasmuch as it has become heated thereby. If a grain of corn was found in the dough, a mass of dough as thick as one's finger should be removed from all around that grain and thrown away, and the use of the rest is permitted.

Care should be taken not to let the dough lie for a moment without working upon it, and as soon as the dough is completed it should be distributed among those who roll it. Care should therefore be taken to make the dough only as big as those who roll it can take care of. And if a part of the unleavened bread remains in the hands of the kneader, the kneading of the dough should be kept up, as it should not lie idle for a moment.

Those who are engaged in rolling should perform their work speedily and not prolong the preparation, and see that there are no particles of dough upon the boards and that none of it stick to their hands; should they find any dough sticking to them, they should instantly cleanse them well.

Immediately after the unleavened bread is prepared, it should be perforated quickly not making any designs and it should be put in the oven as quickly as possible. The utmost care should be taken not to delay it for a moment opposite the opening of the oven, as there it will quickly turn leavened. Hence it is necessary that the one handing the unleavened bread to the baker should be versed in the law and pay scrupulous attention to it.

A God-fearing man should take care, before baking his unleavened bread, to have the oven heated anew and the coals spread upon its entire surface, for who knows whether the one who has baked before him was scrupulous about it.

The baker should most carefully see to it that none of the unleavened bread be doubled up, nor that one should touch the other, for in the place where it is doubled up and touches another one it does not bake quickly and becomes leavened. In the event of one having doubled up or becomes inflated, it is requisite to break off that portion as it is leaven, and it is permitted to use the rest. If, however, they touch each other while still moist in the oven, their use my be permitted *post facto*. The term inflated implies that the unleavened bread was divided at its thick parts, and the hollow part is as thick as a thumb.

Care should be taken not to take the unleavened bread out of the oven so long at it is not baked to such a degree that one may break it without drawing strands of dough therefrom, as previous to that condition it is only like dough which, being taken out of the oven, readily turns leavened. The peel upon which such unleavened bread was taken out, is also thenceforth forbidden to be used for unleavened bread. If it is impossible to tell whether strands of dough can be withdrawn therefrom or not, because of the doubt, the law should be enforced, but if the surface formed a crust the law may be relaxed.

It is proper for every God-fearing man to personally supervise the making and baking of his own unleavened bread and admonish the workingmen to use due care and diligence. This was the method of the great men of Israel, of blessed memory, and this is also the method of the pious in our own times.

The unleavened bread wherewith one fulfills the precept of eating *matzoth* on the two first Passover nights, is called "the unleavened bread of the precept," and it should be made "for the sake of the precept" by an adult male Israelite of intelligence, aged at least thirteen years and one day, or by a female aged at least twelve years and one day, and at each stage of its process, even when drawing water, the worker should say "for the sake of the unleavened bread of the precept."[58]

These laws are some of the basic requirements for baking matzah. The Hasidic community not only fulfills the exact requirements prescribed by the law but observes many additional restrictions to be certain that its matzah is unquestionably "fitting for the most zealous of the zealous." The Hasidic community bakes its matzah from flour that has been guarded against having become leavened from the time of the harvesting of the wheat. The matzah baked from guarded flour is called *shmurah* matzah, "guarded matzah." Only religious Jews who have familiarity with and knowledge of

58. *Code of Jewish Law, loc. cit.,* 110:3–15.

the regulations concerning matzah are engaged in matzah baking; in addition, it is supervised by a religious authority of the Hasidic community.

The Hasidic matzah industry has grown considerably. Today there are many matzah bakeries. Almost every religious organization tries to establish a matzah bakery of its own. The period of baking matzah lasts from four to five weeks, and it gives employment to many Hasidic men who would not undertake similar menial work in another industry. Many Hasidic Jews, especially if they rank high in prestige, consider menial work below their status. But baking matzah, which is a religious article, does not lower their prestige. The people who bake the Hasidic matzah justify this menial labor with the rationale that through their work they are helping more and more Jews to eat real kosher matzah on Passover and thereby to increase their religiosity. It may be noted again that it is not the "white collar" versus "blue collar" distinction that determines the ranking of a certain occupation in the prestige system of the Hasidic community. The prestige of an occupation in the Hasidic community is determined by religiosity. The production of real religious articles (for instance, phylacteries or prayer shawls) is higher in the rank order than the production of articles that have only an indirect religious significance (for instance, Sabbath *Zeiger* or Hasidic clothing). Production of articles that have only an indirect religious significance is higher in the rank order than production of articles that have no religious significance at all (for example, neckties).

The baking of matzah is done either by hand or by machine. There are also two types of matzah. One is the matzah *peshutah,* plain matzah baked from flour that has been specially produced and religiously supervised only from the time of its production. The other type is the previously mentioned *shmurah* matzah. The "most zealous of the zealous" will eat nothing but handmade matzah that has been so guarded. This special matzah costs two dollars and thirty cents a pound, as compared with the commercially produced matzah, which costs about thirty-five to thirty-seven cents a pound.

Because the demand for this special handmade matzah is so great, it encourages many religious organizations to operate matzah bakeries. The following is an advertisement by a matzah bakery that produces this special matzah:

### Guarded Matzah

In the Hungarian House of Baking
Under the supervision of our teacher and master the *Rav* and *Gaon*, the *Tzadik* and Righteous, the *Rav* of Siget, may he live long and happily.
745 Driggs Avenue, Brooklyn 11, New York
We make known that on the first day of the week in which the Torah chapters of *Vayakhel-Pekudei* are read, the first Sunday after Purim, we start with God's will, to bake matzah as in every year. Handmade matzah guarded from the time of harvesting. We beg everybody, especially our customers, make your orders now. Our customers will have preference for that matzah baked on the day before Passover, specially used for the Seder ceremonial.
Jews, especially those from New York, if you want to have matzah for Passover, send your orders right away and you will have them in time.
Guaranteed
For *kashrut* and quality, my bakery is known throughout the year.
With the blessing of a happy Purim and a kosher and happy holiday.
Very respectfully, Josef Ciment, manager
For mail order write to Josef Ciment, 558 Bedford Avenue, Brooklyn 11, New York[59]

Another matzah bakery advertises that its matzah is produced under the "personal supervision" of two Hasidic authorities.

*Congregation of Celim and Papa matzah bakery,*
325 Bedford Avenue between South 8th and South 9th Streets, Brooklyn 11, New York
Telephone EVergreen 8–0771

59. *Der Yid,* April 3, 1959. Translated from the Yiddish.

## Announcement

We make known that the Congregation of Celim and Papa this year also bakes only guarded matzah.

In our own bakery matzah which is guarded from the time of the cutting of the wheat until the end of the baking under the personal supervision of the *Rabbanim, Gaonim,* the *Rav Gaon* from Celim and the *Rav Gaon* from Papa.

This is the only matzah bakery which is under the personal supervision of these great *Rabbanim* and *Gaonim.*

Matzah can be obtained in the bakery and in our store, 35 Avenue B near Roebling Street, Brooklyn, New York

Orders from congregations or individuals or by mail are most promptly filled.

Make your order by mail or phone.

J. Seidenfeld, 90 Wilson Street, Brooklyn 11, New York Telephone EVergreen 8-0771[60]

Another matzah bakery advertises that it is furnished in accordance with all restrictions and that one of the managers has a very attractive *"rebbishe* lineage." Besides this, it has representatives in all parts of New York.

## Important Announcement

*The famous*
*Kereszturer Guarded Matzah Bakery*
makes publicly known to all Jews who are meticulous in the observance of the commandment that our bakery is furnished with all restrictions and splendor—where you can prove it for yourself—besides this, our matzah is thin and thoroughly baked with a delicious taste.

Don't postpone it until the last minute. Call as soon as possible with your order so that we may have the possibility of satisfying you.

For those who cannot be present during the baking, we have—for their comfort—the following stores where they can call for the matzah that is baked in our bakery under the strict supervision of the *Rav,* the *Gaon,* the Righteous

60. *Ibid.*

from Sziget, may God send him good and long years on earth.

In Williamsburg: L. Friedman, 70 Lee Avenue (between Rodney–Ross) EV 8–3145

In Boro Park: M. Grunfeld, 4414–14 Avenue, UL 4–1740 (near the Sephardic synagogue)

In Crown Heights: R. L. Ehrenreich, Central Hebrew Book Store (between Carrol and Crown streets), SL 6–7174.

The guarded matzahs are whole, packed in boxes, which is a guarantee that they remain fresh and whole. Congregations and Yeshivot and wholesalers receive substantial discounts. Kereszturer Matzah Shmurah Bakery 59 Reid Avenue (Corner Lafayette Avenue) Brooklyn, Telephone HY 1–9518

Directions: BMT Jamaica train to Kosciusko Station, or Utica Avenue bus to Reid Avenue. This brings you to the door of our bakery.

[Signed] MOSHE GROS:

The son of the *Rav,* the Righteous from Kroleh, previously from Berbesht and from Ricse

The grandson of the Righteous, the Holy *Rebbe* Yeshajeh'le Kereszturer. May the remembrance of the righteous and the holy one be for a blessing

[Signed] GAVRIEL JUDAH NEISCHLOSS FROM SZERDAHELY[61]

This same matzah bakery distributes business cards, on the back of which is printed:

The advantages our baking possesses:

1. Two new ovens built.
2. A half a yard from the oven it is actually cool.
3. There is a separate room in which the dough is rolled out.
4. There are extra rooms for flour, water, and kneading.
5. A separate room for the cleaning of the rolling pins.
6. Perforators are heated to a glow and changed every 15–16 minutes.
7. The matzah is not turned over in the oven.
8. Three sets of rolling pins are used.
9. A hall is provided for the *hometz* lunches on separate floors for men and women.

61. *Ibid.*

The supervisors are scholars and God-fearing men all under the strict supervision of the *Rav,* the *Gaon,* the righteous head of the religious court in the holy community of Sziget, may he be blessed with long and happy years.[62]

Still another matzah bakery even established its own permanent "specially built" bakery, unlike others that either rent or use transformed bakeries. This organization advertises the following:

### The Satmarer Matzah Bakery

makes known that we have already begun to bake matzah in our specially built guarded matzah bakery. We have erected this year a new mill to grind the wheat so that it is strictly kosher. We have obtained the best quality of flour and the matzah are excellent this year, well-baked and of very good taste, not equaled in former years. We receive orders to be delivered throughout the whole country and also abroad.

Come and see how the matzah bakery looks in matters of *kashrut* as well as in matters of quality of the matzah.

Congregations that want to buy from us must contact us as soon as possible in order that we may assure a satisfactory date for baking.

Congregation Yetev Lev of Satmar

The bakery, 427 Broadway, Brooklyn, New York

Telephone ST 2–9275[63]

This same organization, as noted above, even erected a hand mill for the production of flour for the matzah, so that there should be no question whatever about the strict observance of the law concerning the matzah. They advertise the following:

### Announcement

*Guarded flour from a hand mill.*

I succeeded with God's help in erecting a hand mill of stones; the flour is actually cold and fine in quality. All is

62. From the *matzah* bakery's business card. Translated from the Yiddish.

63. *Der Yid,* April 3, 2959. Translated from the Yiddish.

from fine selected wheat that can be seen to be without any chaff—I invite all in to see it. Give your orders right away so that I shall be able to satisfy you in time because I shall have only a limited amount. The address is:

The Satmarer Bakery, 427 Broadway

Respectfully, Eliezer David
Telephone ST 2-9275[64]

The baking of the machine matzah is conducted in accordance with the same restrictions and prescriptions as the hand matzah. Some people, especially those who are on the margin between Hasidic and "very religious," prefer machine matzah because it tastes better, and they feel that machine matzah can be just as kosher as hand matzah. This matzah is also supervised by a Hasidic *rav,* and the demand for this (still) Hasidic matzah is very high.

Hasidic machine-made matzah is manufactured by the Congregation of (God-) Fearers' Orthodox Matzah Products. This matzah is packed in boxes. On one side of the box, the following is printed:

### *With the aid of God*

This matzah was baked under constant strict supervision of God-fearing Jews with all the restrictions and precisions in accordance with the [Religious] Codifiers. The work is stopped every seventeen minutes. And everyone can enjoy the thoroughly baked and tasty matzah without any *hashash.*

*Hallah* [the "priest's share of the dough"] has been taken according to the religious law.

With the aid of God

Behold, I certify that the matzah baked in the bakery, Orthodox matzah products, are made under excellent and constant supervision.

[Signed] JONATHAN STEIF
Head of the Jewish court of the
Congregation [God-] Fearers.[65]

64. From the original placard. Translated from the Yiddish.

65. From the matzah box. Translated from the Yiddish. It should be noted that in 1960 another label was pasted on the box, because the *rav,* of the congregation had passed away. The label states that the same

On the other side of the box the following is printed:

> Matzah for Passover
> With perfection of *kashrut*
> For the most zealous of the zealous
> Made from excellent choice wheat
> Adath Yereim Orthodox Matzah Products
> 319 Bedford Avenue, Brooklyn 11, New York[66]

While there may be a choice within the Hasidic community between handmade matzah and machine-made matzah, between "plain matzah" and "guarded matzah," there is no one in the community who uses regular commercial matzah that has been produced by bakers in the larger community. That matzah is strictly prohibited.

Hasidic foodstuff has been mainly produced for those Hasidim who insist of consuming food that should be adequate for the "most zealous of the zealous." In Europe, restricted food requirements were associated only with those people who were actually the "most zealous of the zealous" in every respect. Those people were actually very few in number, even among Hasidim. But here in America, because such a great abundance of food exists, extremely restrictive food patterns that satisfy the "most zealous of the zealous" have become popular on a larger community scale. In the Hasidic community, foods that were once associated only with the "most zealous of the zealous" in the literal sense are now the only foods permitted for consumption for everyone. Foods that are considered kosher in the larger Jewish community are not considered kosher in the Hasidic community. Food that has not been prepared by the Hasidim has a *hashash*. No one is trusted with preparation of food,

---

restrictions the *rav* instituted are observed to the fullest. It reads: "We bring it to your attention that all the customs and restrictions which our master, teacher and *rav,* may his memory be blessed, instituted are strictly observed and the matzah is under the strict supervision of the *Rav* Josef Steiner, may his light shine. [Signed] Congregation of the Assembly of [God-]Fearers."

66. *Ibid.*

especially for Passover, except community members who are known for their Hasidic conformity.

There is even a tendency among the members of the Hasidic group to judge the observance of Jews in the larger community by the kind of food they use, making it a major criterion by which religiosity is measured. A non-Hasidic Jew who uses Hasidic foodstuffs is considered a "religious Jew." If an individual is not using Hasidic products, he is practically accused of not eating kosher food.

The following excerpt from an interview illustrates this point:

Last week I was doing electrical work for an American rabbi. I saw that in the rabbi's house non-Jewish milk is used. I told the rabbi that he has no excuse for not using Jewish milk in New York. If he lived outside New York where there is no Jewish milk, and since milk is such an important food without that homes usually cannot put up, I could excuse him for non-kosher milk. But where it is available there is no excuse. I also said to him that even though there are certain religious authorities who may be lenient toward using non-Jewish milk, the *Shulhan Aruch* precisely prescribes that one must drink Jewish milk. This I said to him when I had seen only the milk. But when I saw that he also uses herring packed in sour cream, then I could well imagine what else this American rabbi may use in his house. I had nothing else to say any more. He is already too far gone from his religious observance for me even to make him understand about the importance of using Jewish milk or using those foodstuffs which do not have a *hashash*.[67]

In this category of manufacture and sale of Hasidic foodstuffs belong not only those people concerned with food products that are permissible for consumption, but also those people who manufacture articles that are indirectly connected with food, such as kosher paper bags and tablecloths for Passover. Although these articles are not eaten, the community applies the same restrictions to their manufacture because they come in contact with food. Toothpaste for Passover also belongs to this category, since there is a *hashash* lest it contain substances that are not kosher for Passover.

67. From the files of NHM, 1958.

Since it is taken into the mouth, a person may swallow an infinitesimal amount of food that is not kosher for Passover. The Nut-ola Fat Production Company, Incorporated, produces a kosher toothpaste that a well-known Hasidic lay leader who is president of the company guarantees ". . . has been produced and finished under his hands and that it is kosher for the most zealous of the zealous."[68]

Plastic tablecloths that are used in the household for Passover have a *hashash* that they may have been processed with the aid of alcohol, and since alcohol is a substance prohibited for Passover use, the tablecloth *ipso facto* is considered *hometz* for the most zealous. Now, since plastic tablecloths are *hometz,* and since food comes in contact with them, they are prohibited for use on Passover. The General Dupon Synthetic Company produces a tablecloth under the supervision of *Rav* Raphael Silver that is permissible for use on Passover. On the package of this kosher-for-Passover synthetic plastic tablecloth, *Rav* Silver states:

> I certify that these tablecloths produced by the Favorite Plastic Corporation and sold through the firm General Dupon Company are made under my supervision and they do not contain any mixture of *hometz,* not even an infinitesimal particle. They can be used on Passover without any *hashash* even for the most zealous of the zealous.[69]

Paper bags in which food is wrapped have the *hashash* that they may have been pasted with paste containing *hometz.* Under the supervision of the Central Rabbinical Congress of the United States and Canada, paper bags are made from paste that is permissible for Passover use. Thus, paper bags used on Passover in the various grocery stores, butcher shops, and so on, must be kosher for Passover. The following rubber stamping appears on the kosher paper bags:

> These bags are pasted with paste that is kosher for Passover, made under the supervision of the Central Rabbinical Congress of the United States and Canada.[70]

68. From the toothpaste box. Translated from the Yiddish.
69. From the tablecloth package. Translated from the Hebrew.
70. From the imprint on a paper bag. Translated from the Hebrew.

Another item that comes in contact with food is cleanser for dishwashing. Although cleanser is not eaten, it does come in contact with dishes, and dishes come in contact with food. There is a *hashash* that an infinitesimal part of the cleanser substance may contain *hometz*. Again, under the supervision of the Central Rabbinical Congress of the United States and Canada, the *Mehadrin* Company produces *Mehadrin* cleanser without any *hashash*. The *Mehadrin* cleanser is advertised:

### Important Announcement

After difficult and strenuous effort, thank God, we have succeeded in fabricating *Mehadrin* cleanser to clean all kinds of dishes and sinks [that are used for either] dairy or meat.

Kosher for Passover for the most zealous.

Produced under the strict supervision of the Central Rabbinical Congress.[71]

This category of the manufacture or sale of Hasidic foodstuffs is particularly significant in its functional aspects. The many stringent regulations about dietary habits in the Hasidic community are functional insofar as they are "vital . . . processes . . . which contribute to the maintenance of the organism,"[72] in this case, of the Hasidic community. Hasidic food production has become so vital to the community that without it survival would be questionable. Merton's concepts of manifest and latent functions may be clearly observed in this community. Thus, Hasidic foodstuffs are functional in three ways:

1. They provide community-sanctioned kosher food.
2. They provide one strong means of maintaining social control.
3. They provide insular economic activities.

The Hasidic foodstuffs manufactured in the community are the only foods a Hasidic Jew is permitted to eat. All other

71. *Der Yid*, April 3, 1959. Translated from the Yiddish.
72. Robert K. Merton, *Social Theory and Social Structure* (Glencoe: The Free Press, Inc., 1957), p. 21.

foods either are not kosher or their *kashrut* is questionable. Therefore, the community must provide food because no other food is permitted. The manifest function of food production is that the Hasidic foods are "contributing to the adjustment or adoption of the system which [is] intended and recognized by participants in the system."[73] Without providing this sanctioned food, Hasidic Jews would starve or depart from their deepest values. The community must provide "proper" food in order to maintain its members physically, since all other foods except raw fruit may not be eaten.

The second function of Hasidic foodstuffs is that they provide another strong means of social control. This is a latent function which is neither intended nor recognized in the Hasidic community. Food regulates the behavior of Hasidic Jews to such an extent that with every bite they are consciously aware of the Hasidic dietary observance. They cannot move to another place where they could not obtain Hasidic food; they are actually limited to the area where Hasidic food can be purchased. There were many Hasidic Jews who responded to the question, "Why do you live in Williamsburg?" by indicating that only here could they buy "real kosher food." Although dietary practices re-enforce group values and norms, they were not overtly intended by the community to serve as a means of group control.

Manufacturing and selling Hasidic foodstuff has still a third function which is of greatest importance to the Hasidic economic system. It provides new opportunities for economic activity. Production of food is the most effective way of providing jobs within the Hasidic community. The acceptability or appropriateness of food is determined by the *forleslechkeit* or "community trust" associated with it. Kosher food becomes accepted in the Hasidic community only if it fully meets Hasidic religious standards. Those standards require that "trustworthy" items, such as kosher food, be prepared, manufactured, and supervised by Hasidic Jews. Thus, new jobs are created and protected from outside competition. In the process, the economic base which is essential to the

73. *Ibid.,* p. 51.

maintenance of a socially isolated community is greatly strengthened.

## THE MANUFACTURE OR SALE OF
## NONRELIGIOUS ARTICLES

The category "manufacture or sale of nonreligious articles" includes all occupations connected with the manufacture and sale of articles that are not designated as or used for religious purposes. The manufacture and sale of nonreligious articles is usually directed toward the larger, non-Hasidic community, since these articles are secular in nature. However, in the Hasidic community, even these articles tend to assume semireligious characteristics. An example of such a semireligious article is the wig.

To clarify the semireligious nature of the wig, a short explanation of the Hasidic women's custom of head covering is necessary. The hair of a Hasidic woman must be cut off upon marriage. She is not allowed to wear her own hair uncovered, nor to display any part of her hair in public. Her head must be covered at all times. The "truly modest" Hasidic women do not even uncover their hair when they are alone. Covering one's hair even when in complete privacy is considered an act of chastity. To be able to observe this important ritual of "covering the head," and still appear in public, most Hasidic women wear a *sheitel* (wig), which gives the appearance of one's own hair. Even here, since the *sheitel* gives the appearance of real hair, the "most zealous of the zealous" Hasidic women consider the *sheitel* too modern. Instead of the *sheitel* they wear a headpiece that looks like a wig, except that it is made of some silky material, or they wear a turban. Thus, the headpieces or turbans of the "most zealous of the zealous" Hasidic women are not intended to create the illusion of human hair.

In itself the wig is a nonreligious item, but because the wearing of it in the Hasidic community serves a religious purpose, the *sheitel* maker is considered to be engaged in the manufacture of semireligious articles. It is important that the Hasidic woman beautify herself and make herself attractive to her husband, especially after her "clean days" and the ritual immersion following her menstrual period. Good grooming and an attractive *sheitel* are of utmost importance, so that the lure of the metropolis will have no influence on her husband. The wigs are combed, brushed, shampooed, styled, cut, and dyed by that important figure, the *sheitel macher*.

One *sheitel macher* advertises as follows:

### Sheitelach

Order your wig from Esther's Beauty Salon
58 Lee Avenue, corner Ross Street,
Brooklyn, New York
You can get the most modern style and the most "natural look" and also have a better fitting. Made to order from the finest European hair. Also ready-made for sale in a large selection.
Call for appointment. ST 2-4323[74]

Those Hasidic women who consider the use of the *sheitel* too modern cover their heads with turbans. Some of the women make these headpieces themselves, but the demand has now become great enough so that they are produced commercially. One manufacturer advertises at the various houses of worship with a handwritten and hand-drawn leaflet in which she calls to the attention of the community that:

With the aid of God.
Hasidic women!
Turbans in all styles made to order by
Mrs. Pollock.
80 South 10th Street, EV 7-6201[75]

Like the *sheitel*, other articles made to accord with Hasidic norms are considered semireligious, because they serve religion. For instance, Hasidic women must wear clothing that covers their bodies properly. Dresses must have long sleeves and high necklines and are usually of a dark color.

74. *Der Yid*, February, 1957. Translated from the Yiddish.
75. From leaflet SH2. Translated from the Yiddish.

One dress shop advertises a sale of dresses that meet Hasidic requirements:

> Honig's Bargain Store
> 69 Avenue C, corner East 5th Street, New York
> Big sale of dresses with long sleeves
> Black and blue
> 20½, 18½, 14, 12
> Regular price $15.98—Sale price $2.50[76]

Since covering the body is considered an act of chastity and a symbol of modesty, the dress of a Hasidic woman must cover her properly. She must wear stockings at all times so that her legs will not be exposed to public view. The most zealous Hasidic women wear heavy-gauge stockings, not the sheer nylon ones that are considered to expose her legs. Only with these heavy-gauge stockings is she considered "truly modest" and proper. Thus, dry goods stores are actually selling semireligious items of Hasidic symbolism. The merchants refer to the long black stockings for women not as "long black stockings," but as "Hasidic stockings," indicating the religious significance of the merchandise. One merchant advertises the following:

> You can obtain from us dry goods.
> Baby equipment—children's things
> Also children's and women's dresses with long sleeves, Hasidic shirts and underwear for men. We have just received imported Hasidic black, long stockings for women.
> Best quality at low prices. Come and convince yourself.
> Eliezer Waldman
>     147 Lee Avenue, Brooklyn 11, New York[77]

As discussed earlier, Hasidic men must wear "Hasidic garments," which are status symbols. The more Hasidic a person is, the higher the status he enjoys. The higher the status he enjoys, the more exclusively Hasidic garments he wears.

Thus, there are some Hasidic men who wear "extremely

76. *Der Yid*, November 2, 1956. Translated from the Yiddish.
77. *Der Yid*, August 23, 1957. Translated from the Yiddish.

Hasidic garments" not only on the Sabbath and on holidays but also all week long. Others wear "extremely Hasidic garments" only on the Sabbath, and "less Hasidic garments" on weekdays. Still others wear "less Hasidic garments" on the Sabbath and holidays and *"modernish* garments" on weekdays. Finally, there are some who wear *"modernish* garments" all the time. Despite these differences, there is almost no one in the community who does not wear some Hasidic garment by which he can be externally identified as a Hasidic Jew.[78]

One merchant advertises garments for *rebbes* and for laymen. He advertises various items of Hasidic clothing such as *bekechers, hapotas, halatin,* "chopped *kapotes,"* and even Prince Alberts. He also announces in his advertising that all the clothing he sells is guaranteed not to contain any *shatnes.*[79] This advertisement reads as follows:

> Rabbinical and *balebatishe* clothing.
> I announce to all my friends and customers that all sorts of clothing are available from me.
> Best quality for very reasonable prices.
> Silk *bekechers, kapotes,* table *chalatin,* chopped *kapotes,* Prince Alberts, wool and alpaca, long suits, overcoats, spring coats.
> Special sale of Atlasin *bekechers,* 12 dollars.
> We also make to order with the greatest punctuality all sorts of clothing. All clothing is guaranteed *shatnes*-free.
> With blessings to be inscribed and sealed into the Book of Life for good.
> Gluck Clothing Store
> 210 Broadway, near Roebling Street,
> Brooklyn, New York, EV 7–2004[80]

At another time this merchant ran a special sale in honor of a Jewish holiday. He compared the regular prices to the sale prices, conveying to the community that his prices were reduced "in honor of the holiday." He offered silken *beke-*

78. See pp. 63–69.
79. See pp. 104–107.
80. From leaflet CL3. Translated from the Yiddish.

*chers* and *chalatin,* special garments called "table *chalatin*" because they are worn at the holiday table. He also assured his customers that all his clothing was *shatnes*-free. This leaflet, which was hung in the various houses of worship, read:

### Special Sale

In honor of the Holy Days that come to us for good.

With the help of God, May He be blessed, I announce to all my customers that I have received a great lot of beautiful double-breasted suits, overcoats, spring coats and winter coats made special from imported fine fabrics at amazingly cheap prices.

Suits: Regular price was $48.00, now only $35.90

Spring coats: Regular price was $42.00, now only $36.00

Winter coats: Regular price was $46.00, now only $39.80

Silken *bekechers:* special sale, $32.00

Table *halatin* in various beautiful designs: $9.90

Prince Alberts: $44.00.

We also make all garments to order very punctually by fine, first-class craftsmen for the cheapest prices.

All clothing is guaranteed *shatnes*-free.

Our prices are greatly reduced in honor of the holiday.

Make your purchase in time so that we shall be able to satisfy you the best way and fill all your requests. With blessings to be inscribed and sealed into the Book of Life for good.

    [Signed] Moshe Mordechai Gluck
    M. Gluck Clothing Corp.
    210 Broadway, Brooklyn 11, New York
    EV 7-2004[81]

Still another merchant appeals not only to the "very Hasidic" with extremely Hasidic garments such as table *chalatin* and summer *bekechers* made of Persian silk, but also to the "less Hasidic" with *modernish* garments such as "long Hasidic tropical suits." He also advertises *bekechers* made of nylon, a typical example of how a traditional religion that opposes every possible move leading to secularism

81. From leaflet CL5. Translated from the Yiddish.

adopts technology as a means of furthering religiosity. The advertisement reads:

*With the aid of God*

**Summer Sale**

Tropical suits, wool and Dacron, light as feathers, strong as iron, beautiful workmanship, half-lined with fine Bemberg lining. You buy quality for only $36.00.

Tropical suits from last season, sizes only 38 to 40, $25.00. Overcoats, topcoats, fine 100 per cent wool material, medium gray, dark gray, oxford gray, $42.00.

Long Hasidic tropical suits, $39.00. Table *chalatin* for the summer, $10.00. Summer *bekechers* made from Persian silk, special sale, $36.00. Long rayon jackets, practical in the country, $4.00. Luster topcoats, $18.00 and up.

Single-breasted tropical suits, very beautiful samples, Dacron and wool, $38.00. Single-breasted topcoats, navy and gray, 100 per cent wool, very fine quality, $39.00.

Nylon *bekechers*, $32.00. Light black summer pants, $6.50.

We make all sorts of clothing to order with the best workmanship. Satisfaction is guaranteed.

With honor,
[Signed] Roth & Wollner
145 Division Avenue, Brooklyn, New York
EV 4–4927[82]

It is not enough that a Hasidic Jew be identifiable by others through his external appearance; he must also have other identifying symbols that carry special meaning within his own group. Thus, his undergarments, as well as his outèr garments, must meet Hasidic religious requirements. I was told that a religious functionary, who had all the qualifications for the position of a ritual slaughterer, was not hired in a Hasidic community in Europe because in the ritual baths people noticed that he was not wearing long underpants. It was assumed that if he wore shorts, he had gone too far astray in other religious matters. The truly Hasidic woman must wear a nightgown with long sleeves, regardless of seasonal change, since long sleeves are a sign of chastity.

82. From leaflet CL7. Translated from the Yiddish. Italics added.

The required Hasidic underwear is available at Gluck Brothers and Meyerowitz. They advertise the following:

> *In honor of Passover*
>
> We are in a situation where we can serve you with the most beautiful double-breasted children's suits, in all sizes and colors. First-class fitting without alterations.
>
> We have a large selection of children's and men's shirts. Also, right-to-left underwear, also long underpants, women's gowns with long sleeves, linen, bedding and other things for the home. Boys' and girls' polo shirts in various beautiful colors, and of the best quality.
>
> With blessings for a kosher and happy holiday.
>
> [Signed] GLUCK BROTHERS & MEYEROWITZ[83]

Proper observance of religion is a basis for competition in the Hasidic community. Some merchants try to show that their merchandise exceeds Hasidic requirements. Thus, they imply that they are "holier than thou," that they are aware of the Hasidic restrictions prescribed by the law, that they care lest their customers be exposed to the least possibility of transgression of the law. An illustration of this point can be seen in a clothier's advertisement. This clothier not only has a special department for all rabbinical and Hasidic clothing, he not only sells clothing that is free of *shatnes*, but he also guarantees that his customers will not wear *shatnes* even during the time of the fitting and thus not transgress the law prohibiting the wearing of *shatnes*. The advertisement reads:

### Holiday Sale

> The beautiful new clothing store of Roth & Wollner has prepared a big selection of all sorts of clothing such as: double-breasted suits, shirts, half-long and long overcoats, table *halatin, bekechers,* etc.
>
> In the children's line, we have expanded our stock with husky sizes and also a beautiful selection of overcoats, sizes up to 20. Also very beautiful winter coats, lined with quilted cotton.

83. *Der Yid,* April 3, 1959. Translated from the Yiddish.

Special rabbinical department with all rabbinical and Hasidic clothing. Light table *chalatin,* special only ten dollars. All sorts of clothing are made to order also.

*Stock of clothing is already tested for shatnes. You can be sure about shatnes even during fittings.*

Visit us right away and you will walk out with the fullest satisfaction.

[Signed] CHAIM ROTH AND YONAH YITZCHAK DAVID WOLLNER
145 Division Avenue, Brooklyn 11, New York
Telephone: EV 4-4927
Cheapest prices
We wish to all our friends that they be inscribed and sealed in the Book of Life for good.[84]

One of the most significant status symbols among men in the Hasidic community is the *shtreimel,* made of sable, the average price of it is one hundred dollars. Anyone who wears such a hat is known as a *"Yid mit a shtreimel."* When a Hasidic man puts on a *shtreimel* for the first time (usually at his wedding), it is an indication that he commits himself to a Hasidic way of life, appropriate to one who wears this hat. The wearing of the *shtreimel* and the behavior expected of a person wearing it are simultaneous re-enforcements of the Hasidic norms. A person is expected to behave in a certain manner. When he does, the community permits him to wear a *shtreimel.* Then, because he has a *shtreimel,* he will not commit a breach of trust by not living up to those norms that govern behavior of a person wearing a *shtreimel.* Thus, wearing such a fur hat may identify a person as belonging to a certain status category; but it is not the fur hat itself that puts him there, it is his Hasidic behavior, with which he constantly justifies the wearing of the *shtreimel.*

Since the *shtreimel* is such a important Hasidic status symbol indicating one's religious behavior, it is considered a "religious item" and is available at stores where other religious items are sold. Such hats are manufactured by a *shtreimel macher (shtreimel* maker), who usually has a large selection for sale. One advertises:

84. *Hamaor,* March, 1957. Translated from the Yiddish. Italics the author's.

**"The sabbatical year does not let go until the end,"**

but a *shtreimel* you can buy right away so that you
should have it by the beginning of the year. We
have prepared, in honor of the holy days which
should come to us for goodness, a large stock of
beautiful sable *shtreimlach* for very cheap prices.
Come as long as the stock holds out. You will
be completely satisfied.

With blessings to be inscribed and sealed in the Book of
Life for good.

The House of Trade and Manufacturer of *Shtreimlach*
Kepecs
80 Wilson Street, Brooklyn, New York[85]

The *shtreimel* is an exclusive Sabbath and holiday hat.
People who wear a *shtreimel* on the Sabbath usually wear a
*biber* hat on weekdays. Those Hasidic Jews who wear *biber*
hats on the Sabbath too wear a large black hat on weekdays.
These hats are considered Hasidic hats and are treated as
semireligious articles. Selco Hatter advertises:

**Hats**

*In honor of Passover*
The biggest selection of all sorts of Hasidic or modern
hats. Prices from $5.95 to $20.00
Agency for Stetson hats.
Selco Hatter, Incorporated
337 Roebling Street, Brooklyn, New York
EV 8–6848[86]

It is understandable that clothing may be considered
semireligious in nature; since Hasidic Jews must wear it
for identification. It is more difficult to see how a hardware
store and items sold there can assume religious significance.
Nevertheless, in the Hasidic community articles of hardware
do tend to have a semireligious significance. According to
religious law,

85. *Hamaor,* July, 1958. Translated from the Hebrew.
86. *Der Yid,* April 5, 1957. Translated from the Yiddish.

If one purchases table or kitchen utensils from a heathen, even if they be new, but if they are made of metal or glass, he is forbidden to make any use of them whatsoever, even if they be for cold viands, before he dips them in a well or pool which is fit for ritual immersion of a woman after the period of menstruation, in order that it may be transferred from unholiness . . . to holiness. . . .[87]

Most hardware stores in the Hasidic community have ritual baths on the premises. One of the hardware stores is called *"Barzel"* (literally, "iron" in Hebrew) in order to be identified in the community as a "Jewish iron store." The firm advertises with circulars that are hung in the various houses of worship. A circular reads:

*With the help of God*

**Announcement**

We announce to the dear community that we have taken over the famous *Barzel* house furnishings and hardware store. 115 Lee Avenue, Brooklyn, New York

We have freshened up the store with all kinds of house-wares:

The best enamel and aluminum dishes
Imported and domestic dinner sets
Imported and domestic wonder bakers
The best pressure cookers
All sorts of glassware
All sorts of venetian blinds
The best linoleums, plastics, and inlays
All sorts of electrical appliances
The most beautiful imported crystal

Also other kinds of gifts and various assortments.

We have also a kosher ritual bath in the store for immersing dishes ritually.

We promise the best service and reasonable prices.

Free delivery.

With honor,

[Signed] Mordechai Aharon Weiss and J. M. Bailush
115 Lee Avenue, Brooklyn, New York
EV 7–0992[88]

87. *Code of Jewish Law, loc. cit.,* 37:1.
88. From leaflet HR2. Translated from the Yiddish.

Hardware stores that have a ritual bath on the premises to fulfill religious requirements are thus selling semireligious articles. For example, one hardware store sells *shabbos zeigers*, Sabbath clocks (automatic timers), to turn the lights in the house or in the refrigerator on and off on the Sabbath. It also sells "round and long fish pots" to meet Hasidic household traditions for preparing fish "in honor of the Sabbath and holidays."

There is a ritual manner in which a religious person must wash his hands before a meal. After washing his hands, he must recite:

Blessed are Thou, Lord our God, King of the Universe, Who hast sanctified us with His commandments and commanded us concerning the washing of the hands.[89]

This ritual is called *netilat yadayim*, washing of the hands. In the hardware store as well as in other stores selling religious articles, *netilas yodayim teplach*, washing-of-the-hands pitchers, are available.

Furthermore, a religious woman is required to sift the flour before cooking because there is a *hashash* that the flour may contain moths or maggots. For this purpose, one must use a sifter that will retain possible eggs or maggot larvae. This same hardware store sells "the only real flour sifter" suitable for religiously appropriate sifting of flour. It advertises the following:

> To begin with, we wish you to be inscribed and sealed in the Book of Life for good.
> And then you get everything for the honor of the holiday at
>
> ### Wilhelm's
>
> Big stock of the most beautiful furnishings for young couples.
> Thousands of articles at amazingly cheap prices.
> At amazingly cheap prices also such [articles] as you cannot get elsewhere.
> Gifts for the holiday.

89. *Daily Prayerbook* (translated by Philip Birenbaum) (New York: Hebrew Publishing Co., 1949), p. 14.

Imported dinner sets from five to one hundred dollars.
Unbreakable dishes in the most beautiful designs, whole
  sets and also singles, 50 per cent discount
Heavy aluminum fish pot, round and long
The only real flour sifter
Tea urns with faucets, up to 100 cups
The nicest chrome candelabra and trays,
Amazingly cheap prices
Wonder baker, $3.39
*Shabbos zeiger*
For lights and for the refrigerator to open and close with-
  out any *hashash*
New style washing-of-the-hands pitchers

### *Wilhelm's*

157 Division Avenue, Brooklyn, New York
Telephone, EX 7–5403
103–27 Queen's Boulevard, Forest Hills
Telephone, TW 6–0100
Ritual bath in store for immersing dishes ritually. Orders
are delivered everywhere.[90]

There is even a department store with a ritual bath on
the premises. Since this is a department store, it carries a
number of items of semireligious significance. For instance,
it sells kosher-for-Passover lipstick, cream rouge, and powder,
liquid soap that can be used on the Sabbath, kosher toothpowder, and kosher-for-Passover creams and nail polish. All
these are available at Blatt's Department Store as the following advertisement shows:

### Big Sale in honor of Passover at Blatt's

All sorts of dishes and household furnishings, silverware
  and glassware, electrical appliances of all kinds for the
  cheapest prices
Napkins, one box 9 cents
25-cent coupon, three free with two boxes of waxed paper
Freezer paper only 59 cents instead of 89 cents
Cosmetics, kosher for Passover

90. *Hamaor,* July, 1958, p. 57. Translated from the Yiddish.

Lipstick $1.00, cream rouge 69 cents, powder 75 cents, liquid Sabbath-soap 50 cents, toothpowder 35 cents, creams 45 cents, nail polish 30 cents, polish remover 30 cents, dish wash concentrate, big bottle, 50 cents

Blatt's Department Store

5005 13th Avenue, GE 5-2866, Brooklyn 19, N.Y.

There is a ritual bath in our store for ritually immersing dishes.[91]

In the category of manufacture and sale of nonreligious articles also belong the selling of electrical appliances, silverware, refrigerators, boilers, air conditioners, phonographs, tape recorders, Hebrew typewriters, sewing machines, furs, and so on. None of these items are manufactured in the Hasidic community. The merchants usually advertise in the Hasidic newspapers and on special placards. Since they have difficulty in making their articles appear as semireligious items, or in attaching a semireligious significance to them, they use a different devise to attract the Hasidic community into their stores. They advertise in such a way that the members will identify them instantly as "Hasidic merchants worthy of the community's support."

A Hasidic mattress maker advertises with placards that he hangs in the various houses of worship. He runs a sale, lasting one week, the date of which is signified by quoting the name of the Biblical portion that is read in the synagogue that week. No non-Hasidic mattress maker would indicate the date of a sale with the "weekly portion" read in the synagogue, as does this Hasid, who calls himself a "master craftsman of mattresses." His advertisement reads:

**Sale**

Important announcement from
M. Gross Sleep Shop
152 Lee Avenue
Between Hewes and Penn streets,
Brooklyn 11, New York
Telephone UL 5-1855

91. *Hamaor*, March, 1957. Translated from the Hebrew.

I announce to the dear community that your well-acquainted master craftsman of mattresses, who has many years of experience, has his large customer circles satisfied one hundred per cent with quality and with the price as well. Thank God, I have succeeded in taking in for amazingly cheap prices a large transport of mattresses:

Box springs
High-risers
Hollywood beds
Couches, also orthopedic
Mattresses according to doctors' prescription
Modern styles
All the mattresses come to you from the factory
where everything is made in my presence and
with my supervision.

The sale starts next Tuesday, the third day of *Hukas,* June 24. It lasts until the eve of the holy Sabbath of the portion of *Balak,* July 4. You can get everything for such amazingly cheap prices as for instance: special workmanship demanded, orthopedic mattress together with box spring for as cheap as fifty-five dollars. Hurry—first come, first served.

Come and prove it to yourself.

Your friend,
[Signed] YUDAH MEYER GROSS[92]

Another approach for a merchant who does not sell merchandise of religious significance is to attract the community by identifying himself as a member. Deitsch Paper and Box Company calls itself *"Mendel Shem Tov"* (Mendel of Good Name). *"Shem Tov"* is the famous name of the *rebbe* who founded Hasidism. The company advertises the following:

Do you want the best and quickest service in corrugated boxes, plastic cellophane bags, plain and printed packing supplies, thread, cord, wrapping paper, gummed paper, plain and printed? Moderate prices. Come right to *Mendel Shem Tov.*

Deitsch Paper and Box Company
Closed Saturday. Open Sunday.[93]

92. From leaflet MT2. Translated from the Yiddish.
93. *Der Yid,* August 30, 1956. Translated from the Yiddish.

There are other means of attraction also. Many merchants use a Talmudic quotation in their advertising. In this way a merchant indicates to the community that he has some familiarity with the Talmud. An example of the use of Talmudic quotation is the following:

**"Seeing is not the same as hearing."**

But you must see it; otherwise you will not believe it. Special sale on a nine-piece big dining-room set of genuine walnut. The table enlarges to 96 inches; the chairs have foam rubber seats. $350.00.
Feldheim's Furniture Showroom
Open Sunday[94]

The same merchant uses another quotation from the Scriptures in the following advertisement:

**"The place is too small for me."**

We are limited in space and we must sell.
You can buy now all sorts of samples at prices that you never heard of.
Feldheim's Furniture Showroom, Incorporated
83 Essex, corner of Delancey Street,
New York City
Telephone ST 7–1080
Open Sunday[95]

The use of Biblical quotations is not limited to furniture merchants. A flower shop advertises with a Biblical quotation:

**"It will bloom like a rose."**

Buy your flowers from a Sabbath observer.
The best service and quality. We deliver anywhere. Call GAdney 8–3434.

94. *Der Yid,* November 9, 1956. Translated from the Yiddish.
95. *Der Yid,* January 4, 1957. Translated from the Yiddish.

Rose Flower Shop, 4824 Fort Hamilton Parkway, Brooklyn[96]

There are still other devices besides the use of Biblical quotations that are employed by merchants selling nonreligious articles. Some merchants have special symbols of identification known to the Hasidic community. One of the most important traditional benevolences in Jewish life is the "dowry of the bride," as it is written:

These are the things of which a man enjoys the fruits of this world while the principle remains for him in the hereafter, namely: honoring father and mother, practice of kindness, early attendance at the schoolhouse morning and evenings, hospitality to strangers or visiting the sick, dowering the bride, sending the dead to the grave, devotion, prayer and making peace between fellow men; but the study of the Torah excels them all.[97]

From this quotation it is apparent that dowering the bride is one of the most important acts of benevolence. One merchant who has a bargain store tells the community that he is aware of this quotation from the Mishnah and Talmud. He advertises that he gives special discounts for the groom and bride, indicating that he fulfills this benevolent obligation of dowering the bride:

### Cahan's Bargain Store

93 Stanton Street, corner Orchard Street

You get the biggest bargains from us. Thin sheets, tablecloths, bedspreads, blankets, slip covers, and different dry goods.
Everything very cheap. Special discounts for groom and bride. Free delivery. Come in and convince yourself.[98]

There are still other devices by which the community is attracted. There is, for instance, a merchant who advertises

96. *Der Yid,* September 25, 1957. Translated from the Yiddish.
97. *Daily Prayerbook, op. cit.,* Mishnah Peah, 1:1, and Talmud Shabbat, 127a.
98. *Der Yid,* November 9, 1956. Translated from the Yiddish.

that purchasing from him not only saves money but gives customers an opportunity to perform a *mitzvah*. The Bible says that a person should not cheat his neighbor but "buy from his hands." This merchant uses this Biblical quotation to indicate that it is a "commandment" to buy from one's friends. Thus, a person who buys shoes, rubbers, and pocketbooks from Nathan Schnitzer fulfills a commandment. Nathan Schnitzer advertises the following:

> Do you want to save money? And accomplish a *mitzvah?*
> "Buy from the hand of your friend."
> Come to Schnitzer's Bargain Center, where you will obtain the best in men's and children's shoes. Rubbers and pocketbooks. All sizes at the lowest prices. Come and convince yourself!
> Respectfully,
> [Signed] Nathan Hirsch Schnitzer[99]

The manufacture or sale of nonreligious articles that tend to assume a semireligious character in the Hasidic community is instrumental in three areas: (1) economic activities, (2) social change, and (3) voluntary segregation.

Semireligious articles are instrumental in enlarging the base of the community and in increasing its stability. The religious connotations with which such articles are imbued tend to produce a monopoly in their manufacture and sale for the community.

The second area of interest is social change. It is well known that in America

> We have a shifting technology. Our rapidly changing technical system is constantly making people re-form themselves into new groupings and adopting new thinking after they have learned how to live in a certain situation, which was dictated in part by the former arrangement of technology. . . . There is a constant demand on the individuals . . . to make readjustments. . . . We see in their behavior a disintegrating system to which they strive in vain to adjust themselves. Change is continuous in our social system, for as our technology shifts and our industrial revolu-

99. *Der Yid,* November 2, 1956. Translated from the Yiddish.

tion rapidly increases, the social organization must shift with it.[100]

It may be supposed that such constant change will similarly have a detrimental effect upon the Hasidim. They too may have difficulty in adjusting to the larger society and in maintaining stability. Whether consciously or not, the Hasidic community, by transforming secular items into semireligious ones, has lessened the force of technological change by utilizing it to promote stable religious values. The process suggests that a Hasidic Jew can live in a society where he is surrounded by a secular culture and still maintain his traditional values. His adjustment to technological change is made by assigning religious significance to secular objects. This is one of the ways in which the Hasidim differ from other religious minorities. For example, the Amish, who try to perpetuate their traditional way of life, "resist the new [items] that are continually offered through science and technology."[101] This resistance of the Amish goes so far that they prohibit their members from owning automobiles.[102] If one of their group buys a power washing machine or installs a new gadget, he is looked down upon in the community.[103] In contrast, the Hasidim have been able to utilize technology without violating their religious beliefs. There are, however, many items provided by American technology and used by the Hasidim that have not been converted to semisacred items but that, as time goes on, will probably acquire religious significance. Where a secular object is not converted into a semireligious one, it may at least be used for religious purposes. For example, the Hasidim will not necessarily think of an automobile as a means of getting themselves away from the community and into the outside world, but

100. W. Lloyd Warner. "The Society, the Individual, and His Mental Disorders," *American Journal of Psychiatry,* 94, No. 2 (September, 1937), 281–282.

101. Elmer Lewis Smith, *The Amish People* (New York: Exposition Press, 1958), p. 37.

102. *Ibid.,* p. 189.

103. Charles P. Loomis and J. Allan Beegle, *Rural Social Systems* (Englewood Cliffs, N.J.: Prentice-Hall, Inc., 1950), p. 341.

rather as a vehicle that brings their children to study religion.

The third area in which the manufacture or sale of non-religious articles is instrumental is voluntary segregation. Max Weber has pointed out that: "Toward the outside world Jewry increasingly assumed the type of ritualistically segregated guest people (pariah people). And indeed Jewry did this voluntarily and not under pressure of external rejection."[104]

It must be recognized that the transformation of secular items into religious ones is an instrument through which the demarcation line between Hasidic and non-Hasidic Jews, or between ultra-Orthodox Jews and nonobservant Jews is greatly extended. This is, first of all, because semireligious items have sacred meaning only to ultrareligious Jews. To nonobservant Jews these items have no religious significance whatever. As soon as such objects become religiously meaningful, they promote the development of patterns that govern behavior and thus affect the social relationships between groups. Some of these patterns of behavior become institutionalized as norms and thus help to maintain the Hasidic community's distinctiveness in contrast to the non-Hasidic community, in which these items are neutral and secular in character. Hence, the use of semireligious items aids in voluntary segregation inasmuch as it identifies and unites the actors in one distinct social grouping, and, at the same time, isolates them from those who do not share the values or observe the behavior patterns related to these items. The cumulative effect of such developments is a high degree of social isolation.

## OTHER NONPROFESSIONAL OCCUPATIONS

### Within the Hasidic Community

In the category of nonprofessional occupations within the Hasidic community belong all those positions that involve servicing the Hasidic community exclusively. This category

104. Max Weber, *Ancient Judaism* (translated by Hans H. Gerth and Don Martendale) (Glencoe: The Free Press, Inc., 1952), p. 417.

is divided into two groups: (1) occupations for which some knowledge of religious law is necessary, and (2) occupations for which no knowledge of religious law is required. As has been seen, one of the major requirements for professional service is strong adherence to community norms. Success in nonprofessional occupations, too, largely depends on one's being a Hasidic Jew. In this way these latter occupations also tend to assume a semireligious overtone.

*Nonprofessional occupations for which some knowledge of religious law is necessary* include:

1. The *Mikveh Yid.*
2. The *Mikveh Yiddene.*
3. The matzah baker.
4. The cook in religious schools and restaurants.
5. The undertaker.

The *mikveh Yid* is the person in charge of the ritual bath. He must, therefore, know the law concerning the ritual bath. He must be able to prepare the water for it according to prescription. Besides having this knowledge, he must be a person who is reliable and above and beyond any question so far as his own religious behavior is concerned.

His female counterpart, the *mikveh Yiddene,* is in charge of the ritual bath for women. She, too, must know the law concerning the prescribed immersion of women. She makes certain that women taking ritual baths have completely immersed themselves in the water in accordance with the religious law and that they have properly recited the blessings that are required before ritual immersion takes place. In addition, she must be an observant Jewish woman, as she is looked upon in the community as a semireligious functionary. This is illustrated by the following advertisement:

> Wanted: A pious woman who knows about matters of the ritual bath for women for downtown East Broadway.
> Salary and apartment.
> Interested persons should write to the office of the Editor, Box 97.
> Purity of the Family, on the East Side,
> 145 East Broadway, New York[105]

105. *Der Yid,* August 23, 1958. Translated from the Yiddish.

The matzah baker must have familiarity with religious law concerning the baking of matzah. Cooks in the schools and restaurants must know the dietary laws. Besides this, both must be fully observant Jews who can be trusted with the strict enforcement of the laws.

None of these occupations is unique to the Hasidic community of Williamsburg for all are carried over from Europe. The occupation of undertaker, however, has sprung from the American environment. In Europe, every Jewish community had a ritual society, the so-called *hevrah kadishah* (holy society), which took care of all necessary rituals connected with preparation for burial. In America, where people are busy with jobs that they cannot leave in order to take care of the dead as an honorary activity, it has become necessary to establish funeral chapels or funeral parlors where the dead are given the necessary ritual preparation on a pecuniary basis.

One undertaker calls his establishment the "[God-]Fearer's Funeral Chapel, Incorporated." His announcements tell the Hasidic community that he will satisfy even the "most zealous of the zealous." He points out that his funeral chapel is equipped for Hasidic burial, since not only are the requirements met (that is, the washing of the body and the putting on of ritual shrouds), but there is also a ritual bath in which the body will be immersed. This undertaker hangs a placard in every Hasidic house of worship calling to the attention of the community that people "should arise from their sleep and try to do justice to the person who has passed away" and that this last rite for the dead should be done according to religious law. If the last rite is done in imitation of non-Jewish customs, "one must give account in the world to come." He also tells the community about the inconvenience of this last rite if it is done in one's home: "People are afraid that both they and their floor will get wet."

In this undertaking establishment there is a ritual bath for the purification of the dead. Although in Europe only great and holy men were taken into a ritual bath after death, this undertaker argues that if one can afford it and if it is easily accessible, there is no reason why this privilege should not be given to others in the community. After all, in Europe it was difficult to give this service to everyone, and according to the Talmud if one cannot help himself, the second best must be accepted. But if one can help himself, if one can have better facilities, specifically, if one can have a ritual bath, there is no excuse for not doing so. Besides having this superb religious service, the undertaker argues, it is also "more practical, more sanitary, easier, more kosher, and cheaper." In addition to all these advantages, people will perform the great *mitzvah* of helping one's brother by using this funeral parlor. And their brother he is indeed, and thus he qualifies for their help.

This placard reads as follows:

### With the aid of God

Our brethren of the Jewish people who are anxious to observe the word of God!

The time has come to awake from sleep, to mend the ways by which we give the last rites to the departed, that is, to take care that the "purification" and other rites should be made according to the prescription of the religion and law and in accordance with the honor and the wishes of the departed, and not only for the sake of good appearance. This [desire to give a nice appearance] causes the family to be talked into following the customs of the non-Jews, and the departed who lived all his life as a Jew in the fullest sense of the word, is brought, after one hundred and twenty years, into a chapel where they paint him and powder him, and so forth, which is indescribable, against his will, while he is already helpless.

Is this not a scorn to the poor? And are we not to stand in the world to come before judgment—if after so many years when we have striven to have a kosher place where the purification can be made properly, there are still many leaders of the very religious congregation who allow the departed to be taken to other places?

And what about those who do want to do their duty in giving honor to the departed but are not aware that it is possible to obtain more than "nine measures" [of water for purification] performed in the house of the departed, where the people who handle the dead fear that they and the floor will get too wet. Nothing can be better, more proper, than a kosher *mikveh,* which was made specially for the immersion of the departed. Even if you say that the usual custom was satisfactory until today, it was only because there was no choice, for there were no better ways than what was available. In the Talmud we find written that "where there is no other possibility, the existing circumstances are sufficient." But this does not mean that if we can help ourselves with better conditions, we should not try to improve them. Today [a chapel] has been specially established only for kosher purification to be made in purity of holiness, and in addition it is also more practical, more sanitary, easier and cheaper and besides all this, it is well known from the Talmud and Codifiers that the *mitzva*h of "You shall support him" is the highest degree of charity, that one must support definitely those who are your friends. No impartial person will say otherwise, and only those persons who have a selfish interest will substitute falsehood for truth.

Therefore, everybody is begged hereby that if, God forbid, a departure occurs in your family or among your friends as well as among those who look for a modern chapel, at least let them arrange that the purification be made in a kosher place, which is sanctioned by the greatest rabbis in the land.

[Signed] Receive the truth from the one who said it.[106]

It should be noted that in this placard the name of the funeral chapel is not mentioned. The announcement implies that it is only a "public service" from a "man who cares" about the religious observance of "his brethren." He even signs this public announcement, "Receive the truth from the one who said it." He does not openly identify himself with his funeral establishment. Once the Hasidic Jews are made aware that "the time has come to awake from sleep, to mend the ways by which we give the last rites to the departed," then the undertaker advertises in the Hasidic newspaper:

106. From placard NPS2. Translated from the Yiddish.

### [God-] Fearer's Funeral Chapel, Incorporated

We announce to all congregations and individuals, particularly to Hasidic Jews, that we have erected a chapel to be able to satisfy the most zealous of the zealous persons. When, may the harm not come, it happens that a person departs, God forbid, we are ready to bring the departed to our own chapel where it is most proper to keep the honor of the departed, and do the *taharah* [purification, washing the dead and preparing for burial], and the guarding of the dead person's body until the funeral is performed by pious funeral attendants, observers of the Torah and commandments.

We can purify the departed in a kosher *mikveh*. You can spare yourself the trouble of making the *taharah* at home . . . Everyone is requested when death occurs, God forbid, to contact our chapel, which is recommended by the greatest rabbis in the land.

93 Broadway, Brooklyn 11, New York[107]

There is another undertaker who not only arranges burials in the United States but also makes arrangements for burials in Israel. It has been a tradition among pious Jews to request burial in the Land of Israel. There were many such Jews in Europe who, even before the establishment of the State of Israel, went to live the last few years of their lives in Palestine so that they would be buried there. The Kabbala (mystical literature) introduced the idea that when the Messiah comes, all people will be reincarnated and their souls will "roll" into Israel. To avoid this "rolling" of the souls, some religious Jews request in their wills that they be buried in the Land of Israel. In addition to this Kabbalistic tradition, the Biblical patriarchs, such as Jacob and Joseph, asked that their bodies be taken to the Promised Land. Thus, the very pious man wants to be buried in Israel. Pinchas Mandel makes all the arrangements for this, as his advertisement indicates:

Burial in Jerusalem immediately after departure, may God save us.

Many cases have already been settled with God's help. . . .

107. *Der Yid*, January 31, 1958. Translated from the Yiddish.

Everything arranged in the most honorable way within one and a half to three days until burial in the Land of Israel. Just one call is all that is needed. Moderate prices. Everything is done under strict supervision by a known cemetery expert.

Telephone day or night. Pinchas Mandel, 502 Bedford Avenue, Brooklyn, New York

EVergreen 8–0277[108]

*Nonprofessional occupations for which no knowledge of religious laws is necessary* include:
1. The *Meshulach* (literally, "messenger").
2. The bus drivers for the religious schools.
3. The winery workers.

The *meshulach* is engaged by a charitable organization,. such as a Yeshivah, religious school, or orphanage. He has credentials from the organization by which he is employed and also from some known rabbinical authorities, stating that the organization or the person is "worthy of support." With these credentials, the *meshulach* goes out to various. communities in the United States and collects donations. and contributions for the organization. In doing so, he works for a commission, which is based upon whether he is working for an "established line" or not. "Established line" means. that the organization is well known in many communities in which it has many contributors. If the *meshulach* works for such an organization, he will receive a commission ranging from twenty-five to forty per cent of the donations. If, however, the organization is not so well known, the commission may be as high as seventy-five per cent.

About thirty or forty years ago there were many such meshulachim throughout the United States, going from state to state and from city to city collecting money for charitable organizations. Since that time, most Jewish communities. have organized federated fund-raising agencies so that individual contributors will not have to deal with all types of charity collectors. These organized united charities have reduced the status of the *meshulachim* considerably and have

108. *Der Yid,* March 21, 1958. Translated from the Yiddish.

also reduced their numbers. When the united or federated fund-raising agencies were established, they incorporated into their allocations those charity organizations that were represented by the various *meshulachim*. The Hasidic organizations have been established only recently, and they are not incorporated into the allocations of the Jewish federated charities. To be accepted into these federated charities, the Hasidic organizations would have to become more eminent in the eyes of the secular Jewish communities and the Hasidim would probably have to advocate a more liberal religious philosophy and behavior. But since the Hasidim cannot be expected to take on such advocacy, and since their organizations are not liberally supported, they are in need of "capable collectors" who can increase the funds available for support.

A "capable collector" is sought through an advertisement such as this:

> A famous Yeshivah wants
> Capable collectors—also local collectors
> All established lines
> Call evenings, IN 9–1842[109]

There are some *meshulachim* who distribute charity boxes and solicit members and subscribers for the neighboring Yeshivot. Such a man is sought in the following advertisement:

> A Yeshivah wants a capable man to recruit members in
> the neighborhood, also to distribute charity boxes.
> Call DE 6–2874[110]

Often a collector, because of his many years of association with a certain organization, becomes identified in contributors' minds with that organization. This may tempt the collector to dissociate himself from the organization and collect money for himself. He may just "go it alone." Since he is identified with the organization, however, the donors still think that he is collecting for that organization and con-

109. *Der Yid,* January 31, 1958. Translated from the Yiddish.
110. *Der Yid,* February 14, 1958. Translated from the Yiddish.

tribute accordingly. As far as the collector is concerned, he does not feel that he is deceiving the contributors, because when he asks for money, he does not say that the collection is specifically for the organization. Furthermore, since he knows the route and since the original contact with contributors had been established by him, he does not feel that he is obligated in any way to the organization. In such a case, the organization makes a public announcement that the collector is no longer associated with it so that people will refrain from giving him money intended for the organization. They may give money to him for his own use, but they should be aware that their contributions do not reach the organization. The following is an example of such an announcement:

> Announcement: The Yeshivah and Congregation of Ohel Jacob of Papa, 654 Bedford Avenue, Brooklyn, announces to the esteemed public that our collector, Reb Joseph Benjamin Friedman, may his light shine, has not been connected with our Yeshivah for over a year and has no right to collect funds for our Yeshivah.
> Respectfully,
> Board of Directors of the Yeshivah[111]

It is unnecessary for the *meshulach* to know any specific religious law. However, the organization prefers that he be versed in Talmudical studies and that he be a Hasid, so that the donors will be able to identify him as one who reflects the caliber of the organization. On the other hand, this may antagonize those who are not in full accord with the Hasidic principles which the collector represents. Therefore, a *modernish* type of collector is often preferred by the Hasidic organizations.

The bus drivers of the religious schools take the place of the traditional *behelfer*, who used to take the children to the houses of study. In the United States, where distance is great and the use of automobiles is necessary, Hasidic Jews with beards drive automobiles and buses and take children to and from religious schools. Some of these drivers are also teachers'

111. *Der Yid*, February 14, 1958. Translated from the Yiddish.

helpers and some of them do some instructing, but all of them must be Hasidic Jews.

Winery workers are those who work in the manufacture or sale of kosher wine. It is not necessary for these people to have knowledge of any religious law; however, they must be observant Jews.

In the category of nonprofessional services also fall various hotel services. Hasidic hotels meet with all the requirements that a Hasidic Jew could want. First of all, the hotel must have only *glat* kosher meat, in consequence of which they become known as *"glat* kosher hotels."[112]

A *glat* kosher hotel under the personal management of *Rav* Shlomo Shapiro advertises:

### The American Hotel

Sharon Springs, New York, Telephone 8269
Open before the season under the personal management of *Rav* Shlomo Shapiro, may God send him a long and happy life.

We assure your complete satisfaction, modern installations, comfortable rooms, magnificent grounds with beautiful patio for sun-bathing and rest, *glat* kosher meat, all kosher milk products, real *heimish* [homey] tasty meals, hearty personal care and service, moderate prices. Make reservations right away.

Sharon Springs 8269[113]

Today there are resorts with ritual baths on the premises such as Hoffman's Antel House. Their advertisement reads:

### Hoffman's Antel House

Sharon Springs, New York
I make known to the dear community that you have the best possibility of having all comforts in Sharon Springs. This year I have built onto every room a separate kitchen. Kosher ritual bath on the premises.

EVergreen 4-4593 or ULster 8-2453. These telephones

112. See, for example the advertisements shown below.
113. *Ibid.*

are to be called in New York. In Sharon Springs, New York, 8268.

Your friend,

[Signed] MOSHE HOFFMAN[114]

Another resort, besides having a kosher ritual bath of well water, has a "house of study" on the premises and also something "that has never been before, a Hebrew school with two famous *melamdim*." This advertisement reads:

> Eden Bungalow colony in Ferndale, located between Monticello and Liberty, one block from Route 17
>
> As everyone knows, the Eden colony does not advertise any longer, because our guests already know that all things good are available in our place, such as a house of study, kosher well-water ritual bath, grocery and laundry, and so forth.
>
> We wish to make known to our dear guests that we have this year instituted a good new feature that has never been before, a Hebrew school with two famous *melamdim*.
>
> Simultaneously, we request our customers from last year who would like to have the same rooms to notify us soon because the demand is very great.
>
> We have available one-, two-, and three-room apartments.
>
> Kahan Brothers          Kahan Brothers
> 502 Bedford Avenue       133 Keep Street
> Brooklyn, N.Y.           Liberty Phone 868
> Phone EV 4–3509                    625J1
>          EV 7–0903
> Rooms, bungalows, apartments
> Eden Colony
> Prices are reasonable.
> Route 17, Ferndale[115]

## Nonprofessional Occupations Outside the Hasidic Community

The final occupational category to be discussed includes all those positions that involve servicing the non-Hasidic as well as the Hasidic community. In this category belong those

114. *Ibid.*
115. From the original placard. Translated from the Hebrew-Yiddish.

occupations that, by their very nature, lack particular Hasidic characteristics or are not designed to serve the Hasidic community exclusively. However, because the Hasidim are so structured that almost all behavior is determined by religious beliefs and convictions, even an occupation which is designed to serve the non-Hasidic community is often related to things Hasidic.

An example is the tinsmith whose services are available to both the non-Hasidic and Hasidic communities. The occupation itself has nothing Hasidic about it, but when a tinsmith offers his services to the Hasidic community, he relates them to specific Hasidic requirements. He hangs leaflets in the various houses of worship announcing that for Passover he has sheets of tin to cover the gas range and the sink. These sheets of tin are to prevent the gas range and sink, which have been used throughout the year, from coming into contact with dishes that are used exclusively for Passover. The tinsmith makes basins to protect the Passover dishes from touching the sink. He also makes *megillah* holders (scroll holders) and *mezuzah* holders (doorpost-symbol holders) and pans in which the holiday bread is baked. Thus, even though the occupation of tinsmith is secular in character, he tends to produce articles that are used only by the Hasidic community and related to needs that develop through the special requirements of the Hasidic way of life.

The following is the text of a tinsmith's leaflet:

### With the aid of God

You should order for Passover tin sheets for the gas range and sink now. Call me on the telephone. I will come right away and take the exact measurement, and I will deliver to your home. I make receptacles for the *megillah* and also for the *mazuzah* and also for the *hallah* bakers. All kinds of tinwork for butchers and bakers. I will satisfy you—cheap prices.
With respect,
David Shmuel Schemeltzer
137 Division Avenue (Basement), Brooklyn, New York[116]

116. From leaflet SM10. Translated from the Yiddish.

The gasoline station is a service to the community at large as well as to the Hasidic community. There is no special characteristic that would make a gasoline station Hasidic. Nevertheless, the Hasidic proprietor of a station appeals to the Hasidic community for patronage by identifying himself with the community. Once this has been done, his station will be known as the "Hasidic gasoline station." Not only does the station observe the Sabbath, but the owner tells the community that his gasoline station "closes one hour before the candle-lighting on Friday and opens thirty minutes after the *havdalah* ceremonial at the outgoing of the Sabbath." This additional time before and after the Sabbath is the "Hasidic way" of observing the holiday. Thus, the Hasidic community will know that he is not a mere Sabbath observer, but a Sabbath observer according to Hasidic principles and therefore a person "worthy of support." One such owner advertises in the following way:

> Aaron's Service Station
> Sabbath-observing gas station
> South 8th Street, Corner Driggs Avenue,
> Brooklyn, Telephone EV 4–9749
> Closed one hour before candle-lighting on Friday and opened thirty minutes after *havdalah* at the outgoing of the holy Sabbath.
> We do all repair work. Guaranteed. Responsible. Lowest prices. Twenty-four hour service for steady customers.
> > Respectfully,
> > Aaron Tauber[117]

Dry-cleaning establishments owned by Hasidic Jews are open-to the non-Hasidic as well. Since there is nothing Hasidic in character about such a business, a Hasidic proprietor will make a special appeal to the Hasidic community with a Biblical quotation, indicating that he fully knows the meaning of such linquistic symbols of purification as whiteness and sinlessness. He will tell the community that in patronizing him, they are performing a *mitzvah*, a great religious deed. He will make the community feel that he is giving

117. *Der Yid*, January 3, 1958. Translated from the Yiddish.

them an opportunity to perform such a deed by advertisements such as this:

**"At all times . . . shall thy clothes be whitened."**

I have the honor to announce to the dear public that I have opened a dry-cleaning store. I hope to satisfy my customers completely. At the same time I wish to benefit the public with the performance of a positive commandment . . .

**"And thou shalt uphold him."**[118]

[Signed] MOISHE HOFFMAN
163 Lee Avenue, Telephone EV 8–5574[119]

One dry-cleaning store calls itself "the only Sabbath-observing pick-up and delivery cleaning store." This store takes on a Hasidic character by its claims to observe the Sabbath. Cards with the following text were distributed in the houses of worship:

*With the aid of God*

**Important Announcement**

I make known to the public that I have opened a pick-up and delivery cleaning store for suits and for all kinds of cleaning, and I also take shirts for washing. I also make all kinds of repairs.

You have only to pay for a telephone call, and your clothes will be picked up and delivered when you want them for the same price as if you inconvenienced yourself to bring them to the store. It will save you a lot of time, energy, and worry. Give your order right away.

The only Sabbath-observing pick-up and delivery cleaning store.

118. Leviticus 35:35. The full quotation of the Biblical text reads: "And if thy brother be waxen poor, and his means fail with thee; then thou shalt uphold him: as a stranger and a settler shall he live with thee."

119. *Der Yid,* April 23, 1958. Translated from the Yiddish-Hebrew.

[Signed] The Humble Yitzchak Schwartz
First-Class Pick-up & Delivery Cleaners
168 Division Avenue, corner Roebling Street
Brooklyn, New York—Telephone EV 4–6410[120]

Another service available to the non-Hasidic as well as to the Hasidic community is given by the electrician. He too tries to identify himself with the Hasidic community by appealing for work in the community and by Judaizing his name. Unlike the non-Hasidic community members who tend to Anglicize their names, he does not call himself "Leo" or "Louis" or even "Leib," but he makes sure that he is the one and only "Leibish" Goldberger, as one is properly called in the Hasidic community. He advertises:

### Expert Electrician-Mechanic

We fix refrigerators, washing machines, electric motors, and
    all electric installations.
Good and cheap. Each job is guaranteed.
24-hour service.
[Signed] Leibish Goldberger
85 Wilson Street, Telephone EV 4–4965[121]

Another service available to the non-Hasidic as well as to the Hasidic community is that of trucking and moving. Especially since the Hasidim have been moving back and forth between country resorts or summer camps and Williamsburg, moving service has come to be in great demand. Hasidic men with beards and Hasidic garments are engaged in the trucking business. Although these people work almost exclusively within the Hasidic community in season, their services are nevertheless open to the non-hasidic community. These shippers and truckers are known as the "Sabbath-observing truckers." One of them advertises:

120. From card ZS12. Translated from the Yiddish. This advertisement also appeared in *Der Yid,* January 3, 1958.
121. *Der Yid,* August 23, 1957.

**Sabbath-Observing Moving and Trucking. Insured.**

If you want to move cheaply and safely, just call Ruben-
stein's City-Country Special Station Wagon Service.
140 Hewes Street, Brooklyn, New York
UL 2–3636 and UL 8–0799[122]

Bookbinders also belong to this general category. When
they appeal to the Hasidic community, however, their advertisements make clear both that they are members of the
community and that they perform services specifically applicable to the community. They advertise *spiegel* (mirror)
binding, a certain fancy type of bookbinding with smooth
leather covers that is used for Talmudical volumes of great
value. They also advertise *shul* (synagogue) binding, a con-
ventional and inexpensive type of bookbinding used for
inexpensive prayer books in synagogues. Since many synagogues use uniform prayer books of the same dimensions,
color, and imprint, it is possible to mass produce the bind-
ings. In the actual process of binding these books, conven-
tional mass-production processes are applied. This secular
concept of mass production is called in the Hasidic community "*shul* binding."

The following is a bookbinder's advertisement:

**Leon Bookbinding**

Finest library work, stamping, *spiegel* binding or *shul*
binding. All sorts of paper work for schools. *Shtreimel*
holders are available.
Kalman Friedman
685 Bedford Avenue, New York
Telephone MA 5–2549[123]

When the bookbinders approach the Hasidic community
they signify this by linguistic differentiation. Religious books
are called *sefarim*, (literally, "books" in Hebrew). Secular

122. *Der Yid*, January 3, 1958. Translated from the Yiddish.
123. *Der Yid*, February 28, 1958. Translated from the Yiddish.

books are called *bicher,* (literally, "books" in Yiddish). These
men if bookbinders bind *sefarim,* theirs is a Hasidic occupation; if they bind *bicher,* theirs is a secular occupation.

Another service that belongs in this category is floor waxing and polishing. This, too, is open to the non-Hasidic as
well as to the Hasidic community. This service too identifies
itself as Hasidic because its owners observe the Sabbath. One
advertiser states:

Floor-scraping—waxing and polishing
Twenty-four-hour service except on the Sabbath and holidays
Fully insured[124]

The largest service occupation in the Hasidic community
is that of "operator."[125] Almost everyone who is not an independent merchant but works for another outside the community is an "operator." It is very difficult to become independent after being an operator. It is possible, however,
if one acquires greater knowledge or skill in his particular
trade. For example, the following advertisement was cir-
culated by a person looking for a partner without money.
The only requirement was that the partner be a craftsman
in the needle trade. The advertisement took the form of a
leaflet that was hung in the various houses of worship:

Girl Coat Operators Wanted
Call EV 4–1095
With the help of God
I am seeking a partner without any money on a fifty per
cent basis. He must only be a craftsman who can bring
contracting and who can help in managing. My factory is
newly established, with over forty machines to make girls'
coats or jackets.

Call HY 8–4524 or EV 4–1718[126]

An important aspect of nonprofessional occupations is in
the area of group identification. There is a strong tendency

124. *Ibid.*
125. See pp. 89–90 for a discussion of the use of the term "operator."
126. From leaflet RO16. Translated from the Yiddish.

among the members of this occupational category to identify themselves with the Hasidim by indicating that they share an interest in the "values" of the Hasidic community. The fact that the group ranks lower in the social hierarchy makes it more important for its members to show that their occupation reinforces their identity with the community. Persons who cannot fully participate in community activities cannot assume high status and can easily become the "forgotten men." Therefore, those persons who are occupied outside the community are particularly eager that others recognize them as Hasidic Jews.

The Hasidic identification in connection with their economic activities is not only in order to ask patronage and support in their businesses, but is a positive effort to become identified with the community. This does not mean that individuals who are in this category do not have other identification with the community. They do, of course, behave in accordance with Hasidic norms, but they make a further attempt to be identified as Hasidic Jews through their occupations and to use the services they provide to show their strong feeling of group solidarity. "Operators" in particular, whose occupations do not provide any Hasidic identification, make an attempt to participate in many group activities so that they may be identified as members of the group.

# CHAPTER 12

# A Sociological Analysis

# of the Hasidic Community

$\mathcal{T}$HE PREVIOUS CHAPTERS have described a community whose affairs are guided primarily by religious considerations. So strong are religious sentiments that not only religious affairs but secular activities as well are controlled and directed mainly by religious prescription and authority. In the Hasidic community religion as a unified system of beliefs and practices[1] exerts a cohesive integrating influence upon the actions and thoughts, both public and private, of its members. It creates a reciprocity between religion and all other community affairs. Religion determines the characteristic form of most activities, so much so that even secular activities have come to acquire a religious meaning.

The sociological significance of such an orientation can perhaps best be understood in terms of Kingsley Davis's cate-

1. Emile Durkheim, *The Elementary Forms of Religious Life,* translated by Joseph W. Swain (Glencoe: The Free Press, Inc., 1947), p. 47.

gorization of the function of religion. Davis has elaborated Durkheim's position[2] to summarize these functions as follows:

Religion then does four things that help to maintain the dominance of sentiment over organic desire, of group ends over private interests.

First, it offers, through its system of supernatural belief, an explanation of of the group ends and justification of their primacy.

Second, it provides, throughout its collective ritual, a means for the constant renewal of the common sentiments.

Third, it furnishes, through its sacred objects, a concrete reference for the values and a rallying point for all persons who share in the same values.

Fourth, it provides an unlimited and inseparable source of rewards and punishments—rewards for good conduct, punishment for bad.

In these ways, religion makes a unique and indispensable contribution to social interpretation.[3]

The Hasidic community can be comprehended almost in its entirety in terms of these four basic functions of religion. Supernatural beliefs are the only consistent explanations of Hasidic behavior, anticipation, and goals. These are "self-evident" convictions. The main object of the group's existence is the perpetuation of *Yiddishkeit*, traditional religious Judaism, through Hasidic behavior. The strong conviction of the reality of supernatural beliefs justifies to the group its attitude of primacy. By considering itself first in rank and in importance, the group maintains the stimulus to direct most of its activities along the religiously oriented lines which differentiate and define Hasidism. Acting religiously in all activities constitutes the heart of the group norms. Although some of these norms have immediate functions in the everyday interaction of group life, above this level of immediate utility there is always a more fundamental meaning. This meaning constitutes what elsewhere has been

2. *Ibid.*, pp. 416–417.
3. Kingsley Davis, *Human Society* (New York: The Macmillan Co., 1948), p. 529.

called the "superordinate meaning system."[4] It is the upper-
most level of human conceptualization and provides the specific motivation behind community norms that are exercised
at the level of community interaction.

The second function of religion, as given by Davis, is that
"it provides through its collective ritual, a means for the
constant renewal of common sentiments." It is obvious from
the previous description that in the Hasidic community
many activities assume the form of a collective ritual. Beside
the usual practices of Orthodox religious Jews, many additional rituals are required of the Hasidim. Indeed, most of
the daily activities are prescribed by the religious laws so
that these uniform ritualistic practices provide the basis for
renewal of the common sentiments. Common rituals in the
Hasidic community are not restricted to those that are
publicly expressed but include all religious rituals, public
and private, that are uniformly observed during the course
of the day. However, these Hasidic rituals have gradually
become part of the general community norms. As compared
with other Orthodox Jews, the Hasidim must observe stricter
food habits and practices. Prescribed ritualistic observance
must be kept constantly in mind; the duration of prayer in
the morning, afternoon, and evening is long; greater expressions of piety are required in religious performances; external appearance is prescribed; and the Sabbath and religious holidays last longer. In short, there are a host of rituals
exclusive to the Hasidic community, the performance of
which serves as a means of identification and ultimately as
the basis of full group acceptance of individuals.

Davis's third function of religion is to serve "through its
sacred objects [as] a concrete reference for the values and a
rallying point for all persons who share in the same values."
This is particularly true in the Hasidic community. Many
objects that elsewhere have no relationship with religion are
here given religious significance. Objects that appear to be
secular in nature are transformed to assume sacred character.

4. Charles Y. Glock, "The Sociology of Religion," in Robert K.
Merton, Leonard Broom, and Leonard S. Cottrell, Jr. (eds.), *Sociology
Today* (New York: Basic Books, Inc., 1959), p. 156.

Such objects are concrete references to community values. They are so many in number that community values are constantly in sight. As has been seen, a timer becomes a *shabbos zeiger*,[5] a water pitcher becomes a *netilas yodaim tepl*,[6] a heavy-gauge stocking becomes a "Hasidic stocking,"[7] and so forth. All these items are religious symbols that, among the Hasidim, are attached to ordinary and habitual activity, and which constantly serve to reinforce religious values.

Davis's fourth function of religion is that "it provides an unlimited and inseparable source of reward and punishment —rewards for good conduct, punishment for bad." This involves the basic elements of group control. Reward and punishment refer not only to the afterworld but also to the present. In the Hasidic community, in contrast to the usual American community, overt disapproval for minor deviation occurs frequently. An insignificant deviation from prescribed ways may draw reproaches from friends and associates, who may even call upon the rabbi to reproach an individual authoritatively. On the other hand, persons who conform to the norms are constantly rewarded by recognition with honors in the house of worship, at the *rebbe's* meal ceremonials, and by all who know them as observant Jews. Furthermore, those who conform to community norms achieve greater economic success because they are given preference in patronage and community support over people lower in the religious status rank order. Thus, a continuous system of reward and punishment reinforces the community norms.

These four major functions of religion operate in every society, but in the Hasidic community they are infinitely more forceful than in other Jewish communities. Here, the institution of religion is clearly the major encompassing force behind all other institutions. Particularly in economic affairs, the contrast with the large American society is marked. Robin Williams says of the American economic system that

5. See pp. 101–102
6. See pp. 222–223.
7. See p. 214.

[It] has acquired such independence from other areas of life that if often give the appearance of being self-generating and self-perpetuating. Economic activity has become so sharply differentiated from the containing social structure that it is deceptively easy to think of "purely economic" activity to identify economic institutions with the common sense category "making a living."[8]

In the Hasidic community, however, economic institutions achieve no such independence of other institutions. Here, religion determines the items to be produced, the items to be consumed, and even the occupations one may hold. The latter function is especially important because in the United States a person is commonly identified by occupation rather than by other personal characteristics. He is a doctor, lawyer, teacher, or plumber,[9] and his status is most commonly based on his job.[10]

But in the Hasidic community one is identified not by occupation but by religious performances, and it is by the intensity and frequency of religious observance that he gains status in the community. Many Hasidic men have much higher status in the community than their occupations would indicate to outsiders. For this reason, when members of the group move outside their community (from Williamsburg, for example, to a resort in the mountains), they will ostenta-

8. Robin M. Williams, Jr., *American Society,* revised ed. (New York: Alfred A. Knopf, Inc., 1960), p. 150.

9. Lyle Saunders, *Cultural Differences and Medical Care* (New York: Russell Sage Foundation, 1954), p. 126.

10. Cecil C. North and Paul K. Hatt of the National Opinion Research Center, "Jobs and Occupations: A Popular Evaluation," *Public Opinion News,* 9 (1947), 3–13; reprinted in Reinhard Bendix and Seymour Martin Lipset (eds.), *Class Status and Power* (Glencoe: The Free Press, Inc., 1953), pp. 411–426. See other occupational indices such as the "Edward's Occupational Index," "Minnesota Occupational Scale," "Center Occupational Index," in Theodore Caplow, *The Sociology of Work* (Minneapolis: University of Minnesota Press, 1954), p. 31; *Sixteenth Census of the United States: 1940 Population; Occupation Statistics for the United States, 1870–1940* (Washington, D.C.: United States Government Printing Office); and Richard Centers, *The Psychology of Social Classes* (Princeton: Princeton University Press, 1949), pp. 48–51.

tiously engage in those religious activities that establish their status as Hasidim in the eyes of other Hasidim.

Occupation in the Hasidic community is, however, an important means of furthering one's religious activities, since occupation determines how well one is able to perform his religious obligations.[11] This, too, contrasts with the situation usually found in the United States, where, as Parsons says, an occupation's

. . . most essential feature is the primacy of functional achievement. This implies the selection of people on the basis of their capacities to perform the task, of innate ability and training, not by birth, or any other antecedent element of status. It further implies the segregation of the technical role from other aspects of the incumbent's life, most of which are in the nature of the case governed by other types of standards.[12]

Because occupation plays such an important role in the individual's life in the American society, and because of high geographic mobility, the community may easily lose control over the individual. He need not depend upon the community for moral or psychological support since he may find these in his occupational associations. Thus, Parsons feels that:

One [consequence] is the involvement of people in systems of social relationship of very great complexity which, because of their newness and rapidly changing character, cannot be adequately governed by established and traditionalized norms.[13]

Perhaps this might also be assumed about the Hasidim. Rapid growth inevitably affects occupational opportunities as well. As more members of the community move into a greater variety of occupations and as the types of occupations increase, there may be more extensive involvements in external systems of social relationships. The more social mobility the members gain through occupational spread,

11. See p. 59 ff.
12. Talcott Parsons, *Essays in Sociological Theory* (Glencoe: The Free Press, Inc., 1954), p. 311.
13. *Ibid.*, p. 312.

the more the community may lose control over them. It can be argued that as time passes the possibility for members of the group to assimilate and lose their identity as Hasidic Jews will increase. This is greatly feared by the present leaders. They believe that if the members of the Hasidim engage in secular occupations, even though these are not irreligious, assimilation will be hastened. They fear that in an urban setting like New York City, where the members are exposed to many activities and values foreign to them, where there is no wall isolating the Hasidim from the general community, assimilation and even amalgamation may occur. This fear is related largely to the occupational involvement of Hasidic members in nonreligious undertakings.

However, the urban setting does not necessarily limit or arrest the Hasidic way of life; it may even contribute positively to its growth and development. Judaism, as Max Weber has pointed out, is an urban religion.[14] The Jewish people have adapted themselves with singular success to city life.[15] It is true that Hasidism had its roots in the Carpathian Mountains and in rural Polish, Galician, and Hungarian communities. But Hasidism, as we know it today, exists only in an urban setting. The Hasidim of Williamsburg have taken advantage of the existing economic system in their new environment and have grown in strength and number. Were they not now in an urban community, the Hasidim could not, in fact, establish themselves so firmly as a thriving religious group.

As I shall try to demonstrate, the economic system of the Hasidim rests mainly upon the following characteristics:

  1. Specialized occupations.[16]

14. Max Weber, *General Economic History* (translated by Frank H. Knight) (Glencoe: The Free Press, Inc., 1950), p. 317.

15. This contention is borne out in the United States by a census survey of March, 1957. The data show that among major religious bodies Jews are the most highly urbanized. As of 1957 no less than 96.1 per cent were living in urban areas, of which 87.4 per cent were living in cities with a population of 25,000 or more. See Table 23–4 in Donald J. Bogue, *The Population of the United States* (Glencoe: The Free Press, Inc., 1959), p. 694.

16. See p. 127 ff., "Religious Professional Services."

2. Specialized articles and shops.[17]

3. Accessibility of jobs in the general labor market outside the Hasidic community.[18]

4. A great variety of goods.

5. The transformation of manufactured goods into religious articles.[19]

6. Invention of new articles.

7. Creation of new jobs.[20]

8. The establishment of markets for religious articles.[21]

9. Competition in the "reliability" of kosher goods.[22]

10. Profit in wholesale-retail distribution.

11. A high degree of interdependence.[23]

All these characteristics reflect the urban setting. A system based on such specialization and interdependence of parts is possible only in an urban community. The opportunity for the manufacture and sale of articles is greatly heightened by the accessibility of raw materials at all times and by a sizeable market for products in the urban community. For example, the manufacture or sale of Hasidic foodstuff[24] could not be established on an elaborate basis in a rural community. In rural Hungary only one or two large animals were slaughtered during any one week. If the ritual external examination of the slaughtered animal raised some question of blemish, the animal was not considered *glat*[25] and many Hasidic Jews refrained from eating meat until an animal that was *glat* could be secured. In the United States, where there is a great abundance of animals and a large slaughtering industry, people can afford to produce and to purchase *glat* kosher meat. This could not be a regular economic activity if it were not possible to dispose of those animals which do

17. See pp. 157–158, "Leaven Searching Sets."
18. See p. 231 ff., "Nonprofessional Occupations."
19. See pp. 101–102, the "Frig-o-Matic Sabbath *Zeiger.*
20. See pp. 104–107, the "*Shatnes* Laboratory."
21. See pp. 153–175, "Manufacture of Sale of Religious Articles."
22. See pp. 189–196, the *hashash* phenomenon.
23. See p. 191, "bloodless egg noodles."
24. See p. 175 ff.
25. See p. 178.

not meet the Hasidic requirement. Such disposal, and therefore such specialized production, is possible only in an urban community where there is a market for all kinds of meat. In a rural setting one of two things would happen. Animals that were not *glat* would be rejected, with consequent economic waste and less economic support available for religious activities. Or animals failing to meet requirements would come to be eaten anyhow, thus weakening the religious base of the Hasidim.

The economic activities of the Hasidic community are organized, then, in a way that is compatible only with an urban community. Two hypothetical questions may be raised: (1) Can the Hasidim re-establish themselves in a rural community? (2) Can the Hasidim become economically successful in a rural area? The answer to both of these questions is negative. Whereas the Hasidim may take up residence in a rural area, their economics must continue to depend on urban organization. There has already been a demonstration of this. To avoid the strange cultural influences of the metropolis and to be able to bring up the children in an exclusively Hasidic atmosphere, a community of about sixty Hasidic families formerly from Williamsburg has been established near Monsey, New York. It is known as New Square (named after Squarer *rebbe*). After its fifth year of existence, this community is still culturally, socially, and economically part of the Williamsburg Hasidic community. Most of the male adults in New Square commute daily to New York. Even its *rebbe* and other religious functionaries and its religious schools are maintained by the Hasidic Jews of New York.

As to the question of whether the Hasidim can become economically successful in a rural area, the answer is still negative. First, unlike the Mennonites, the Hasidim are not farmers, nor did they pursue agriculture in Europe. Although some of them do come from rural areas, none of them were farmers. Thus, the Mennonites, who were farmers in Europe and are farmers in America, to whom "economic success in farming has come to represent . . . the work in character,"[26] have found their social adjustment on the farm. When as individuals they move away from the farm, they tend to lose all identity and to assimilate. The Hasidim, however, are people whose economic activities have always been urban; that they can and do make a good social adjustment in an urban setting has been demonstrated. Engaging in urban economic activities does not cause the loss of their identification, because such activities are so organized as to reinforce religious values and norms within an in-group setting.

Second, the urban life, in the Hasidic community as elsewhere, is so structured as to create a high degree of interdependence based on an extensive division of labor. Hence, there is a constant demand for new articles and new jobs. For example, one of the ingredients in the "Leaven-Searching Set" is feathers. Busy urban persons have no time to go to a poultry slaughter house to obtain these. As a result, a "Leaven-Searching Set" has become a consumers' good.[27]

Third, the urban forces that threaten the community provide additional economic activities. For example, the function of the Hasidic foodstuffs is not only to provide community-sanctioned kosher food, but also to exert a strong measure of social control. A Hasidic Jew cannot move to a place where he cannot obtain Hasidic food. To do so he would have to withdraw from the group, which is the source of his deepest beliefs and greatest satisfactions. Since only Hasidic Jews are trusted at any stage in the preparation of kosher food, the manufacture of Hasidic foodstuffs according to religious prescriptions serves to provide jobs for the community, and, at the same time, to help to maintain the social isolation of the Hasidic workers.

Because of the strong secular influences of the larger New York community, it might be expected that there would be signs of assimilation among the Hasidim, which might point to the disintegration of the group. But no such signs are yet visible, perhaps because urban living contributes positively to the maintenance of this community. Its economic activ-

26. Melvin Gingerich, *The Mennonites in Iowa* (Iowa City: The State Historical Society of Iowa, 1939), pp. 207–208.
27. See pp. 156–159 for more extensive treatment.

ities, which are basically urban in character, are religiously motivated. Judaism has, however, always had enough flexibility to make adequate adjustment to changing situations in its economic activities. Throughout the ages Jews have found ways to engage in business and still comply with religious requirements. This ability to reconcile business practices with the prescriptions of Judaism was sufficiently marked to lead Sombart to the conclusion that Jews had an important influence upon modern capitalism.[28] The Hasidim have been able to find economic activities that not only do not require violation of religious laws but that actually complement and supplement religious observance while providing an acceptable living for individual community members and economic support for the community's religious activities.

Substantiating this argument, it should be pointed out that in the Hasidic community religion is very well adjusted to the economic institutions of the capitalistic system. Profit-making is considered entirely moral and legitimate. It is legitimatized to such an extent that religious congregations sponsor butcher stores and from their profits support religious schools. Even the salaries of the butchers and ritual slaughterers are paid by the religious organization itself. The Congregation of Yetev Lev of Satmar advertises that by eating *glat* kosher meat, one "supports the Torah and the fear of God." The following part of an advertisement clearly indicates the religious sanction of such economic activity:

> Good tidings for those who most zealously observe strict *kashrut.*
> Eat *glat* kosher meat in order to strengthen the Torah and the fear of God.
> *Glat* kosher beef and poultry from
> The slaughtering and butcher stores of Kehal Yetev Lev
> The establishment of our master and teacher, the *Gaon* of Satmar, may he live long and happily.
> We are extremely happy to inform all our friends and sympathizers that a few days ago we opened a new butcher

28. Werner Sombart, *The Jews and Modern Capitalism,* translated by M. Epstein (Glencoe: The Free Press, Inc., 1951), pp. 71–73.

store in Boro Park, in order to supply beef and poultry from the slaughtering of Kehal Yetev Lev to all our friends and customers in Boro Park.

The opening of this new butcher store is a result of the establishment of a new branch of the Yeshivah "Torah Veyirah" in Boro Park because, thank God, in a short time it has increased by several hundreds of students, may they multiply, and the income of this butcher store, as well as of the one in Williamsburg, serves only and exclusively for supporting the Yeshivah and strengthening its education and training.

It is known to all that the holy Yeshivot of Torah Veyirah, whose number of students is now, with God's help, more than two thousand, may they multiply, is basically maintained with the income of the *meshulachim* [collectors] and

Particularly do they depend upon the income of the butcher stores, which were established only and exclusively with this holy purpose, that all their income should serve for the support of the holy Yeshivot of Torah Veyirah. Consequently, those using the meat from our butcher stores give a supporting and helping hand to the strengthening of the holy Yeshivot Torah Veyirah, and aid in the improvement of the financial circumstances of the hundreds of poor students of our holy Yeshivot.

Concerning the slaughtering of Yetev Lev, it is well known that it is the most original of its kind, since all the slaughterers and butchers are under the supervision of the Congregation Yetev Lev and receive their salary from the congregation's treasury. All this is in accordance with the custom of our forefathers in the holy communities in Europe, as it has been always.

Beside the fact that all of the meats in our butcher store are from the slaughtering under the supervision of the Congregation Yetev Lev of Satmar, we assure our customers that they will get for their money the very best merchandise available in quality and freshness of the meat.[29]

Another illustration will indicate the ways in which the Hasidic community gives religious sanction to modern eco-

29. *Hamaor*, December, 1958. Translated from the Hebrew.

nomic practices. A religious Jew cannot charge interest,[30] a matter with which the *Code of Jewish Law* deals extensively.[31] The Hasidic community demands that the law of interest be observed even today. The following is the English content of a circular that was hung in every house of worship in the community:

> It is forbidden to lend or borrow with interest.
>
> The seriousness of this injunction is expressed in the severity of its penalty. The person who takes interest is termed by our Sages as a disbeliever in God [sic] (Baba Metzia 71A) and he is destined not to be resurrected.
>
> As a result of ignorance, many Torah-true Jews unwittingly violate this law. We find it therefore, necessary to offer the community the following information:
>
> 1. Buying from a Jew on the installment plan that requires interest payments is forbidden.
>
> 2. If a seller states his selling price and stipulates a higher price if it is a credit purchase, this constitutes interest taking.

30. The following are the Biblical passages prohibiting charging interest:

"If thou lend money to any of my people, even to the poor with thee, thou shalt not be to him as a creditor, neither shall ye lay upon him interest. (Exodus 22:24)

"And if they brother be waxen poor and his means fail with thee; thou shalt uphold him: as a stranger and a settler shall he live with thee. Take thou no interest of him or increase, but fear thy God, that thy brother may live with thee. (Leviticus 25:37)

"Thou shalt not give him thy money upon interest, nor give him thy victuals for increase. (Leviticus 25:37)

"Thou shalt not lend upon interest to thy brother; interest of money, interest of victuals, interest of anything that is lent upon interest. (Deuteronomy 23:25)"

31. *The Shulhan Aruch-Yoreh Deah* deals with the law concerning charging interest in the following chapters: 159 (three paragraphs), 160 (twenty-three paragraphs), 161 (eleven paragraphs), 162 (five paragraphs), 163 (three paragraphs), 164 (four paragraphs), 165 (one paragraph), 166 (three paragraphs), 167 (one paragraph), 169 (twenty-seven paragraphs), 170 (two paragraphs), 171 (one paragraph), 172 (six paragraphs), 173 (nineteen paragraphs), 174 (eight paragraphs), 175 (eight paragraphs), 177 (forty paragraphs), in total eighteen chapters and 173 paragraphs.

3. Interest paid to a Jewish person on account of a mortgage is forbidden.

4. The ban on interest-taking includes the lender who receives the interest, the borrower who pays it and the guarantor or co-maker who makes possible the transaction. All three share equal guilt.

5. Under certain circumstances, a *"Shtar Isske,"* a special contract can be drawn up to allow a transaction involving interest. As details of this contract are complicated, a Rabbinical authority or Rabbinical Organization must be consulted.

> [Signed] Torah U'mitzvot
> 203 Lee Avenue, Brooklyn 6, New York
> EV 7–8520[32]

In a society where the medium of exchange is money, it is difficult to conceive of the operation of economic establishments without loans and without charging interest. Not even the Hasidic community can run its economic affairs without money as the medium of exchange. Therefore, the community must resort to the traditional way within the technical legality of the *Code of Jewish Law* whereby monetary return for loans is permissible even for the "most zealous of the zealous."

Those Hasidic business establishments that are financially sound and can secure loans from legitimate banks have no difficulties in meeting religious requirements, for such loans are permissible. But those Hasidic establishments that are small and whose business techniques and methods are "Hasidic" are poor credit risks. They have to borrow money from other members of the Hasidic community who know them and are willing to risk the possibility of financial loss. According to Jewish law, the lender is not allowed to charge interest but he *is* permitted to become a partner in the business for which the money is being used. Once he becomes a partner, he is allowed to draw a profit from the business. The amount of profit is based upon the amount of money lent. The borrower also signs a promissory note to make the assurance of repayment stronger.

32. Undated circular.

This business transaction establishing a partnership as a substitute for lending money at interest is done through a written document, signed by the borrower and two witnesses. The blank form for this transaction is available at religious book stores. The following is the translation of such a document:

*With God's help*

**Permit for Business Purposes**

I, the undersigned, acknowledge that I received from the sum of                     for business purposes from today until the day of                     so that the profit will be shared by us, half for myself and half for                     (the above). Damages, God forbid, will be shared by us half and half. It is agreed between us that nothing will be accepted as loss except that which is verified and proven by a legitimate and honest witness, according to our holy Torah. As to the profits, I pledge that at the end of the term I will testify under oath that there were no more profits than I have declared. But we also agreed that I have the right to buy the part of the profit belonging to                     (the above) for                     per cent of the above mentioned sum yearly. In case these percentages that I give him are higher than the capital sum, he can never have any claims against me, for then the entire profit belongs to me. And as long as I have not returned the entire sum, even after the above date, it will remain in my possession for business purposes, according to the above basis of agreement. I also confirm that I have received payment for my trouble and I also have given a "Bill of Exchange" or a note according to the laws of the state.

Day                          Weekly Portion
Year                         City

                                        Witness
                                        Witness

The Money Receiver                                   [33]

In the Hasidic community, the greatest virtue is still to "serve God with study and worship." If a person works, he

33. From the original document. Translated from the Yiddish. (Published by M. Pollak's Hebrew Book Store, New York, no date.)

has no time to study and worship. Yet, one must work in order to maintain himself and his family so that they may serve God. Thus, work is only a means to an end—study and worship, but work in itself is of no great virtue. However, work has a higher status in the United States than in Europe probably because of the fact that in Europe the economic circumstances of a worker were not as favorable as in the United States. In Europe, laborers were not learned in Jewish law and for this reason alone they were of lower status. But in the United States, the majority of Hasidic Jews are engaged in occupations that involve working with their hands. They may be well rewarded, and because physical labor is more rewarding than in Europe, and because Hasidic laborers are able to and do participate in the cultural and religious affairs of the community and show familiarity with religious laws, their occupations do not determine their status in the community. Rather, their status is determined by the extent of their religious participation and observance. Members fall within the hierarchical range, from the lower stratum of conforming Hasidic Jews to the upper stratum of the "most zealous of the zealous" in religious observance. Thus, bearded Jews are not necessarily practicing rabbis or other religious functionaries but may be laymen engaged in a variety of economic pursuits. Through their religion they have developed specialized functional roles by which they are identified. Their social structure provides them with culturally defined goals, purposes, and interests which become the objectives for all members of the Hasidic community. At the same time, the community "defines, regulates and controls the acceptable modes of reaching out for these goals."[34] Thus it becomes a cohesive community in which the cultural goals and the institutionalized norms operate jointly and effectively in shaping even its economic practices. Urban culture has had its greatest influence upon the Hasidic Jews in the area of economic activities, which potentially may lead toward assimilation, yet such activities

34. Robert K. Merton, *Social Theory and Social Structure* (Glencoe: The Free Press, Inc., 1957), pp. 132–133.

have also been effectively used to promote Hasidism. As one respondent stated:

> Once one learns the American ways of doing business, he can make a better living, and to make a better living is conducive to Hasidism. [Q. How?] If you make a better living, you can be a better Hasid by giving more money to the Hasidic causes; by buying more kosher phylacteries; by buying a more beautiful *esrog;* by having more time to study.[35]

Thus, the participation of even learned Hasidic Jews in physical labor may be seen to represent still another economic adjustment to an urban society.

Besides the urban influence, there are five other aspects of American society that are important to the growth and development of this sacred society. These are: (1) economic security, (2) democracy, (3) separation of church and state, (4) cultural and religious diversity, and (5) the existence of a non-Hasidic community.

The Hasidic community could not flourish equally well in a society characterized by economic hardship. Economic security contributes to the maintenance of Hasidic values by creating conditions conducive to religious observance. It gives the Hasidic Jew more time to devote to the cultivation of Hasidism and promotes an atmosphere that sets the stage for the support of all kinds of Hasidic interests and activities. This would be impossible in a poverty-stricken society where even food was hard to come by or in one where members of a minority group lacked the freedom to create their own job opportunities.

Democracy also contributes to the maintenance of the Hasidic community. In the United States the idea of the existence of minority ethnic and religious groups is not new but is actually an accepted aspect of the social structure. In the United States cultural and religious diversity strengthens the separation of church and state. Conversely, separation of church and state allows and greatly encourages cultural and religious diversity. Under such conditions it is relatively easy for a minority group to function. In a society where

35. From the files of LPS, 1958.

there is homogeneity or perhaps a very few minority groups, it is likely that the focus of discrimination and prejudice would be directed toward any minority group so that the group would ultimately disappear. But in America, where there are many minority groups, one additional group can live practically unnoticed. It is true that internal cohesion may sometimes best be achieved by attack from the outside, as in the case of the Doukhobors, who have created issues with the government and provoked conflict in order to create an external pressure which has contributed to their social solidarity.[36] But this is not the case with the Hasidim. First, they do not need to provoke such outside pressures because the "undesirable" behavior patterns of the nonobserving Jewish community already does this. Second, because there is the non-Hasidic Jewish community between the Hasidim and the larger non-Jewish community, "standard" American values do not penetrate easily to the Hasidim. And, finally, group cohesion is positively attained by inside identification. In other words, the voluntary identification with Hasidism and with the Hasidic community has a stronger effect in regulating and controlling the acceptable modes of behavior than outside forces have.

Therefore, American democracy is more conducive to Hasidism than even a Jewish state. In a state where all Jews are identified with Judaism, the one religion, it is unlikely that a deviant group like the Hasidim would be tolerated.[37] This sentiment has been expressed by many Hasidic Jews, a number of whom have said that it is easier to be Hasidic in the United States than in Israel. One Hasid relates:

In America if a person does not observe Jewish law, we can say to our children that this person is a *goy*. But in Israel where everybody is a Jew, what do we say to our children? We cannot tell them that they are *goyim*. Neither can we tell them that they are Jews because they will ask why they do not observe the religion. We cannot tell our children that there are two kinds of

36. Pauline V. Young, *The Pilgrims of Russian Town* (Chicago: University of Chicago Press, 1932), pp. 237–251.

37. The author is planing to conduct a similar study in Israel of the *Neturei Karta*, the counterpart of the Hasidism of Williamsburg.

Jews; one who observes and one who does not, because they may think that if one is still considered a Jew without observing the religion, why shouldn't they do the same? But we do not have this problem in America.[38]

The final aspect of American society that contributes to the existence and further development of the Hasidic community is the existence of a non-Hasidic Jewish community. This community helps the Hasidim maintain itself economically. It provides a market for Hasidic products, jobs for community members, and help in maintaining Hasidic institutions such as the religious schools, houses of worship, ritual baths, and so forth. Whereas the existence of an outside group might have a deteriorating effect upon the religious life of the Hasidic community, it is actually utilized for economic maintenance. Hence, one of the greatest survival values of this community lies in its ability to orient the socially sanctioned values and goals of its religious life to utilize urban secular economic activities.

38. From the filed of JF, 1957.

# APPENDIX

# Some Problems in Studying

# the Hasidic Community

I T WOULD PERHAPS BE USEFUL to begin this discussion by relating some of the many difficulties I encountered in my attempt to gain entrance into the Hasidic community. In the beginning, many individuals showed distrust and resentment at my presence. I do not live in the neighborhood and I do not wear Hasidic clothing or a beard or sidelocks, as most of the male members of the community do. Among the group I was a stranger, regardless of my Jewish background.

From 1934 to 1937 I attended a Hasidic rabbinical school in Papa, Hungary, with some Hasidic Jews now in Williamsburg. This fact helped me, of course, in comprehending the group norms and the significance of various Hasidic activities. It gave me a necessary orientation at the exploratory stage of my study. However, my previous affiliation with a Hasidic group did not in itself help me because to those people who had known me previously, I was "already too far gone," and my friendship was of no particular value to them.

Thus, many tried to shy away from me during my initial attempts at contact. All in all, there was nothing in my appearance or in my activities that conveyed my background to those persons I hoped to interview. To them, I looked like a stranger and the group does not trust strangers. Some of them expressed this resentment by posing the following dilemma: "If you are one of us, you ought to know what Hasidism is. There is no reason why you should go around and ask questions about us. If you are not one of us, it should not be your concern to know how the Hasidim live." A similar sentiment was expressed by another Hasidic Jew: "No one goes around asking questions without any motives, but if someone does ask questions without motives, he must be a *meshugener* (insane) and why should anyone bother with a *meshugener?*"

At the earliest stage in the study, I tried to convince some of the informants that I was part of the group. This did not help. I was told quite plainly that if I knew the group and considered myself part of it but did not conform to its customs, ceremonies, and rituals, I could only be a person who had left the fold. And why should anyone associate with such a person? "No good can come from a person such as this, anyway." When, on the other hand, I told some of my informants that I was an outsider, this did not help either. Their reply was:

Don't you believe in human decency? Don't you believe in privacy? . . . You want to come in and make a study of these pious people and you want to describe that? These people are pious and holy. There are certain things in life that are indescribable and that should be kept that way. You have absolutely no right to come in here and disturb or even ask about the conduct, behavior, and form of life these people are leading. This form of life is their whole existence, this is their totality of being. You dare touch that? . . . These people are sacrificing much and depriving themselves of many of the wonderful things that life could offer, purely because of their deep dedication to their religion. You cannot do it. . . . You should not do it.[1]

1. From an interview, ZL3, 1956.

Taking still another approach, I told the group that I was a writer who wanted to write on the subject of Hasidism. I was promptly called an atheist. I was told that anyone who looked like me and wrote about Hasidism must be an atheist.

It should be everyone's duty to guard himself against atheists. Only a Hasidic Jew has a right to write about Hasidism. . . . You may write or you may not write about atheism, but I can tell you only this much, that if you write about Hasidim, it is bound to be atheistic. The mere fact that you are doing the writing, that in itself makes it atheistic. . . . The way you are, the way you look, the way you talk, if you write about Hasidism, it is and it must be atheism. If you follow my advice, you won't write about Hasidim. If you are such a good writer, why don't you write about other things? Why should you write about Hasidim?[2]

When I told some informants that I was making a study to contribute to scientific knowledge, the reply made it obvious that they had no comprehension whatever that it was in any way possible to contribute to science for its own sake. They said that only the Talmud, the Bible, and other religious works can be studied for their own sake. It was extremely difficult to establish my role in the community. In an anthropoligical study,[3] Hortense Powdermaker made use of the title of "visiting teacher," given her by the Department of Education at Jackson, Mississippi. This provided an easy introduction to local white and colored educators. In fact, they sponsored her study and introduced her to other members of the community. I could not say that I was gathering material for teaching purposes, because this would have antagonized some informants. Neither could I establish myself as "one who asks questions," the term applied to an anthropologist among one group of Navaho Indians,[4] be-

2. From an interview, ZFI, 1957.
3. Hortense Powdermaker, *After Freedom* (New York: The Viking Press, Inc., 1934).
4. Benjamin D. Paul, "Interview Techniques and Field Relationships," in Arthur L. Kroebar, *Anthropology Today* (Chicago: University of Chicago Press, 1953), p. 434.

cause in the Hasidic community "one should show inquisitiveness in Talmud only."[5]

The group is careful to guard against sensationalism. Many newspaper reporters have taken advantage of the Hasidim and have written about Hasidic life in a journalistic manner. This type of writing has been strongly resented by the group. Many of them expressed their dissatisfaction with an article in *Life* magazine that described the group with "uncomplimentary remarks." The article had stated:

Carryovers from the archaic Jewish way of life can be seen today in a shabby-looking section of Brooklyn called Williamsburg. There, amid drug stores, service stations, and delicatessens, move strange figures that seem to belong to another age —bearded men with side curls and long black coats.[6]

It is the sincere conviction of the members of this community that they are the "true religious Jews." They felt that this article should have made fun of the nonobservant Jews who have left the traditions of their forefathers, but instead it made fun of them, the "truly religious." They objected to being called "archaic," "strange figures" who "belong to another age," just because they have remained true to their traditions. As a result, they wanted to know what would be said about them and how it would be said.

Many Hasidim were reluctant to give any information about themselves. They said that the group has been seriously misrepresented and that many lies have been promulgated even in the Yiddish press. There was, they insisted, no way to protect themselves from these lies and misrepresentations. "The people of the newspaper know that we do not read their newspapers and that we do not take up issues against them whenever they misrepresent us. But we must be very careful with whom we speak and to whom we give information."[7]

5. From an interview, RHL, 1956.
6. Life, 38, No. 24 (June 13, 1955).
7. Interview with the personal secretary of D's, 1956.

Establishing rapport, then, presented one of the greatest problems in carrying out this study. The informants wanted to know my answers to many questions before they would consider answering. They wanted to know who I was, what I was doing, what my occupation was, where I lived, what my religious viewpoints were, whether I was an observant Jew, whether I knew anything about Hasidism, what my affiliations were, and to what associations I belonged. Typically, one said:

> Before I give you information, I have to know who you are, what you are, what you are doing. You have to give me an account about yourself in a detailed explanation so that I will know that I can trust you. . . .[8]

Such illustrations are adequate to indicate the distrust that the group displayed and the difficulties I had to overcome in order to gain entrance and obtain information.

To overcome these difficulties it was necessary to develop specific approaches for the study of this group. I had to adjust to each situation, manipulate events and, in general, allow great flexibility in approach in order to reach the various members of the community.

My initial contact with a member of the Hasidic community was made through the aid of what I called a "reference person." He was a religious non-Hasidic Jew who was tolerant about the study I was making. After I had established good rapport with him, I asked him to introduce me to a Hasidic Jew he knew. Again, when I had established good rapport with this new informant, I asked him to introduce me to still other Hasidic Jews. In turn, this new informant introduced me to someone else, thereupon becoming my new "reference person." I asked him to say a few complimentary words about me or my study to the person to whom he had introduced me and to assure him that "everything is all right." I found that each additional informant whom I met through a reference person was less suspicious of me because he associated me with my reference person, whom he trusted. In my conversation I often mentioned this person to re-

8. Interview with NBI of Keap Street, 1956.

affirm the rapport and to aid me further to reduce suspicion. As soon as I had made contact with key people in the Hasidic community, I was able to refer to them during various interviews. This was particularly helpful when important or delicate issues were touched upon. This reference to key leaders was exceedingly profitable inasmuch as the informants then became more willing to discuss even personal matters.

It was important that an informant be met through the introduction of another person who was known to the new prospect. The mere fact that I was introduced by a person whom the informant knew well was an indication that I was not a complete stranger. However, it was often most productive to interview people under circumstances such as at a wedding or other festivity where they were willing to talk freely. On these occasions, I usually made a remark that begged for a reply and led to a conversation.

I tried to create situations in which I was able to do some favor for a Hasidic individual, such as lending him money or contributing to the institutions or organizations to which he belonged. This "morally" obligated the person to reciprocate in some way, and the least he was able to do was "to talk." Careful steps had to be taken to contribute the money appropriately so that no suspicion of "ulterior motives" behind my charitable performances was created. The interval between my "benevolence" and asking one to reciprocate was sufficiently long so as not to create the feeling that the two were related, but sufficiently short so as not to let him forget my action.

Each time I attended, contributed to, or purchased something in the community, I made certain that the people involved would remember me. The following various steps will indicate how this was accomplished: When I made a purchase of the weekly published speeches, I first discovered who sold them; I then met the person who sold them through the aid of some three or four other people; I next inquired about the person who edited them; I asked about their accuracy — I wanted to know if they contained the exact words of the *rebbe* — finally, I subscribed to all future publications.

At the same time I inquired about the specific copies which the seller did not have at his disposal at the moment, and asked when these copies could be obtained. I practically performed "much ado about nothing," and tried to make a "big fuss," and attached importance to a simple purchase of the leaflets. It gave me an opportunity to see certain persons more often and to be seen by others more often in favorable circumstances. This was important because everyone was a possible informant. I carried these leaflets in my hands when I came to some of the scheduled interviews if I thought they would be recognized and would make a "favorable" impression.

The group as a whole does not speak English. Some of the Hasidim say that they speak "a little English." However, a vocabulary of "yes," "no," "okay," "money," "check," "job," "business," and "operator" is by no means adequate for communication. The group as a whole speaks Hungarian-Yiddish. It is not the same as the Russian-Lithuanian-Yiddish which is the standard Yiddish in America. The fact that the great majority of the group speaks Hungarian did not cause any difficulties. On the contrary, it helped a great deal, since I speak Hungarian fluently. It is very interesting to note that as soon as I was able to display knowledge of the group's language (including accent and dialect), a "familiar chord" was struck. This they indicated by saying, "Oh, you too are a Magyar," or "Oh, you speak Hungarian!" This was an indication to them that I was not "somebody spying on them."

In connection with the group's language, a technique I called "Simultaneous Usage of Multiple Languages" seems to have been a very profitable tool. This technique works in the following way. When I asked a question in Yiddish, I immediately repeated the question in Hungarian. After asking the question, I did not wait for the informant's reply but repeated the question in another language, constantly using familiar terms in Yiddish, Hungarian, Hebrew, and also familiar English terms. The respondent had a chance to formulate his thoughts during the time consumed by the repetition in the complementary languages. In addition, this gave the informant a broader comprehension of the question, and it also constantly lessened antagonism and lowered barriers.

There were, however, certain phrases that the Hasidic community used that were not familiar to me. I carefully noted these phrases and inquired about them from others with whom I came in contact. I asked for clear definitions and examples of how they are used. But I never risked using a phrase inappropriately in a way that would obviously have shown that I was a "stranger." Once I knew the proper translation and interpretations of the phrases, I used them as frequently as possible, whenever the situation was appropriate.

One of the favorite pastimes in the Hasidic community is "politicking," that is talking "politics" about the various Hasidic *rebbes*. One Hasidic Jew may be an ardent follower of a particular Hasidic *rebbe* whom he considers to be the holiest man on earth. At the same time, he may think and speak ill of another *rebbe*. It was necessary for me to gain information about the Hasidic "politicking," about the agreements and strife among the various factions centered around the *rebbes*. Once I had obtained information about these underlying antagonisms, I used this in my conversation to indicate full familiarity with the inner workings of the Hasidic community. I tried to put forth challenging questions, because once the Hasidic informant had been persuaded to talk, he opened up and conversed freely, especially about the subject matter that encompassed his major life interests. As soon as I was able to reach this point, it became obvious that the Hasidic Jew liked to talk about himself and the ideas and philosophies that he held in highest esteem.

I found it profitable to appear a little naive, though not too much so, because that could have made the informant distrustful or afraid that his answers would not be understood. Thus, the informant had the psychic gratification of "instructing the ignorant" in the subject matter in which he was an expert. Even when I knew a great deal about something, I made my respondent feel that his detailed knowledge was giving me additional information. The informants generally displayed the attitude that they lead a life of idealism, that they are performing "great things," "real things," and the "right things," that they are "sacrificing their whole being on the altar of idealism," and that they are lofty in all their undertakings. Letting the informants engage in this oratory served as a "warming up" for obtaining more precise information.

I did not conduct "standardized interviews" with a list of questions decided upon in advance of the interview and asked with the same wording and in the same order of all respondents.[9] Instead I engaged in "unstructured interviews,"[10] in which I did not follow a list of questions, and in "focused interviews,"[11] in which I employed an interview guide with supportive questions but with considerable flexibility. I engaged those respondents whom I met casually in various situations in unstructured interviews. However, I used the focused interview for respondents with whom a time and place of meeting had been prearranged.

Because of the unstructured nature of the interview and because of the latitude an informant had in engaging in oratory, he sometimes digressed from the issue under discussion. In these cases I let the informant conclude his statement and brought him back to the main line of our conversation by saying, "There is still something not clear to me . . ." and repeated or paraphrased the question at hand.

If an informant contradicted a point he had made earlier in the interview, I again waited until he had concluded his statement. I did not remind him that he had contradicted

9. Eleanor E. Maccoby and Nathan Maccoby, "The Interview: A Tool of Social Science," in Gardner Lindzey (ed.), *Handbook of Social Psychology* (Reading, Mass.: Addison-Wesley Publishing Company, Inc., 1954), Vol. I, p. 451.

10. C. R. Ropers, "The Non-directive Method as a Technique for Social Research," *American Journal of Sociology*, 50 (1945), pp. 279–283. The distinction between "structured" and "unstructured" interviews, or between "active" and "passive" interviews is fully treated by C. Kluckhohn, "The Use of Personal Documents in Anthropology," in L. Gottschalk, C. Kluckhohn, and R. Angell (eds.), *Social Science Research Council Bulletin*, No. 53 (1945), pp. 79–173.

11. Robert K. Merton and Patricia L. Kendall, "The Focused Interview," *American Journal of Sociology*, 51 (1946), pp. 541–557.

himself but instead I said, "I do not recall exactly . . . but someone recently told me such and such . . ." or, "Is it possible that this can be looked upon from another viewpoint?" and repeated or paraphrased the statement he had previously made. I was very careful not to antagonize him. At no time did I let him know that I was probing, or that he had contradicted himself.

If his information was contrary to what other informants had told me, I mentioned that "others have told me such and such," something contrary to what he had described. Or I repeated the same question and pretended that he had not answered it. Or I used expressions such as, "I never heard of this," or I asked only one word in Hebrew, "Emes?" (literally, "truth"). Thus, many times the informant felt it necessary to modify his statements. Again this question was asked in amazement and not in tones that could have been an offensive challenge.

The best method I had of evaluating the accuracy of any statement was, however, through consultation with a few Hasidic Jews with whom I established a close and intimate relationship. When I heard a bit of information for the first time or when an informant made a statement contrary to those made previously by someone else, I asked my intimate friends to investigate its accuracy in the community. For example, if an informant quoted a *rebbe* as saying something, or if he made a generalized statement about the Hasidic community that I had never heard and that seemed unlikely, I asked my friends to find out through their close contact with other Hasidim whether or not the statement was generally known to be true. All facts, except those about the individual informant's personal life, were confirmed by others. These intimate informants also served to gather certain information in areas where it was difficult or unwise for me to enter.

I recorded all interviews in one of the following ways: (1) write-up from memory, (2) verbatim note-taking, and (3) mechanical recording. At the prearranged interviews I used a dictating machine (Edison Voicewriter). The informants were asked permission for my use of "the gadget." This machine was used usually at the second meeting after a good rapport had been established between the informant and me. During other interviews, only notes were taken because asking for permission to use dictating instruments during the interview was too great a risk. Some of these verbatim note-takings were so successful that at times informants said: "Take this down, this is very important," or "What did you write down? Let me hear." Then, after I had read it back, they supplied additional information.

There were interviews when even taking notes seemed to be a great risk, particularly when the informants were *rebbes* or *Shtickel rebbes* and very high in the Hasidic hierarchy. In these cases, where no verbatim notes were made, I tried to record as soon as possible every word that had taken place during the interview. I attached the dictating machine to the cigarette lighter in my automobile through the aid of an electrical transformer, and after the interview I went to my car and dictated every word I could remember that had been spoken during the interview. The content of this dictation was later transcribed on paper with great care, and missing links added from memory or from additional interviews. Such recording was extremely helpful in reproducing the content of interviews.

Besides interviewing, I observed the various Hasidic activities. I visited all the places of worship during some of the social, religious, and ceremonial activities and observed the group in action. During some of these activities I was a participant-observer. I visited many of the retail stores and purchased most of the Hasidic products. In many food stores I became a regular customer, just to gain entrance and to collect the various labels on the food products.

Although I participated in and attended many of the Hasidic activities, my final role in the community was that of an "author who is going to write about the Hasidim." Since I was not considered offensive and since I was seen in and out of the community for thirteen years, during which time nothing was seen of my publication, I was tolerated and considered a "harmless busybody who is just snooping around."

Besides my personal contacts, I subscribed to the weekly

newspapers and monthly rabbinical journals, through which I carefully followed the announcements of social events and advertisements for Hasidic products. I collected all announcements available in the houses of worship. I purchased or otherwise acquired the placards and bulletins that were displayed. I also collected all papers, speeches, published resolutions, leaflets, advertisements, and documents that were known to me. Most of these communications were in Yiddish or in Hebrew, and I have translated them from the original copies in my possession.

In conclusion, in this appendix an informal exposition of the techniques used in this study is given. It has been pointed out that because of the members' distrust of any ousiders I had to be extremely flexible in my approach and techniques. For this reason the more orthodox techniques which might normally be more effective in studies of this kind could not be used at the time. This flexibility has proven to be most advantageous in gathering data, particularly in those areas of the inquiry where community members exhibited great reluctance and unwillingness to cooperate.

# Glossary

*Adat Yereim* (Hebrew). The Congregation of [God-] Fearers.

*Antragen* (German). To introduce the idea of marriage between particular individuals regarded as suitable for each other.

*Arbah Minim* (Hebrew). Literally, the "four kinds." During the Holiday of Tabernacles a Jew must recite a prayer over the "four kinds," that is, palm branch, citrus fruit, myrtle, and willow branch.

*Arugat Habosem* (Hebrew). Literally, "garden bed of spices." Name of a religious organization.

*Ashkenazishe Yiden* (Yiddish). Literally, "Ashkenazic Jews." Those Jews who observe the various religious rites and rituals according to the Germanic (Ashkenazic) tradition (vis-à-vis the Sephardic Jews).

*Ausgegrunt* (German). Literally, "the green has worn off."

*Ausgleichen* (German). Literally, "compromise." An agreement.

*Avlah* (Hebrew). Literally, "injustice."

*Baal Habayis* (Hebrew). Literally, "house owner." A full-fledged member of the community.

*Baal Tefilah* (Hebrew). Literally, "master of prayers." Conductor of prayers during a public worship or, reader of the religious worship.

*Baer Hetev* (Hebrew). A commentary on the *Shulhan Aruch* (*The Code of Jewish Law*).

*Balebatishe Yiden* (Hebrew-Yiddish). Literally, "house-owner Jews." The full-fledged community members who participate in most of the local affairs and who are considered "well off."

*Bar Mitzvah* (Hebrew). Literally, "son of the commandment." The initiation of a Jewish male child into adulthood at the age of thirteen.

*Bat Mitzvah* (Hebrew). Literally, "daughter of the commandment."

The initiation of a Jewish female child into adulthood at the age of twelve, as adopted by Conservative and Reform Jewish congregations.

*Bat Onshin* (Hebrew). Literally, "punishable daughter." Girls reaching the age of physical maturity, approximately at twelve, automatically become responsible for the observance of the negative commandments according to Jewish law.

*Batlan* (Hebrew). Literally, "idler." A person who frequents the houses of study and studies and has no other occupation. Also, a professional scholar.

*Bechezkat Kashrut* (Hebrew). Believed to be or regarded as being kosher.

*Bedikat Hometz Lecht* (Hebrew-Yiddish). Candles used in the ceremonial search for leaven the night before Passover.

*Bedikat Hometz Set* (Hebrew-English). A ritual kit that contains all the necessary articles for the ceremonial search for leaven the night before Passover.

*Begleibter Yid* (Yiddish). Literally, "a trustworthy Jew," with proper observance of Jewish rituals.

*Behelfer* (Yiddish). A person who took the children to the houses of study. (This occupation was prevalent in Eastern European Jewish communities.)

*Bekecher* (Yiddish). A long Hasidic coat made of silk or silken material in which the pockets are in the back.

*Ben Torah* (Hebrew). Literally, "son of Torah." It refers to a relatively young scholar in Talmudic matters.

*Beshalach* (Hebrew). A portion of the Torah read in the synagogues during a particular week.

*Bet Shalom* (Hebrew). Literally, "the house of peace."

*Biber* hat (Yiddish-English). A large-brimmed hat made of beaver [*biber*] worn by *rebbes, shtickel rebbes, sheiner Yiden, talmidei hachamin,* and *balebatishe Yiden.*

*Bikur Holim* (Hebrew). Literally, "visiting the sick." A social organization.

*B'nei Yisoschor* (Hebrew). Literally, "the sons of Issachar." A religious organization.

*Bord* (Yiddish). Beard.

*Der Yid* (Yiddish). Literally, "the Jew." The name of a Hasidic newspaper.

*Die Yiddishe Woch* (Yiddish). Literally, "The Jewish Week." The name of a Hasidic newspaper.

*Din Torah* (Hebrew). Literally, "Torah justice." Rabbinic arbitration.

*Echteh Americans* (Yiddish-English). Literally, "real Americans."

*Ehrlicher Yid* (Yiddish). Literally, "honest Jew." Honest-to-goodness Jew who behaves appropriately according to Jewish law.

*Ehrlicher Yid Durch und Durch* (Yiddish). Literally, "honest-to-goodness Jew through and through." It refers to an extremely pious Jew.

*Eigener Baal Habayis* (Yiddish-Hebrew). One's own boss.

*Elul* (Hebrew). The name of a month in the Jewish calendar corresponding approximately to August-September.

*Emes* (Hebrew). Literally, "truth." If used in an interrogatory form, it means "truly."

*Esrog* (Hebrew). "The fruit of goodly trees." A citrus fruit, one of the "four kinds" used on the Holiday of Tabernacles.


*Ferherer* (Yiddish). Examiner.

*Ferleslicher Yid* (Yiddish). Trustworthy Jew.

*Fersheidene gesheften* (Yiddish). Various businesses.

*Fleishig* (Yiddish). Meat and meat products.

*Frei* (Yiddish). Free, at liberty; or unconfined, uncontrolled and loose.

*Frei land* (Yiddish-English). Free country.

*Frumer doctor* (Yiddish-English). Pious or observant doctor.

*Frumer Yid* (Yiddish). Pious or observant Jew.


*Gabbai* (Hebrew). Literally, "treasurer." The manager of a synagogue or the secretaries and managers of the *rebbe's* household. *(Gabbaim.* Plural.)

*Gaon* (Hebrew). Literally, "grandeur." A title applied to the heads of the Sura and Pumpedita Talmudical academies in Babylonia. It is a title given to an outstanding Talmudic scholar. (*Gaonim.* Plural.)

*Gemeinschaft* (German). A closely related community.

*Geribener Ying* (Yiddish). A shrewd fellow with experience and a touch of arrogance.

*Gezegenen* (Yiddish). Literally, "to take farewell." A Hasidic ceremonial. When one comes to the *rebbe* with a request and before leaving, the *rebbe* extends his hand and wishes or prays for the welfare of the visitor. The visitor shakes or kisses the *rebbe's* hand and leaves the *rebbe* some money.

*Glat Kosher* (Yiddish-Hebrew). Literally, "smoothly kosher." It indicates that the meats or the meat products are kosher without any shadow of doubt.

*Goldene Medinah* (Yiddish-Hebrew). Literally, "golden land."

*Goy* (Hebrew). Literally, "nation." A non-Jew. (*Goyim.* Plural.)

*Goyeh* (Yiddish). A non-Jewish married woman.

*Goyishe Goyim* (Yiddish-Hebrew). Non-Jewish non-Jews as distinct from non-observant Jews (called *Yiddishe goyim*).


*Hadassim* (Hebrew). Myrtle twig, one of the requirements of the "four kinds" that are used on the Holiday of Tabernacles.

*Halachic* (Hebrew). Pertaining to Jewish law.

*Halatin* (Yiddish). Hasidic garments or Hasidic jackets.

*Halav Tameh* (Hebrew). Literally, "unclean milk." The milk of a non-kosher animal.

*Halav Yisrael* (Hebrew). Literally, "Jewish milk." Milk that has been milked under the supervision of a "trustworthy Jew."

*Hallah* (Hebrew). Also, *Challah*. Literally, "the priest's share of the dough." A religious ceremony performed over the finished dough; also, the popular name for the Sabbath or holiday bread.

*Hamaor* (Hebrew). A Hebrew journal on Jewish law and customs.

*Hanukah* (Hebrew). Also, *Chanukah*. Feast of Lights.

*Hanukah Lecht* (Hebrew-Yiddish). Also, *Chanukah Lecht*. Candles lit on the Feast of Lights.

*Hashash* (Hebrew). Apprehension or doubt.

*Hasid* (Hebrew). Literally, "pious." A member of the Hasidic community. Indicates a particular type of religious behavior. (*Hasidim*. Plural.)

*Hasidisher Yid* (Yiddish). Hasidic Jew. (*Hasidishe Yiden*. Plural.)

*Havdalah Lecht* (Yiddish). Twisted candles lit at the ceremonial at the outgoing of the Sabbath.

*Hazan* (Hebrew). Cantor.

*Heimisher Yid* (Yiddish). Literally, "homey" or "indigenous Jew." A person who is originally from Europe and who observes the *Shulhan Aruch* according to the tradition. (*Heimishe Yiden*. Plural.)

*Hevrah Kadishah* (Hebrew). Literally, "holy society." An organization that takes care of all the necessary rituals concerning the preparation for burial.

*Hevreh man* (Hebrew-Yiddish-English). Literally, "a man of the organization." Indicates cleverness in a derogatory sense.

*Hitachdut Harabanim D'Artzot Habrit V'Canada* (Hebrew). The Hasidic rabbinical organization called in English, "The Rabbinical Congress of the United States and Canada."

*Hometz* (Hebrew). Also, *chometz*. Literally, "leavened." Things that are prohibited for Passover use.

*Hoshanos* (Hebrew). Literally, "willows of the brook." One of the "four kinds" used during the Holiday of Tabernacles.

*Hukat* (Hebrew). A portion of the Torah read in the synagogue during a particular week.

*Isur Hasagat Gevul Yadua* (Hebrew). Literally, "beware of the prohibition against trespassing the property of another." A written form of property protection which serves as a copyright.

*Kabalah* (Hebrew). Literally, "receipt." A certificate stating the God-fearingness, skill in slaughtering, and knowledge of the law of the ritual slaughterer.

*Kadish* (Hebrew). Literally, "sanctification." The customary prayer to be said after a parent's death.

*Kaftan* (Yiddish). A black overcoat, a Hasidic garment.

*Kahal Arugat Habosem* (Hebrew). The Congregation of Garden Bed of Spice.

*Kahal Torat Haim* (Hebrew). The Congregation of Torah of Life.

*Kapote* (Yiddish). A long overcoat, usually black and not quite as fancy as the *Bekecher*.

*Kashrut* (Hebrew). Pertaining to the observance of the dietary laws.

*Kislev* (Hebrew). The Jewish month corresponding approximately to November-December.

*Kitzur Shulhan Aruch* (Hebrew). The abridged *Code of Jewish Law*, arranged and edited by Solomon Ganzfried.

*Kosher* (Hebrew). Literally, "ritually permitted," "valid," "fit for consumption," "proper to use."

*Kosher alibe d'chol haderet* (Hebrew). Things considered kosher according to the opinions of all the religious authorities.

*Koshere Milach* (Yiddish). Kosher milk, milk which is ritually supervised.

*K'vod Hachamim* (Hebrew). The honor and respect accorded to wise men.


*Lamed Vov Tzadikim* (Hebrew). The thirty-six unknown righteous men upon whose virtues the whole world exists.

*Leshata* (Aramaic). For the time being.

*Lulav* (Hebrew). Branch of a palm tree. One of the "four kinds" which are used on the Holiday of Tabernacles.


*Madanim* (Hebrew). Literally, "delicacies."

*Maggid* (Hebrew). Literally, "preacher."

*Mahmir* (Hebrew). Literally, "one who is strict." Refers to persons who interpret the *Code of Jewish Law* in a strict sense. (*Mahmirim.* Plural.)

*Magen Avraham* (Hebrew). A commentary on the *Shulhan Aruch*.

*Mashgiach* (Hebrew). Literally, "supervisor." An overseer of religious matters.

*Matzah* (Hebrew). Literally, "unleavened bread." A flat, cracker-like baked product made of flour and water.

*Matzah Peshutah* (Hebrew). Plain matzah baked from flour that has been especially produced for the purpose of baking matzah.

*Matzah Shmurah* (Hebrew). Literally, "guarded matzah." Matzah baked from flour that has been carefully tended from the time of the cutting of the wheat.

*Megillah* (Hebrew). Literally, "scroll." It usually refers to the Book of Esther. (*Megilot.* Plural.)

*Mehadrin* (Hebrew). Zealous in religious observance.

*Mehadrin Min Hamehadrin* (Hebrew). The most zealous of the zealous in religious observance.

*Mekel* (Hebrew). One who is lenient. It refers to persons who interpret Jewish law in a milder sense.

*Melamed* (Hebrew). Instructor, usually in religious matters. (*Melamdim*. Plural.)

*Meshugener* (Yiddish). Crazy, insane.

*Meshulach* (Hebrew). Literally, "messenger." A person who collects donations and contributions for a religious or charitable organization.

*Metargem* (Hebrew). Literally, "translator."

*Mezuzah* (Hebrew). A religious symbol which is permanently placed on the upper right doorpost of the Jewish home. (*Mezuzot*. Plural.)

*Mikveh* (Hebrew). Ritual bath.

*Mikveh Yid* (Yiddish). Literally, "A Jew of the ritual bath." The person who is in charge of the ritual bath.

*Mikveh Yiddene* (Yiddish). A woman who is in charge of the ritual bath for women.

*Milchig* (Yiddish). Dairy and milk products.

*Mishna[h]* (Hebrew). Literally, "[oral] study." The collection of laws upon which the Talmud is based.

*Mishnah Berurah* (Hebrew). An abridged *Code of Jewish Law*.

*Mitzvah* (Hebrew). Literally, "commandment." A prescribed religious performance, or, a good deed.

*Modeh Ani* (Hebrew). Literally, "I thank." The first prayer said in the morning upon awakening.

*Modernish* (Yiddish). Modern.

*Mohel* (Hebrew). Circumciser.

*Moleh Rahamim* (Hebrew). Literally, "full of compassion." A prayer said for the deceased.

*Moleh Zoger* (Hebrew-Yiddish). Literally, "*Moleh*-sayer." The person who recites the *Moleh* prayer in the cemeteries.

*Moser* (Hebrew). Literally, "informer" or "traitor."

*Naches* (Hebrew). Literally, "happiness" or "contentment."

*Nerot Shel Shavah* (Hebrew). Literally, "candles of wax."

*Netilat Yadayim* (Hebrew). Ritual washing of the hands upon awakening and before meals.

*Obgehitener Yid* (Yiddish). Literally, "the guardian Jew." The so-called ultra-Orthodox Jew who is extremely conscientious in the observance of religion.

*Ohnzepenish* (Yiddish). Literally, "hanging on." Refers to a person or thing that hangs on to somebody or something and is considered a nuisance which is hard to get rid of. The term is used for a person who becomes a nuisance in a given circumstance.

*Parochet* (Hebrew). Curtain for the Holy Ark in the synagogue.

*Parve* (Yiddish). Neutral food that contains neither meat nor milk. This food is permissible for use with either meat or dairy products.

*Pasul* (Hebrew). Ineligible for ritual usage.

*Pesach* (Hebrew). The Holiday of Passover.

*Payes* (Hebrew). Sidelocks.

*Pidyan* (Hebrew). Literally, "redemption." The money followers give their *rebbe* at the *gezegenen* ceremony.

*Pittum* (Hebrew). The stem of the *esrog*.

*Purim* (Hebrew). The Holiday of Lots as described in the Book of Esther.


*Rabbi* (Hebrew). A non-Hasidic spiritual leader or minister of a Jewish congregation or other religious organization, usually graduated from and ordained by the educational institution he attended. It usually implies in the Hasidic community that the rabbi is a modern religious leader who has little training in Jewish law and that his religious conduct is not traditional. (*Rabbis* Plural.)

*Rav* (Hebrew). A religious leader of a religious Jewish congregation who was ordained by well-known religious scholars and who has great familiarity with the Jewish law and conducts himself in a traditional manner. (*Rabbanim*. Plural.)

*Rebbe* (Hebrew). The religious leader of a Hasidic community.

*Rebbishe Gesheften* (Yiddish). Occupations which are connected with being a *rebbe, rav*, and their assistants.

*Rebetzin* (Yiddish). The *rebbe's, rav's*, or rabbi's wife.

Rosh Hashanah (Hebrew). The Jewish New Year.


*S'chach* (Hebrew). Tabernacle top used on the Holiday of Tabernacles.

*Sefer* (Hebrew). Literally, "book." Among the Hasidim, a book of religious content. (*Sefarim*. Plural.)

*Sefer Torah* (Hebrew). Torah scroll.

*Shabbos Lecht* (Yiddish). Sabbath candles.

*Shabbos Zeiger* (Yiddish). Literally, "Sabbath clock." An automatic timer which turns the electric current off and on.

*Shadhan* (Hebrew). Professional or semiprofessional marriage broker.

*Shamash* (Hebrew). A religious servant in charge of the house of worship.

Shavuot (Hebrew). Feast of Weeks or Pentecost.

*Sheiner Yid* (Yiddish). Literally, "beautiful Jew." Very observant person, usually religious professionals in the Hasidic community.

*Sheitel* (Yiddish). Wig.

*Sheitel-macher* (Yiddish). Wig maker.

*Sheliach Tzibur* (Hebrew). Literally, "emissary of the congregation." The reader at a religious worship.

*Shich und Zocken* (Yiddish). Literally, "shoes and socks." *Shich* are slipper-like shoes, and *Zocken* are white knee-socks into which the breeches are folded. They are a Hasidic status symbol.

*Shiduch* (Hebrew). A marriage or a match for marriage.

*Shmurah Matzah* (Hebrew). Literally, "guarded matzah." see *Matzah Shmurah.*

*Shohet* (Hebrew). Ritual slaughterer.

*Shohet-Gassim* (Hebrew). Ritual slaughterer of large animals.

*Shohet-Ofot* (Hebrew). Ritual slaughterer of poultry.

*Shomrei Torah U'Mitzvot* (Hebrew). Literally, "Observers of the Torah and Commandments." It refers to persons who observe Jewish law in the strict traditional manner.

*Shtetl* (Yiddish). Literally, "village." A small European Jewish community.

*Shtickel Rebbe* (Yiddish). "Somewhat of a *rebbe.*" A rank is not as high as the *rebbe's.*

*Shtreimel* (Yiddish). A fur hat made of sable. A Hasidic status symbol.

*Shul* (Yiddish). House of worship or synagogue.

*Shulhan Aruch* (Hebrew). *Code of Jewish Law.*

*Sidur* (Hebrew). Prayer book. (*Sidurim.* Plural.)

*Sofer* (Hebrew). Scribe of religious letters and documents.

*Succah* (Hebrew). A temporary booth or tabernacle built for the Holiday of Tabernacles.

*Succot* (Hebrew). The Holiday of Tabernacles.


*Tachrichim* (Hebrew). Shrouds.

*Taharah* (Hebrew). Literally, "purification." Washing of the dead and preparation for burial.

*Talit-Katan* (Hebrew). Literally, "small prayer shawl." It is worn by a religious Jew under the jacket as part of his apparel.

*Talmid Hacham* (Hebrew). Literally, "the wise man's disciple." It refers to a learned man of Torah and Talmud. (*Talmidei Hachamim.* Plural.)

*Talmud* (Hebrew). Literally, "teaching" or "study." It refers to the Amoraic discussion of the *Mishnah.*

*Tameh* (Hebrew). Literally, "unclean" or "polluted."

*Tefilin* (Hebrew). Literally, "phylacteries." A religious object worn by the observant Jew every day, except on the Sabbath, and religious holidays during the Morning Prayers.

*Tishri* (Hebrew). A Jewish month corresponding to September-October.

*Torah* (Hebrew). Literally, "instruction" or "teaching." It usually refers to the entire Jewish law.

*Trefah* (Hebrew). Literally, "torn." An animal which otherwise is permissible to eat but upon slaughtering is found to have some organic defect is prohibited for consumption and is described ·as *trefah.*

*Tzadik* (Hebrew). A righteous man or an extremely religious man.

*Tzedakah* (Hebrew). Literally, "righteousness." The popular expression for charity.

*Tzitzis* (Hebrew). Fringes upon the prayer shawls.

*Tzon Kedoshim* (Hebrew). Literally, "Holy Herd." It refers to the Jew in the mystical literature.

*Ungarishe Yiden* (Yiddish). Literally, "Hungarian Jews."

*Yarmelke[h]* (Yiddish). Skull cap.

*Yahnzeit* (Yiddish). The anniversary of a death.

*Yahrzeit Lecht* (Yiddish). Candles lit on the anniversary of a death.

*Yerei Shamayim* (Hebrew). God-fearing.

*Yeshivah* (Hebrew). A religious school. (*Yeshivot.* Plural.)

*Yid* (Yiddish). Literally, "Jew." (*Yiden.* Plural.)

*Yiddish* (English). Jewish.

*Yiddishe Goyim* (Yiddish). Nonobservant Jews.

*Yiddisher Mama* (Yiddish). A Jewish mother.

*Yiddisher Tochter* (Yiddish). Literally, "Jewish daughter." A young woman who behaves appropriately in the community.

*Yiddishkeit* (Yiddish). Literally, "Jewishness." It refers to the basic religious dogma of traditional Judaism.

*Yom Kippur* (Hebrew). Day of Atonement.

*Zechut Avot* (Hebrew). The merits of the forefathers.

*Zehr Hasidish* (Yiddish). Extremely Hasidic.

# Bibliography

## of Works Consulted

### BOOKS

Allen, Edward J. *The Second United Order among the Mormons*. New York: Columbia University Press, 1936.

Anderson, Nels. *The Desert Saints: The Mormon Frontier in Utah*. Chicago: University of Chicago Press, 1942.

Blum, Raphael. *Tal Hashomayim*. New York: Hadar Linotyping and Publishing Co., 1958.

Bogue, Donald J. *The Population of the United States*. Glencoe: The Free Press, Inc., 1959.

Caplow, Theodore. *The Sociology of Work*. Minneapolis: University of Minnesota Press, 1954.

Centers, Richard. *The Psychology of Social Classes*. Princeton: Princeton University Press, 1949.

*Code of Jewish Law (Kitzur Shulhan Aruch)*. Compiled by Solomon Gansfried and translated by Hyman E. Goldin. New York: Hebrew Publishing Co., 1927.

*Daily Prayerbook*. Translated by Philip Birenbaum. New York: Hebrew Publishing Co., 1949.

Davis, Kingsley. *Human Society*. New York: The Macmillan Co., 1948.

Durkheim, Emile. *The Elementary Forms of Religious Life*. Translated by Joseph W. Swain. Glencoe: The Free Press, Inc., 1947.

Eisenstein, J. D. *Ozar Dinim u-Minhagim (A Digest of Jewish Laws and Customs)*. New York: Hebrew Publishing Co., 1938.

Gerth, Hans H., and C. Wright Mills. *From Max Weber: Essays in Sociology*. New York: Oxford University Press, Inc., 1958.

Gingerich, Melvin. *The Mennonites in Iowa.* Iowa City: The State Historical Society of Iowa, 1939.

Hawthorn, Harry B. (ed.). *The Doukhobors of British Columbia.* Vancouver: University of British Columbia and J. M. Dent & Sons (Canada), Ltd., 1955.

LaPiere, Richard T. *A Theory of Social Control.* New York: McGraw-Hill Book Company, Inc., 1954.

Loomis, Charles P., and J. Allan Beegle. *Rural Social Systems.* New York: Prentice-Hall, Inc., 1950.

McNiff, William J. *Heaven on Earth.* Oxford, Ohio: The Mississippi Valley Press, 1940.

Merton, Robert K. *Social Theory and Social Structure.* Glencoe: The Free Press, Inc., 1957.

Moore, Wilbert E. *Economy and Society.* New York: Doubleday & Company, Inc., 1955.

Ogburn, William F., and Meyer F. Nimkoff. *Sociology.* Boston: Houghton Mifflin Company, 1958.

Park, Robert E., and Herbert A. Miller. *Old World Traits Transplanted.* New York: Harper & Brothers, 1921.

Parsons, Talcott. *Essays in Sociological Theory.* Glencoe: The Free Press, Inc., 1958.

Powdermaker, Hortense. *After Freedom.* New York: The Viking Press, Inc., 1934.

Radcliffe-Brown, A. R. *The Andaman Islanders.* Glencoe: The Free Press, Inc., 1948.

Roth, Cecil, *Jewish Life in the Middle Ages.* London: Edward Goldston, 1932.

Saunders, Lyle. *Cultural Differences and Medical Care.* New York: Russell Sage Foundation, 1954.

Simpson, George E., and J. Milton Yinger. *Racial and Cultural Minorities.* New York: Harper & Brothers, 1958.

*Sixteenth Census of the United States: 1940 Population; Comparative Occupation Statistics for the United States, 1870–1940.* Washington, D.C.: United States Government Printing Office, 1943.

Smith, C. Henry. *The Story of the Mennonites.* Newton, Kans.: Mennonite Publication Office, 1950.

Smith, Elmer Lewis. *The Amish People.* New York: Exposition Press, 1958.

Sombart, Werner. *The Jews and Modern Capitalism.* Translated by M. Epstein. Glencoe: The Free Press, Inc., 1951.

*Statistical Abstract of the United States, 1959.* Washington, D.C.: United States Government Printing Office, 1960.

Stouffer, Samuel A., *et al. The American Soldier: Adjustment during Army Life.* Vol. I. Princeton: Princeton University Press, 1949.

Ujvári, Péter (ed.). *Magyar Zsido Lexikon.* Budapest: Pallas Irodalmi és Nyomdai Részvénytársaság, 1929.

Volkart, Edmund H. *Social Behavior and Personality, Contributions of W. I. Thomas to Theory and Social Research.* New York: Social Science Research Council, 1951.

Weber, Max. *Ancient Judaism.* Translated by Hans H. Gerth and Don Martindale. Glencoe: The Free Press, Inc., 1952.

———. *General Economic History.* Translated by Frank H. Knight. Glencoe: The Free Press, Inc., 1950.

———. *The Theory of Social and Economic Organization.* Translated by A. M. Henderson and Talcott Parsons. Glencoe: The Free Press, Inc., 1947.

Williams, Robin M., Jr. *American Society.* New York: Alfred A. Knopf, Inc., 1960.

Young, Pauline V. *The Pilgrims of Russian-Town.* Chicago: University of Chicago Press, 1932.

# ARTICLES

Davis, Moshe, "Jewish Religious Life and Institutions in America," in Louis Finkelstein (ed.), *The Jews, Their History, Culture, and Religion* (Philadelphia: The Jewish Publication Society of America).

Deutsch, Gotthard, "Aharonim," *The Jewish Encyclopedia* (New York: Funk & Wagnalls Co., 1906), pp. 283–284.

Festinger, Leon, "A Theory of Social Comparison Forces," *Human Relations,* 7 (May, 1954), pp. 117–140.

Glock, Charles Y., "The Sociology of Religion," in Robert K. Merton, Leonard Broom, and Leonard S. Cottrell, Jr. (eds.), *Sociology Today* (New York: Basic Books, Inc., 1959).

Greer, Leland Hargrave, "Mormon Towns in the Region of Colorado," *Anthropological Papers,* No. 32 (Salt Lake City: University of Utah Press, May, 1958), p. 3.

Kelley, Harold H., and Martin N. Shapiro, "An Experiment on Conformity to Group Norms Where Conformity is Detrimental to Group Achievement," *American Sociological Review,* 19 (December, 1954), pp. 667–672.

Kluckhohn, C., "The Use of Personal Documents in Anthropology," in L. Gottschalk, C. Kluckhohn, and R. Angell (eds.), *Social Science Research Council Bulletin,* 53 (1945).

Maccoby, Eleanor E., and Nathan Maccoby, "The Interview: A Tool of Social Science," in Gardner Lindzey (ed.), *Handbook of Social Psychology,* Vol. I (Reading, Mass.: Addison-Wesley Publishing Company, Inc., 1954).

Merton, Robert K., and Patricia L. Kendall, "The Focused Interview," *American Journal of Sociology,* 51 (1946).

North, Cecil C., and Paul K. Hatt, "Jobs and Occupations: A Popular Evaluation," *Public Opinion News,* 9 (1947), pp. 3–13. Also reprinted in Reinhard Bendix and Seymour Martin Lipset (eds.), *Class Status and Power* (Glencoe: Free Press, Inc., 1953).

Parsons, Talcott, "Age and Sex in U.S. Social Structure," *American Sociological Review*, 7 (October, 1947), pp. 610–613.

Paul, Benjamin D., "Interview Techniques and Field Relationships," in Alfred L. Kroebar (ed.), *Anthropology Today* (Chicago: University of Chicago Press, 1953).

Ropers, C. R., "The Non-directive Method as a Technique for Social Research," *American Journal of Sociology*, 50 (1945).

Sklare, Marshall, "Aspects of Religious Worship in the Contemporary Conservative Synagogue," in Marshall Sklare (ed.), *The Jews* (Glencoe: The Free Press, Inc., 1958).

Steinhertz, Jakab, "Magyar Nyelv A Zsinagogaban" ["The Hungarian Language in the Synagogues"], *Magyar Zsido Szemle*, Vol. 3:6 (June, 1886), pp. 340–342.

Warner, W. Lloyd, "The Society, the Individual, and His Mental Disorders," *American Journal of Psychiatry*, Vol. 94, No. 2 (September, 1937).

Zemplényi, Jakab, "A jesibák állapota hazánkban," *Magyar Zsido Szemle*, Vol. 3:6 (June, 1886), pp. 415–419.

## OTHER MATTER USED AS REFERENCES

Bressler, Marvin. "Jewish Behavior Patterns as Exemplified in W. I. Thomas' Unfinished Study of the Bintl Brief." Unpublished Ph.D. dissertation, Graduate School of Arts and Sciences, University of Pennsylvania, 1952.

Deets, Lee Emerson. "The Hutterites: A Study in Social Cohesion." Unpublished Ph.D. dissertation, Faculty of Political Science, Columbia University, 1939.

*Hamaor.* Various issues, 1956 through 1959.

*Life,* Vol. 38, No. 24 (June 13, 1955).

*Der Yid* [*The Jew*]. Various issues, 1956 through 1960.

# Index

*Esrog,* 164, 281
 business in, 165
 dealer of, 165
 season for, 164
*Esrogim,* 165, 166
Esther, Book of, 142
Europe, Eastern, 22
 Orthodox elements from, 27
Examiner, in religious school, 135
"Expected of women," 53
External appearance, 16, 87
External pressures, 20
External symbols, 91

**F**

"Faith strengtheners," 108, 112
Familial norms, 55
Family, 26, 55, 58
 defects in, 45
 life, Hasidic, 52, 53, 58
 line, 26
 living, 52
 norms, 53
Farmers, 7
Fayetteville, 6
*Ferherer,* 135, 281
*Ferleslicher Yid,* 187, 188, 281
*Ferleslichkeit,* 146
Fight against assimilation, 85
Finkelstein, Louis, 21
*Fleishig,* 176, 281
Focused interview, 275
Food product, 49
Freedom, 20
*Frei,* 38, 281
Frig-O-Matic Sabbath Zeiger, 101, 102, 255
*Frum,* 148
*Frumer* doctor, 148, 281
*Frumer Yid,* 148, 281
Functional roles, 263

**G**

*Gabbai,* 119, 281
Galicia, 17

Ganzfried, Solomon, 60
*Gaon,* 39, 122, 124, 173, 281
*Gemeinschaft,* 100, 281
General Jewish Congress, 13
*Geribener Ying,* 130, 281
Gerth, Hans H., 126, 230
*Gezegenen,* 118, 281
Gingerich, Melvin, 8, 257
"Glamor girl" role, 53
*Glat,* 185, 255
*Glat* kosher, 178, 186, 281
 butcher, 178, 179, 186
 catering places, 180
 food, 180, 181
 food products, 181
 hotel, 182, 230
 meat, 178, 179, 180, 182, 183, 184, 185, 239, 255, 258
 for the "most zealous of the zealous," 182
 products, 183, 185
 restaurants, 181
 sausage, 179
Glazer, Nathan, 27
Glock, Charles Y., 250
God-fearing young man, 90
*Goldene Medinah,* 37, 281
"Good companion" role, 54
Gottschalk, L., 275
Government, 5, 6
*Goy,* 27, 41, 112, 281
*Goyeh,* 27, 28, 281
*Goyim,* 15, 41
*Goyishe Goyim,* 41, 281
"Grace after Meals," 72
Greek Orthodox Church, 5
Greenwald, Leopold, 13, 18
Greenwald, Rabbi Moses, 109
Greer, Leland H., 7
Group behavior, 4
Group beliefs, 9
Group cohesion, 4, 11, 104, 265
Group consciousness, 35
Group control, 32, 80, 251
Group identification, 8, 10, 246
Group norms, 4, 211
Group values, 4, 8, 211

110, 128, 129, 134, 138, 146,
169, 227, 258, 286
justice, 131
loyalty to, 24
scrolls, 141, 142
Traditional garments, 25, 26
Traditional Jewish laws, 42, 45,
81, 129
Traditional Judaism, 19, 42
disorganization of, 42
Traditional observance, 24
Traditional practices, 29
Traditional rituals, 26
Traditional values, 229
Translator, 128
Transylvania, 9
*Trefah*, 286
Trustworthy Jew, 180
*Tzadik*, 119, 286
*Tzedakah*, 286
Book of, 75
*Tzitzis*, 17, 153, 287
*Tzon Kedoshim*, 134, 287

## U

Ujvari, Peter, 13
Ukraine, 9, 17
Ultra-Orthodox, 25, 26, 27, 28, 81,
230
Undertakers, 155, 231
*Ungarishe Yiden*, 30, 287
Union of American Hebrew Con-
gregations, 22
Union of Orthodox Rabbis, 23
United Synagogue of America, 22,
24
Unleavened bread, 198, 199, 200
Unmarried women, 91
Unstructured interviews, 275
Unterland, 17
Upward social mobility, 81
Urban community, 256
Urban culture, 263
Urban life, 257
Urban religion, 254
Utah, 6, 7

## V

Vacation Fund for Poor and Or-
phaned Children, Inc., 76
Values, 266
Vienna, 119
Violations of the law, 42
Volkart, Edmund H., 33
Voluntary segregation, 228, 230

## W

Warner, W. Lloyd, 229
Washington, 7
Wealth, 60, 61, 62, 68
Weber, Max, 125, 126, 230, 254
Wedding ceremony, 41
"Welcoming the Sabbath," 72
Welfare activities, 75
Welfare organizations, 74, 79
Williams, Robin M., Jr., 251
Williamsburg, 3, 26,
"natives" of, 27
Winnipeg, 9
Wire workers, 17
Women, 31
religious status of, 24
World Jewry, 230
World War II, 3, 19, 27
Worldly rewards, 61
Worshipers, donations of, 118

## Y

*Yahrzeit*, 174, 287
*Lecht*, 159, 287
Yanev, 165, 166
*Yarmelke[h]*, 153, 155, 287
*Yerei Shomayim*, 128, 287
*Yeshivah*, 26, 53, 151, 174, 179,
236, 287
*Torah Vodaath*, 29
*Yeshivot*, 19, 90, 156, 287
students of, 19
*Yid*, 287
*Yid mit a Shtreimel*, 219
Yiddish, 12, 28, 30, 49, 287
language, 107
newspapers, 32, 34, 78